Hunger and Shame

To My Best Friends,

This is your book – putting up with me all these years – insisting) on good writing – helping) me avoid simplistic interpretations – and much more. Hope you'll feel proud. Love Forever,

Mary

Hunger and Shame

Poverty and Child Malnutrition on Mount Kilimanjaro

~

Mary Howard and Ann V. Millard

Routledge
New York and London

Published in 1997 by

Routledge
29 West 35th Street
New York, NY 10001

Published in Great Britain by
Routledge
11 New Fetter Lane
London EC4P 4EE

The text was set in Minion.
Printed in the United States of America on acid-free paper.

Library of Congress Cataloging-in-Publication Data

Howard, Mary Theresa.
Hunger and shame: child malnutrition and poverty on Mount Kilimanjaro /
Mary Howard and Ann V. Millard.
p.   cm.
Includes bibliographical references.
ISBN 0-415-91613-5 (hc : alk. paper). — ISBN 0-415-91614-3 (pbk. alk. paper)
1. Malnutrition in children—Tanzania—Kilimanjaro Region.
2. Chagga (African people)—Nutrition. 3. Kilimanjaro Region
(Tanzania)—Economic conditions. 4. Kilimanjaro Region (Tanzania)—
Social conditions. 5. Chagga (African people)—Economic conditions.
6. Chagga (African people)—Social conditions. I. Millard, Ann V.
II. Title.
RJ399.M26H69 1997   96-46937
363.8'2'0967826—dc21   CIP

Contents

∼ Illustrations

～ Tables

Foreword

Robert B. Edgerton

It is self-evident that the quest for food is crucial for all living organisms, humans very much not excepted. Most of our ancestors who lived by hunting and gathering usually managed to feed themselves reasonably well. It was with the advent of the cultivation of food crops and reliance on cereal grains that malnutrition became a widespread problem. Even so, rising fertility led to such population growth that there are now some six billion people on earth, fully one billion of whom suffer from major forms of malnutrition (Jelliffe and Jelliffe 1989:2).

Hunger, malnutrition, and starvation have not escaped the often pained scrutiny of anthropologists as they have described the lives of people throughout the world. They have written about subsistence strategies, the sacralization of food, and the dreadful consequences of prolonged hunger. This work is fundamental to our understanding of the evolution of human cultures just as it is to the problems of the contemporary world. Yet few of these works leave so vivid a mark as *Hunger and Shame*, by Mary Howard and Ann V. Millard.

The book is a report about malnutrition among the Chagga of Tanzania, a people who live on the southern slopes of beautiful Mt. Kilimanjaro. The natural beauty of their world hides the dismal reality that their rate of child malnutrition is among the highest in the country, itself one of the poorest in the world. We first meet the Chagga in the mid-1970s, when they were still suffering the effects of a profound famine that had struck the area. After nearly two decades, famine had ended but malnutrition had ravaged many poor families among this often prosperous African people. We are forced to meet parents who cannot feed their children or themselves and to visualize stunted bodies tormented by diseases involving malnutrition. The filth of their urine-soaked living quarters, their ragged clothing, and their dead eyes make an unforgettable impression. Much of the book's value lies in the impact of these images of human misery as the physical pain of hunger is joined by the sense of shame and loss of dignity that such poverty brings.

The book is more than a vivid introduction to malnutrition, shame, and death. It also provides a detailed analysis of the meaning of poverty among the Chagga and of the economic and political factors that have so weakened the kin networks that poor Chagga were earlier able to rely upon. Population growth and land shortage are obvious contributors, but the dichotomy between rich and poor is also a function of access to modern education, creating an enduring gap between rich and poor. Wage labor is another potent factor. Many men must migrate in search of wage-paying employment, leaving their wives to care for their farms and their children, a burden that leaves some women too exhausted to do either one well. More-subtle aspects of Chagga culture contribute to the plight of the malnourished as well. Finally, we are introduced to NURU, the Nutrition Rehabilitation Unit established among the Chagga in 1972. Paid for by private American funds and staffed by doctors from the United States and Europe, NURU provides an instructive example of the cultural complexities that must be confronted if nutrition rehabilitation is to succeed.

Half a century ago, a young anthropologist named Audrey Richards wrote a book entitled *Land, Labor, and Diet in Northern Rhodesia*, which examined nutrition in an African society. Since Richards wrote, the ravages of malnutrition in Africa are worse, not better. *Hunger and Shame* forces us to confront the problem, and while it offers no easy solutions, it opens the door to better understanding and, not least, to greater compassion.

Reproduction, Social Relations, and History: Approaches to Child Malnutrition

Ann V. Millard and Mary Howard

The entry of Chagga farmers into coffee production is a contested part of their history. Around the turn of the century, the colonial regime coerced Chagga to work as laborers on Europeans' plantations and blocked their entry into competition as coffee producers. Nonetheless, coffee was to become the major cash crop of Chagga farmers, who made it important to the national economy as well.

One story told on Mt. Kilimanjaro says that a Roman Catholic priest first gave coffee seed to the Chagga people, who thus began their own coffee plantations. Another version of the story focuses on a high-ranking Chagga official who privately bought seed from an Italian settler and began a farm, later to sell seed to other officials and the chief.

In the first version, the main actor is a European missionary taking the role of a generous interventionist who refused to favor the economic interests of European plantation owners. The story characterizes Chagga farmers as depending on European leadership for the key to their future. The second version depicts the Chagga as controlling their own destiny and successfully adopting a European cash crop while thwarting the monopolistic maneuvers of European farmers and other colonialists.

According to historians, both stories carry some truth (Iliffe 1979:154). In the 1890s, Chagga catechists did acquire seeds from Christian missions, but a long, drastic downturn in the world market made coffee farming unprofitable in that decade. Early in this century, however, during a market upswing, when Europeans were forcing the Chagga people to adopt cash, work on plantations, and forgo many aspects of customary rule by their chiefs, the Chagga began coffee farming on their own initiative (ibid.).

These stories contrast sharply in their depiction of the shapers of Chagga destiny: kindly European idealists or intelligent Chagga strategists. A contrast of this sort often underlies debates over the roles accorded to rural people in less developed countries in determining their course of economic development (on stereotypes of peasants and of people in less developed countries, see Maclachlan 1983; Moore 1994; Said 1979; Scott 1985). The actions of the poor on Mt. Kilimanjaro challenge a modern myth that rural people in developing countries, frequently called "peasants," blindly follow tradition and do not willingly change their ways. They are assumed to let ill children die out of ignorance or because "life is cheap." According to the stereotype, they are passive people meekly accepting fate, going about their daily lives unthinkingly, and harming their children unknowingly. Although "peasant" is a term that has a technical significance in anthropology, we avoid it in this book because it carries implications that are quite misleading for the general reader. Instead, we use the term "farmer" to include those with large coffee plantations, those with few coffee trees, and still others who cultivate only food crops for their own table.[1]

The tendency to view rural people as docile followers rather than active innovators pervades work on child malnutrition. Many health programs assume that parents are generally complicit in their own impoverishment and the suffering of their children (see Vaughan 1991). In this volume, we argue that Chagga problems with child malnutrition result not from the backwardness ascribed to peasant societies but largely from institutional changes tied to major forces sweeping through East Africa during the twentieth century: colonialism, Christianity, capitalism, and, in Tanzania, two decades of socialism. The interaction of the Chagga people with these forces has sustained the high rate of child malnutrition on Mt. Kilimanjaro. We address child malnutrition in a broad context, including its biological, social, and cultural aspects, and analyze the misunderstandings that sustain it. With the twentieth-century erosion of the authority and economic cohesiveness of the Chagga patrilineage, some researchers might expect a trend away from a male-dominated society toward greater gender equality (Caldwell 1982; but see Leacock 1981:18–20; Sacks 1979), which was advocated by the socialist government of Tanzania. Economic, political, and religious structures introduced by Europeans and reshaped on Mt. Kilimanjaro, however, have ensured the persistence of male authority. Men remain owners of nearly all farmland, recipients of income from coffee harvests, and holders of most political offices.

The burdening of women on Mt. Kilimanjaro with increased responsibilities to provide for themselves and their children (Kerner and Cook 1991; Gladwin 1991; Swantz 1985; Swantz et al. 1975; Von Freyhold et al. 1973) is a pattern found throughout Africa and in many other parts of the world (Brown 1995; Deere and Leon de Leal 1982; Eide and Steady 1980; Lukmanji et al. 1993; NCC/CSPD 1993:ix, 81; O'Brien and Gruenbaum 1991; Schoepf and Schoepf 1990; Turshen 1991; Collier and Yanagisako 1987; see also Devereaux 1987; Strathern 1987; Zeitlin, Ghassemi, and Mansour 1990). In many rural societies in developing countries, class differences interact in a complex way with gender inequality (Morsy 1978; see also DeWalt, Kelly, and Pelto 1980; Hirschmann and Vaughan 1983), putting impoverished women and men in similar social and economic positions, with no farmland and little access to other economic resources.

Actions of male relatives, neighbors, and local politicians who intervene to stave off child death tend to be unexplored. We provide detailed information about such efforts as well as those of mothers and fathers coping with malnourished children.

In addition to challenging myths about "peasants" and "patriarchy," this book also addresses assumptions about international economic development and medical prevention programs. In analyzing the ways that the Chagga people actively shape their own lives, we find that many are trying to cope with forces beyond their control, whether in their own society, in their nation, or abroad.

The international market is part of what determines the global distribution of poverty, creating a context in which economic development policies must address people living in hardship (on problems with the concept of "development," see Warren and Bourque 1989). The global economy is not simply a system of trading relationships; it is also a system of social relations in which powerful people control world resources and determine development policies. Such people are often influenced by common myths about the causes of poverty and malnutrition, and their views have powerful consequences for child survival.

Although some researchers focus blame for high rates of child mortality on local cultures, our work questions whether the main (or only) onus should lie on the "knowledge, attitudes, and practice" of poor people. By considering in detail Chagga knowledge of child hunger, we put an emphasis on Chagga culture, society, and economy that may imply to some readers that the major culpability for high rates of child malnutrition lies with the people of Mt. Kilimanjaro. Such a reading would be in error, however. The Chagga example shows that it is the interaction of customary practices with forces originating outside Mt. Kilimanjaro that has led to the deepening of poverty and isolation of the poor, resulting in high rates of child malnutrition on the mountain. The international and ethnic division of labor (apparent in the coffee trade on Mt. Kilimanjaro but not taken up in this book) is often mistaken for a set of relationships determined by cultural differences, again making poverty seem to be the construction of the people living in it.

Medical programs designed to prevent child malnutrition are too often saddled with responsibilities beyond their capacities (on the complexity of malnutrition, see Jelliffe and Jelliffe 1989; Williams, Baumslag, and Jelliffe 1985). Medical institutions often have an apolitical image, enhanced by the respectable aura of high technology (Davis-Floyd 1992; Jordan 1978; Rothman 1982), rendering them acceptable to authorities in dealing with health issues that are potentially politically explosive, such as malnutrition and social inequality. Unfortunately, health professionals usually lack the training in social science issues and the political authority needed to reverse the poverty that is the fundamental cause of high rates of child malnutrition.

Reproduction and Social Relations

This volume deals most generally with reproduction and social relations. "Reproduction" in this context involves the biological and social aspects of continuity with the next generation, through childbearing, providing for a household, and caring for its members. Biological factors that affect the survival of young children encompass maternal and child nutrition and health, including birth spacing (Hull and Simpson 1985; Cosminsky 1985), all of which have changed over the course of this century (Feierman and Janzen 1992; on the "household production of health," see Berman, Kendall, and Bhattacharyya 1994; Coreil et al. 1994; Harkness and Super 1994; Schumann and Mosley 1994). Relevant processes in social relations involve the distribution of food, land, and work as well as the relationship of Chagga society to the larger world, including Tanzania and the global economy.

The background for this study includes the work of many scholars who have studied child malnutrition and food crisis (e.g., de Garine and Harrison 1988; Dettwyler 1994; Dirks 1980; Harrison 1988; Newman 1990). Some anthropologists have opened up vigorous debates by taking controversial perspectives, especially concerning parental intentions toward their malnourished children. The works of Turnbull (1972), Scrimshaw (1978), Cassidy (1980), LeVine and LeVine (1981), Nations and Rebhun (1988), Scheper-Hughes (1984, 1992), and Castle (1994) debate the intentions of mothers whose children are malnourished, the facilitation of malnutrition by certain cultures or power relationships, and the effects of demographic pressures on culture and parental behavior.

In related research, Edgerton (1992) shows that small-scale "traditional" societies generally have histories of causing culture-specific forms of human suffering; many governments of more developed countries contrast in the scale but not the depth of destruction wreaked upon other human beings. His work calls for more careful scrutiny of the ethnographic record in place of a romantic approach that expects members of "traditional" cultures to live in harmony (see also Newbury 1991).

This volume contributes to the effort to understand child malnutrition on Mt. Kilimanjaro in terms that are realistic instead of romanticized. In trying to avoid glossing over or disguising conflict on Mt. Kilimanjaro, we are critical of some Chagga for their stance with regard to malnourished children. Such criticism is presented with an acute awareness that many societies, including our own, place hardships on young children and other dependents (e.g., Howard 1990; Millard 1990).

Sen's work in India shows that even in a society with sufficient food, some people are forced into food crisis when they lose their "entitlement" to food as customs of redistribution and reciprocity erode (1981). Raikes (1988) describes a pattern of loss of entitlements in many regions of Africa and finds that rates of child malnutrition tend to peak in Africa's mountainous areas, where cash crop production has been most successful. The shift to commodity food production has been accompanied by weakening reciprocity between the poor and their community leaders, by an increasing gap between rich and poor, and by the growing poverty of many households faced with shortages of farmland and landlessness.

Some analysts see the commercialization of agriculture as the only hope for people in developing countries (e.g., Seavoy 1989). The predicament of the poor after seventy years of Chagga farmers' involvement in the international coffee trade, however, leads us to question that claim. Clearly, deep involvement in commercial agriculture does not solve the problem of poverty (Gamassa 1991; Ljungqvist 1993:233; Vahlquist 1972; Whiteford and Ferguson 1991). Numerous studies find that the global economy is an important force in shaping the worldwide pattern of poverty and related rates of child malnutrition (Berg 1972; Downs et al. 1991; Huss-Ashmore and Katz 1989, 1990; Huss-Ashmore and Thomas 1988; Messer 1989; Semiti 1972; Susser, Watson, and Hopper 1985:49–131; see also Kelly and Reardon 1995). While international trade ties places such as Mt. Kilimanjaro to wealthy industrial centers around the world (Wallerstein 1986), these links are seldom considered in relation to the problems of the rural poor. Many people in more developed countries are "afraid that increasing numbers in the Third World will one day demand their due and lower our own standard of living; fearful that the pressures of population may finally demonstrate that the 'only solution is revolution'" (George

1983:45; see also analyses by Arnold 1988:40; Dirks 1992; Foster 1992; Shields 1995; Watts 1991).

The current revival of Malthusian perspectives and social Darwinism (e.g., Herrnstein and Murray 1994; Rushton and Bogaert 1989) provides a way of justifying the status quo, a way of explaining the plight of the poor as due to something intrinsic to them and thus their fault, not the fault of those who are better-off (Gould 1981; Leslie 1990; Shanklin 1994; see also Clifford 1988; Fernandez 1990). The analysis in this book brings us to question this formulation regarding the poor in more developed countries, depicted as unthinking or uncaring about their children, inured to terrible living conditions (and conditions of dying), and not particularly even noticing the tragedies of their lives (see also Chavez 1992; Piven and Cloward 1993).

The distress of the poor bears significance for policy, politics, and social theory. The controversy over how to think about impoverished people raises questions about research methods and other aspects of epistemology. The traditional anthropological methods of participant observation and intensive interviews can allow people to express their emotional reactions to hardship, from intense passion to resignation, and discuss their ways of coping with adversity (Bennett 1990; Engle 1990; Jerome 1980; Messer 1990; Rogers 1990; Scrimshaw 1990). The contemporary anthropological effort to record and interpret the emotions and interactions of community members and researchers (Bell, Caplan, and Karim 1993; Caplan 1993; Lutz 1988; Rosaldo 1980; Taussig 1992; Wikan 1990; Winkler 1995), particularly in times of crisis, has allowed for greater attention to the views of people who are the focus of ethnographic research, a crucial step in examining child malnutrition. Ignoring people's experience renders them mute and passive, apparently incapable of strategizing about their problems, and this depiction leads to paternalistic approaches to their situations (Coles and Coles 1989; Finerman 1995). Although survey methods are valuable for some purposes, the restricted range of potential responses is part of what has led many anthropologists and others to shift to different approaches to analyzing child malnutrition and other crises.

Scholars of food crisis have begun to create a "comparative phenomenology" of hunger and famine (Arnold 1988:2), treating hunger as "a complex process, not an event" (Watts 1991:36), and it is our aim to contribute to that effort. During this study, the people of Mt. Kilimanjaro expressed a range of views about the reasons for child malnutrition, and our analysis takes account of their different social and economic positions. We incorporate the emotions of those struggling with child hunger on Mt. Kilimanjaro, including impoverished parents, their better-off relatives, health care professionals, government officials, and researchers.

Mary Howard's research on Mt. Kilimanjaro provided the main source of information in this book. By including her dramatic first-person interactions with people struggling with ailing children and other adversity, we engage the readers in a problem-posing approach (Freire 1985; Hope and Timmel 1984). In the process of writing, we have drawn from our different backgrounds in anthropology and other disciplines and from our commonly held conviction that it is possible to improve the theories and programs dealing with child malnutrition.

On a practical level, we think that people in government, academia, and business can help open doors to allow the rural poor to gain control of their lives and ensure the survival of their children. We also recognize the reluctance of people in positions of authority at many levels to concede anything that might seem to threaten their positions in a familiar social order. As outsiders to Chagga society, we have only a partial understanding of contemporary life on Mt. Kilimanjaro, and we offer this account only as an introduction to Chagga culture and history without pretending to capture all of its complexity.

We do not claim to know the answer to preventing child malnutrition on Mt. Kilimanjaro, but we are persuaded that it lies partly with the Chagga people themselves and partly with policymakers who need to take cognizance of the breadth of the problem and discard useless stereotypes of the poor. By reconsidering the significance of culture and the world economy, and by considering all the requirements of reproduction, it is possible to arrive at a better understanding of child malnutrition. In this book, we explore Chagga culture and social relations in the form of the interaction of people on Mt. Kilimanjaro with forces on the regional, national, and global levels, culminating in the high rates of child malnutrition on the mountain.

Acknowledgments

I am deeply grateful to Ohio Wesleyan University for its financial and collegial support. Over the years, I have benefitted from Thomas E. Wenzlau Faculty Development Grants to return to Tanzania in 1989 and 1993; funding for a student assistantship provided by donations from Peter and Eleanor Kleist; and an extra scholarly leave to complete the manuscript. Many thanks to Laurie George and Janice Schroeder who assisted me with word processing and my colleagues in the Department of Sociology/Anthropology who have been especially supportive throughout the writing process. I am also grateful to the Michigan State University CICALS program which granted me travel funds to consult with Ann Millard in East Lansing.

I had the good fortune to do social research and planning on child health problems in the Kilimanjaro region during the 1970s with Marja-Liisa Swantz, Berta Marenga, Michaele Von Freyhold, Ulla-Stina Henricson, Katherine Sawaki, Irmgard Lindner, and Bo Baldin. I am indebted to Marja-Liisa Swantz for her pioneering research methodology, which integrates research with social activism. I am also deeply appreciative of the good fellowship and direction of Bo Baldin and Ulla-Stina Henricson in the Pediatrics Department and the Community Health Program at the Kilimanjaro Christian Medical Center.

I owe special thanks to Tom Zalla with whom I experienced the difficulties of beginning a family far away from home during very stressful times. I worked with Tom on a large economic survey of household milk production in the Kilimanjaro Region and he lent his data and expertise to those of us researching child health problems. Tom and I enjoyed the friendship and support of Emmanuel and Margaret Gotlieb and Sally and Jim Kocher in our visits to the University of Dar es Salaam. I am most grateful for Sally Kocher's sensitive photography in our book, which adds so much to the imagery of families during the 1970s.

Faculty in the Department of Anthropology at Michigan State University were helpful in untangling the often conflicting and contradictory information I obtained while doing Ph.D. research in Tanzania. Arthur Rubel (now at the University of California, Irving) was instrumental in my reintegration into academic life after a long period away and Cheryl Ritenbaugh (now at the University of Arizona) advised me to expand my field notes and journals into descriptive narratives which were used to write the dialogues in our book. Cheryl, Ann Millard, and Sara Quandt were helpful with the analysis of child malnutrition and with the editing of my dissertation. Harry Raulet introduced me to interpretive anthropology and challenged me to integrate it with political-economic analyses.

I owe much to my friend Libbett Crandon-Malamud whose book *From the Fat of Our Souls* has been a model and an inspiration. Libbett encouraged me to publish my dissertation and she continued to check on my progress and boost my confidence until shortly before she died. Robert Edgerton has also been very kind and encouraging of my research and work on another problem related to stigma and shame—that of mental retardation. I am very grateful for the time he took to write the insightful forward to our book.

I wish to thank the many friends and colleagues who read either a few chapters or the entire manuscript and contributed useful, critical feedback. Foremost among them is Patricia Whittier who edited our book and gave us many astute criticisms in substance and style. I am also appreciative of Patricia and Herbert Whittier's and Isidore Flores's friendship and tolerance as they allowed our project to invade their homes. At Routledge, Marlie Wasserman helped steer us away from pedantic writing and encouraged the first person narratives found throughout our book. Chung Min Chen and Jim Peoples patiently reviewed many early rough drafts of Chapters 1, 2, and 3 and were especially helpful with the analysis of Chapter 4. We were fortunate to be able to draw from Sally Falk Moore's illuminating scholarship on the social life of the Chagga people. Her comments on a draft of Chapter 6 reminded us of the importance of considering time and regional variation on Mt. Kilimanjaro, while Donna Kerner reviewed Chapter 8 and added insights on the problem of gender stratification within Chagga culture. Thanks to two Ohio Wesleyan students from Tanzania: Robert Nyonyi who assisted me with written Swahili, statistical analysis, and word processing;

and Ferry Oriyo who contributed personal observations of the Kilimanjaro scene and provided useful criticisms. I'm also indebted to Berta Marenga, the nurse in charge of the nutrition center on Mt. Kilimanjaro. Berta's comments and criticisms of our final draft, and her willingness to share her knowledge of child health and Chagga culture stemming from a lifetime of work with malnourished children and their families, have proved invaluable.

Other crucial sources of commentary and criticism came from Erika Bourgignon, Judith Gussler, Betty Messinger, Corinne Lyman, Anna Macias, Jan Smith, Theodore Cohen, Akbar Mahdi, Uwe Woltemade, Harry Raulet, Emmanuel Twesigye, and Thomas, Matthew, and Christopher Zalla. We have altered the text in response to many of our readers' concerns when it was possible to do so, but we claim all errors of fact and interpretation as our own.

My greatest debt of gratitude is to the Chagga people for their openness and hospitality and their patient tolerance of my cultural naiveté. Many individuals took the time to teach me important lessons about pregnancy, child care, health, and farming while sharing years of daily life on our *shamba*. I wish to thank Lazarro, Maria, Josephi, Agnesi, Patrice, Anna, Sikina, Mohammed, Tarde, Omari, Gogo, Abdi, Yesiah, Moshi, and Edwardi for their friendship and their support of me and my family. Our cooperative farm benefitted from the largesse of many friends including Natalia and Harry, Faye, Reverend Paul, Donesta, and my dear friend and companion, Maryanna.

And then there are the men, women, and children from the mission area whose stories are told within this book. Their willingness to share vivid expressions of suffering gave me insights into the painful feelings of shame associated with hunger and poverty. I dedicate this book to them and to my closest loved ones, my sons Matthew and Christopher, my sisters Rita and Ann, my brother Tom, and my friend Chung Min.

MARY HOWARD

I thank my colleagues for productive discussions of child malnutrition, especially Claire Cassidy, Anne E. Ferguson, Margaret A. Graham, Sharon Hoerr, Stanley Khaila, Kathryn Kolasa, Russell M. Reid, Debra A. Schuman, and Susan C.M. Scrimshaw. I sought no funding for this work and finished it during a sabbatical leave for which I thank my colleagues at Michigan State University. Additional thanks to Judy Pugh, Harry M. Raulet, and Loudell F. Snow, with whom I have taught in the Medical Anthropology Program.

Along with my co-author, Mary Howard, I thank Michael Gembremedhin at UNICEF in Nairobi and Mansweth and his family on Mt. Kilimanjaro for their hospitality and aid during our recent East African trip. We also thank those who took us into their housing compounds, clinics, and offices to explain their views of life on Mt. Kilimanjaro.

For comments on chapters, we are grateful to the following people, who are in no way responsible for the flaws: Isidore Flores, Molly Lauck, Nancy Millard, Bernard Ortiz de Montellano, Harry M. Raulet, Debra Rothenberg, and Barbara Rylko-Bauer. We are particularly grateful to Patricia Whittier for comments, criticisms, encouragement, and words of calm throughout our writing.

I dedicate this book to all those who struggle with malnutrition in daily life, clinical work, and research. More personally, I dedicate it to my husband, Isidore Flores, for his support and to my granddaughter, Elena, for her instruction as an infant during the writing of many passages about her age mates in this book.

ANN V. MILLARD

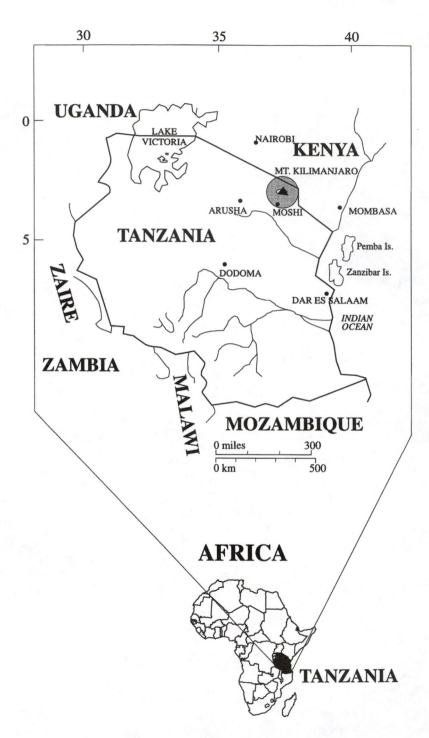

~ Figure 1 *Location of Mt. Kilimanjaro*

Chapter One

The Shame of Hunger

⌇ On the slopes of Mt. Kilimanjaro, Francis Lema struggled to contain his anger as he spoke about his two dead children and two living sons, both severely stunted by malnutrition. Only one of the five children, a daughter, was healthy. As he protested the tragedies of his life, tears welled in his eyes, while Bibiana, his wife, sat quietly with a pained look on her face. "Can you tell me why this had to happen?" he asked. ⌇

A man of dignity, Francis strove to maintain his composure while telling me about the loss of his children. He had gone to great lengths to save them but to no avail. At this point in our relationship, he was starting to question many of the principles by which he had lived his life; I had never before seen him so close to exhaustion and despair.

Francis's haunting question provoked the writing of this book.[1] The story of his family is an account of hunger and shame. The multiple causes of his children's deaths included the family's poverty, a cause of shame that impedes efforts of parents to find adequate food and medical care for their children. While Francis and Bibiana's poverty was stigmatic, their children's malnutrition brought even more shame.

The experience of the Mt. Kilimanjaro people with hunger and the role of shame in shaping it has grown out of their social life, economy, and history. Their children's malnutrition is rooted in the rhythms of everyday life—farm work, life in the family compound, and local commerce, which ties them to the global market. In this everyday context, we explore the meaning of child hunger and the shame it causes.

In addition, we examine the biological and cultural aspects of child malnutrition to understand the systematic forces and misunderstandings that sustain them. Colonialism, Christianity, capitalism, and socialism have all played roles in the high rates of child malnutrition and in intensifying its stigma. Francis and Bibiana Lemas' problems with child malnutrition result not from the

~ Figure 2   *Francis Lema, in 1989*

backwardness ascribed to farming societies in less developed countries, we maintain, but from the relentless erosion of poor people's political power in the face of these institutions.

As we describe the Lemas' and other parents' struggles with their children's hunger, we analyze in depth the failure of a medical institution designed to prevent and treat child malnutrition. The Nutrition Rehabilitation Unit, NURU, was developed by experts who combined a biomedical approach with education in nutrition and agriculture, all based on an ideology of community participation. Although NURU saved lives, we examine its failure at malnutrition prevention to contribute to the growing work in institutional ethnography (Escobar 1995; Fiske 1989; Scott 1990). It is our hope that such a critique will contribute to the development of more culturally sensitive, inclusive, and sustainable approaches to the prevention of child malnutrition.

~ Figure 3   *Bibiana Lema with her daughter Nuya in 1974*

"These People": Constructing Kin as Other

The Lemas belong to a group known as the Chagga, a relatively prosperous farming people whose homeland is Mt. Kilimanjaro, Tanzania (Figure 5). Many Chagga are successful entrepreneurs, farming the fertile volcanic soil on the mountain and growing fine arabica coffee to be exported all over the world. They established one of the first farming cooperatives on the African continent in 1925 (Iliffe 1979:276–79). Through

～ Figure 4   *A View of Mt. Kilimanjaro.*   After Moore 1986:16

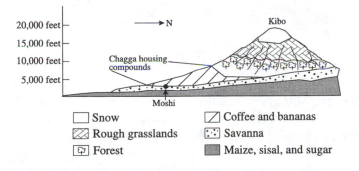

～ Figure 5   *Profile of Mt. Kilimanjaro.*

After Moore 1986:16
Kimberly Nickols

Christian mission schools, the Chagga became the most highly educated people in the country (Kerner 1988; see also Samhoff 1979), and many have entered professional positions and government service as a response to the growth of the population and an acute shortage of land. In spite of their prosperity, however, the Chagga have at times over the last thirty years had the highest rate of child malnutrition in Tanzania (Hai Nutrition Campaign 1987; Kreysler 1973; Lindner 1972; Shayo 1981; Women and Children in Tanzania 1990).

I first came to know the Lemas in 1974 during home visits for an evaluation of NURU. A team of Chagga researchers and I carried out the study, which took place during the height of a severe famine that devastated agriculture in most of East Africa. Known locally as the time of *njaa* (hunger), the famine disrupted the lives of everyone on the mountain. It was triggered by a long period of drought; a crippling disease of the main cash crop, coffee; a drop in world coffee prices; and global inflation. At the height of the famine, as many as fifty thousand households — 40 percent of those on the mountain — sought emergency food aid from the government (Swantz et al. 1975). People today still shudder as they recall the anguish of this period.

I went to Kilimanjaro in 1970 to do anthropological research on the causes of child malnutrition. It wasn't until the fourth year of my stay, during the NURU study, that I became fully aware of the impact of the shame and stigma associated with poverty and child malnutrition. One of my first insights into the social ostracism of impoverished families came from Gladys Kimario, a university-educated Chagga researcher whom I would replace on the study team. She decided that she had had enough of "these people." *Hawa watu* (these people) was a common referent to the poor — sometimes used by their own kin to convey a sense of distance or otherness from themselves. Mrs. Kimario, as she preferred to be called, took me and the principal investigator, Dr. Marja-Liisa Swantz, to meet some of the families in the study.

1974

〜 Mrs. Kimario seemed to be a knowledgeable and competent investigator, and she gave us a great deal of information on "the cases" I was about to inherit from her. She led us to a Roman Catholic mission in the upper reaches of one of the poorest districts on the mountain. We were introduced to some Church and government officials and then proceeded to the Lema family compound. We wanted to talk to Francis and Bibiana Lema about their son Hamisi, a six-year-old boy who had been treated at NURU.

As we approached their compound, Mrs. Kimario commented, "This family can't do anything right, and they don't seem to care. I'm tired of their backwardness and apathy! Come! I'll show you." Neither Francis nor Bibiana was home at the time. She led us into their house—an unthinkable intrusion on Kilimanjaro under most circumstances but apparently excusable in Mrs. Kimario's mind that day.

We entered the Lema house, which was an untidy mud structure with a roof thatched with banana leaves and patched with flattened tin cans. The doorway provided the only light inside the one-room house. At first, we could barely make out Hamisi, but eventually we saw that he was still malnourished after returning from NURU. His four brothers and sisters also had symptoms of malnutrition. The children whimpered for lack of camouflage in their barren surroundings as they scurried to escape the glare of the strangers who had so rudely entered their home.

A stench of urine coming from the children's bedding began to overwhelm us. We put our hands over our noses and mouths and left quickly. "This is outrageous!" Dr. Swantz said after we got out of earshot. She was shocked by the contrast with her pleasant memories of Mt. Kilimanjaro from years earlier, when she had worked as a teacher in one of the better-off districts on the mountain. She added sorrowfully, "What in the world could have caused this?"

Equally disturbing to her was the attitude of Mrs. Kimario toward impoverished members of her own community. Dr. Swantz hoped that face-to-face contact with poor people would encourage empathy in the university students and inspire them to find solutions for their problems. The students were supposed to work alongside poor women as equals and help them form income-generating cooperatives; in this way, their research would be in accord with the ideals of the socialist government. Dr. Swantz's strategy worked in most cases, but not in Mrs. Kimario's. Addressing a group of poor women at NURU, Mrs. Kimario had declared, "You embarrass me! Why are your children without food? Your laziness and ignorance are causing them to be ill! You can go out and earn wages and prevent malnutrition. You're giving all of Kilimanjaro a bad name!"

I would hear poor people publicly reprimanded in this manner many times by professionals and other better-off members of their community on Mt. Kilimanjaro. ⌁

The Human Face of Poverty

We tell the stories of people whose children were starving to illustrate their struggles with hunger and strategies for dealing with it. Drawn from field notes, recollections, diaries, and visits to the area over a twenty-five-year period, the stories include dialogue, emotion, and sketches of living

〜 Figures 6, 7, and 8   *Economic variation among neighboring Lema households*

〜 Figure 6   *Paulo and Sylvia Lema and their seven surviving children lived in the thatched house.*

〜 Figure 7   *Edwardi and Philippe Lema's compound with the cattle barn to the left (it was better built than most of the surrounding home's of Edwardi's kin).*

〜 Figure 8   *A typical modern house with cement blocks, tin roof, and glass windows. The Kilimanjaro people take pride in their flower and vegetable gardens.*

conditions to provide a sense of the social and psychological realities of child malnutrition. I include my own thoughts and feelings at times to illuminate the assumptions, motives, and actions of health planners, researchers, and medical staff as some of the many actors in this drama of human suffering.

Francis Lema's struggle takes center stage in several chapters—as the father in a patrilineal system in which the family wealth passes through males, Francis largely determined the fortunes of his household.[2] His wife, Bibiana, who was both pitied and held in contempt for the condition of her children, had less time available to assist me in the research process. She was too busy caring for her children and cultivating the family's food crops.[3] Francis worked as a day laborer at the Roman Catholic mission where I found lodging during the NURU study, and through proximity and personal compatibility, we became friends.

I saw that, in contrast to Mrs. Kimario's report, Francis and Bibiana were not apathetic about their children's health. The couple cared deeply for each other, their children, and neighbors who were also struggling with hunger and illness. Out of concern, they arranged meetings for me with families living in conditions they considered worse than their own.

They first took me to a clearing about a hundred yards from their house. There stood the small mud dwelling of Francis's first cousin, Nathaniel Lema, and his wife, Cecilia. I was stunned to learn that they had lost all five of their children.

The two couples later brought me to help their ailing cousin Paulo Lema, who lived next door. Paulo's wife, Sylvia, was pregnant with her thirteenth child, while the twelfth was malnourished and still unable to walk at two and a half years of age. Five of their children had died.

I accompanied all of the Lemas to the house of still another ailing neighbor, Lucas Towo, who could not afford medical treatment. Lucas was very ill, and he died shortly after my visit. Two of the four children in his home were severely malnourished and eventually died.

We take up the situations of the three Lema households and other impoverished families and their neighbors who lived close to the mission. We describe their histories, their connection to one another, and the reasons for their failure to prevent their children's deaths. Their failures resulted in part from their society's shift from subsistence farming and kinship-based social relations to a new way of life based on a cash economy and *maendeleo* (progress). Most of the Kilimanjaro people had ambitions to achieve *maendeleo* but lacked equal access to its material benefits.

The impoverished Lema families' homes were clustered near a sprawling house and farmyard owned by their wealthy first cousin, Edwardi Lema (see Figure 9). He owned four imported milk cows that lived luxuriously in comparison to his poor kin. He also owned a large coffee grove, and he was

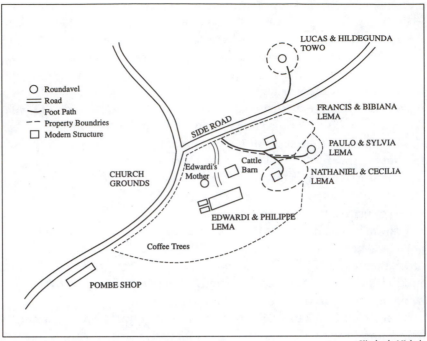

~ Figure 9   The Lema neighborhood

Kimberly Nickols

a local chairman of the coffee cooperative. The proximity of impoverished households to kin who were much better off presents a vivid example of economic extremes in a patrilineage. The good health of Edwardi's nine children and his plans to provide secondary education for all of them sharpened the contrast with his neighbors. He refused to speak with me and later threw his wife, Phillipe, out of the house when he found out she had become involved in my research.

Differing responses, such as those of Edwardi and Phillipe, to poorer neighbors' needs were common during the famine. Some better-off people, such as Phillipe, tried to help their poorer kin and neighbors. The Chagga community was still strongly integrated economically, and people still expected assistance from their kin, who often provided it during good times. Others, such as Edwardi, turned their backs even when their own relatives' children were slowly starving to death. Such a shocking deviation from Chagga cultural ideals begs explanation. Whereas short-term disasters may bring people of all income levels together, the time of *njaa* lasted for years and continued to cast a shadow over the impoverished that tested customs of mutual support among kin. In the period of food crisis, many sought to protect the members of their own households by denying assistance to poorer kin who had little to offer in return in the cash economy.

In this account, the actors are neither victims who are all pure of heart nor villains motivated solely by self-interest and greed.[4] The realities on Mt. Kilimanjaro defy such a simplistic formula. Some professional Chagga and other better-off neighbors were as outraged as Dr. Swantz about the development of abject poverty on Mt. Kilimanjaro and continued to battle it in spite of enormous obstacles. Occasionally, I also observed poor individuals seizing opportunities that might harm others while benefiting themselves. On the other hand, during the height of the food crisis, poor families could offer their time or labor in place of elusive money, and they often assisted one another. Francis Lema, for example, knew that I had some access to medical and government resources and that our friendship might benefit his family and his poorer kin.

Each day on my way to visit other families, I passed the Lemas' home and stopped to get their reactions to various issues. Francis had a penchant for reflecting on society and freely expounded on his ideas, partly in reaction to the daily troubles he faced. He seemed at times able to stand outside his own suffering, like a bystander at the scene of an accident. He wasn't simply passive, however; he also took action and prompted me to help organize poor men in the neighborhood into a commercial cooperative. Our experience with local Church officials and politicians involved in this effort provided me with fundamental insights into the barriers poor people face on a daily basis.

In spite of the scorn of some in the community, Francis struggled to maintain his hope and dignity and expressed no bitterness or resentment toward his wealthier relatives who lived next door. Instead, he was a model of compassion, and he taught me much about the problems of poverty and malnutrition from his perspective.

1989

∼ When I left Tanzania after my first stay, I was aware of child malnutrition as a complex, troubling, and enigmatic process. My return to Kilimanjaro in 1989 for an unrelated study was an opportunity to visit the families I had met two decades earlier.

While I waited for a bus to take me back up the mountain, my thoughts turned fondly to Francis and Bibiana. There had been another food crisis in 1984, and conditions in Tanzania had worsened in many ways during the 1980s. "Will they remember me?" I worried. "Who am I to have gotten involved in their problems only to disappear and then return, unannounced, years later?"

When I arrived at their house, I found Francis sitting outside on a mat. His feet were badly swollen.

"Dear God, where have you been?" he demanded as I approached him. His voice began to quiver, and tears moistened his eyes. Remembering to be hospitable, he then warmly stretched out both hands but skipped over the usual lengthy salutations.

"I'm sorry I can't stand to greet you. Sand fleas," he added immediately, and looked down at his feet. He was incapacitated by a sand flea infection. The stench drew flies to the oozing sores on his feet, swollen to twice their normal size. He could not walk unassisted. Without prompting, Francis began to describe his life, picking up the themes of our conversations of fifteen years earlier as if they had happened only the day before.

Francis's living conditions had deteriorated from years before. There were holes in the mud walls and the tin section of the roof had been replaced hastily with banana leaf thatch. As the primary provider of the family's food, Bibiana had no time to repair the house after working in the fields and caring for her husband and children. Francis's illness claimed a great deal of Bibiana's energy. She half-carried him when he went to the banana grove to relieve himself.

Referring to their children, Francis said, "Hamisi died, and so did Adija." Bibiana looked away at the mention of the names of their oldest son and daughter, who had died in spite of the efforts of all three of us to save them. Only the youngest child, a girl, experienced no apparent ill effects from the time of *njaa*.

The two surviving sons, curious about my visit, lounged in earshot next to their tiny makeshift sleeping quarters, a one-room house barely large enough for two people to lie down. Francis pointed to them and began to lament their situation. "Look at my sons. They have not grown as they should have," he exclaimed as they disappeared in embarrassment into their house.

I was startled at how stunted the two were. Remembering my own two sons born in East Africa years earlier, Francis continued, "How do they compare to your boys? *Mungu wangu* [My God]! What will be their chances in life when we can't afford to marry them off?" Before I could respond to his questions, for which I had no adequate answer, Francis added, "Can you tell me why this had to happen?"

When I said goodbye, I pressed a large sum of money into his hands to cover medical expenses and other needs—a gesture that would have embarrassed both of us fifteen years earlier but which provided relief for Bibiana, the boys, Francis, and me. ⌒

That day's encounter troubled me deeply. While he had graciously accepted my charity, the tone and substance of Francis's questions displayed the anger he may have felt years earlier. Francis had returned to his community in middle age after converting to Islam. In a solidly Catholic region of Mt. Kilimanjaro, he had acted humbly and tried to make a go of it. He had inherited a coffee farm from his father, and his acquiescent strategy may have helped him to keep his farm, even though his neighbors might want to buy him out.

When we traveled to Mt. Kilimanjaro in 1993 to visit the families who would appear in this book, we went first to the mission close by the Lemas' home. The parish priest informed us that "the poor pagan," Francis, had died of a sand flea infection and that we "shouldn't worry" because "he died after accepting Christ in baptism."

Clearly concerned about this tragic episode in his parish, the priest spoke with a tone of pity that nonetheless added to the social exception better-off people made of Francis over his lifetime. It saddened me, even as a Roman Catholic, to hear of Francis's religious acquiescence on his deathbed. I had vivid memories of Francis interacting with more-powerful people in an acquiescent manner while being quietly esteemed by his poorer kin for his wisdom and leadership. In the eyes of the larger community, Francis was never able to rid himself of the shame of his poverty and his children's malnutrition.

Hunger and Shame

The various explanations given by Francis and other Chagga during the period of *njaa* form the heart of our interpretation of the local significance of child malnutrition. Examinations of the history, political economy, social structure, culture, demography, and ecology of Mt. Kilimanjaro also enter into our interpretation (see also Huss-Ashmore and Katz 1989, 1990; Downs et al. 1991). We show how the social and economic safety net, or system of entitlements (Sen 1981), once provided by kinship obligations tore under the impact of twentieth-century political and economic change ushered in by European colonialism.

Throughout their history, the Chagga have been involved with the outside world. Beginning with trade with Arab caravans in the eighteenth century and continuing today with international tourists who come to climb Mt. Kilimanjaro, the Chagga are viewed as an enterprising and modern people. A population explosion increased the number of Chagga from a hundred thousand to almost a million during this century, contributing to a shortage of farmland (Gamassa 1991). Various pressures from the cash economy continue to widen the gap between better-off and poor and create vulnerability to global market fluctuations.

Education provides the primary escape route from dependence on farming for those who are unlikely to inherit enough farmland to support a household. Families who invest their cash in their children's education increase the likelihood that their children will have better-paid employment, yielding funds for remittances to aging parents. Some parents, though, cannot afford to send their children to school; they cannot purchase the basic supplies, clothes, and transportation to school, and they need their children's labor on the farm.

Demands for cash are driving the transition from subsistence farming to cash cropping and wage labor, creating a polarization of wealth and poverty. Though expanding, the scale of wealth is small compared with income disparity in the United States and Europe. In the 1970s, some Chagga, whom we refer to as "wealthy" or "better-off," were poor by U.S. standards. Edwardi's annual income, for example, was probably under $10,000. About 15 percent of the people at the top had incomes estimated to range from $1,000 to $6,000, which was considered ample when combined with subsistence farming. Such families were able to keep up investments in their coffee crop and could afford improved housing, imported commodities, perhaps a car or motorcycle, and more eduction for their children. Most people with middle incomes, estimated to be about $400 to $900 annually, shared the material ambitions of their better-off kin even though they were seldom able to realize them. The bottom 15% of the population, into which the households of Francis, Nathaniel, and Paulo fell, generally had little or no land, lived in housing made from freely gathered materials, and had incomes estimated to be below $300 a year.[5] Economic failure could force them to sell their land to kin and neighbors and become totally dependent on low wages earned at seasonal jobs in a society with intense fears of poverty and a shortage of farmland. In the 1990s, incomes have stagnated with the exception of the small fortunes of a few wealthy people who have amassed them from business ventures or remittances from well-educated children living overseas.

Means of escaping customary kin obligations derive from new values associated with being modern. Today, Chagga society has a variety of moral codes and social customs intensifying differences among people of different livelihoods, lineages, and regions on the mountain. This pluralism leads to varying standards for poor and wealthier people, but regardless of moral code, the shame and stigma of poverty contributes to social marginalization throughout Chagga society. Structures imposed from outside, including Christian churches, socialism, and capitalism, have not been effective substitutes for the old kinship safety net. While charitable organizations and government programs have a veneer of helpfulness, they fail to prevent poverty and sometimes even exacerbate it.

The shame of poverty is compounded by child malnutrition. Referred to locally as *kuvimba* (to swell) and "kwashiorkor," malnutrition in a child signifies many things, including the failure of parents to keep from having children in quick succession—a shameful lapse according to Chagga custom. Christianity, especially Roman Catholicism, is linked to reduced intervals between births and rapid population growth (Moore 1986:110), which has reduced the size of land holdings. We explore the ways in which customary and Christian beliefs are manipulated to blame the impoverished, and we examine the cultural meanings from which their shame is constructed.

Changing responsibilities of men and women have also accompanied the transition from a self-sufficient subsistence economy to a cash economy. These changes lead to confusion and ambiguity and often result in conflict between men and women and between generations (see Cook and Kerner 1989; Mbilinyi and Mbughuni 1991; Swantz 1985; Turshen 1991). Women are exhausted by taking on their husbands' tasks as men migrate in search of wage labor. This leaves little time and energy for child care, rendering some children, especially weanlings, vulnerable to illness. The tensions that arise out of these situations can result in alcoholism, curse, and accusations of sorcery, which are given as further explanations for *kuvimba*.

Child care under normal, everyday circumstances and explanations about the disfavored status of some malnourished children appear in ethnographic accounts about child care in the past (Gutmann 1926; Raum 1940). In a complex process, some children may become marginalized in their own families while their siblings thrive. My attempt to save a child brought to my attention by Francis illustrates the strengths and weaknesses of NURU and the inability of medical intervention to solve social problems.

A long period of reflection on my life on Mt. Kilimanjaro and my involvement with NURU and the families with malnourished children are the primary sources of my insights. As painful as many of these experiences were, I have attempted to be frank about my own misunderstandings in interactions with Chagga friends and neighbors. Through both the planning and evaluation of NURU, I sought to find a helping role in the midst of the food crisis and discovered the hard way that outsiders' solutions are often inappropriate for solving local problems (see also Dirks 1992; Escobar 1995; Feierman and Janzen 1992).

Though Francis Lema and most of his children have perished, he returns in the pages of this book as a gentle guide through the harsh realities of famine and want. The stories he and his neighbors and kin tell help us understand the forces on Mt. Kilimanjaro and those coming from abroad that continue to cause child malnutrition. They illuminate wider issues facing Tanzania and other developing countries—the legacy of colonialism, cultural pluralism, loss of kin entitlements,[6] competing ideologies of economic development, rapid population growth, and poverty. They also shed light on widespread responses to times of crisis when people either provide assistance or blame those who suffer. There are parallels to this story wherever wealth coexists with poverty.

Chapter Two

To the Mountain and an Early Confrontation with Death

⁓ Could anyone truly believe that I cursed a child and caused his death? His mother had been ignoring me, and I tried to warn her that the child's life was at stake. How could I have chosen the very words that, in local custom, cast a spell condemning him to die? ⁓

A year after my arrival on Mt. Kilimanjaro, an infant, Roberto, died at my small cooperative farm. Everyone, including me, was blamed. I was not immediately aware that I had cursed Roberto, but relations with my community became so strained that I was forced to confront aspects of Chagga culture that had been dismissed as superstitions by my educated Chagga friends. I was distraught over Roberto's death because I had frequently taken care of him, and I was angry and saddened that anyone could ascribe evil intent to me.

The accusation of sorcery was the last thing I could have imagined the previous year, as I was preparing to travel to Mt. Kilimanjaro with my husband, Tom Zalla. His major professor in agricultural economics had received a request from the Tanzanian government to study dairy farming in the Kilimanjaro region and asked him to do the project as his research for the Ph.D. degree. It was a great opportunity for both of us to live outside the United States and carry out research. We had read of *ujamaa* villages (government-sponsored rural socialist communities) and hoped to join one. The timing of the trip, however, was somewhat at odds with my own graduate program since it was too early in my studies to officially begin research for my Ph.D. degree. I intended to assist my husband in his study, carry out my own project, and start having children. In retrospect, I am not surprised that we took nearly five years to accomplish all this.

With my faculty committee, I planned to carry out a study without knowing for certain whether it would be my for Ph.D. Anthropologists, including my advisor, had been refused permission to do research in Tanzania; I hoped that government sponsorship of my husband's research would improve the chances of government clearance for my own study. In fact, I was relieved to leave campus, where classes were constantly disrupted because of political protests tied to the U.S. invasion of Cambodia. As a huge state university with tens of thousands of students and major involvement in counterinsurgency efforts in Vietnam (Hinckle et al. 1966), Michigan State University was a microcosm of the volatile and increasingly violent argument in our society. I looked forward to living in a country that aspired to peace, equality, and collective economic development. Julius Nyerere, the first president, was an eloquent spokesman for these ideals as he guided Tanzania through the early years of African socialism.

My readings about child health in less developed countries identified bottle feeding as leading to high rates of infant death. With widespread use of unsafe water and unsterilized bottles by the rural and urban poor, it was a deadly alternative to breastfeeding (Van Esterik 1989). In the literature on Tanzania, I found the paradox that the Kilimanjaro region had both the highest per capita income and the second highest rate of child malnutrition in the country. I developed a research proposal to study child illness and bottle feeding, and we left for Tanzania in 1970.

My field methods class had been interrupted by teach-ins, and I resolved to learn on my own in the field in Tanzania. I note my shortage of training not as a form of confession but to draw attention to my perspective as I began my research. My reaction to Roberto's illness and death reflect a naiveté typical of a well-intentioned student with a rather unsophisticated understanding of cultural dynamics, poverty, and malnutrition on the other side of the globe. My initial assumption that I would focus on a single, major cause of malnutrition was leavened by interactions with Chagga friends and study participants and by work with nutrition programs, and I began to develop a sense of the complexity of child malnutrition.

When we arrived in Tanzania, we first looked for an *ujamaa* village, a government innovation in which members were to collectively own and farm land granted by the Tanzanian government. We were surprised to find very few *ujamaa* villages on Mt. Kilimanjaro. As we discussed the possibility of living in one, our Chagga acquaintances responded to our inquiries with hostile remarks about the *ujamaa* concept and socialism in general.

True to our optimism, we decided to establish our own cooperative farm. We eventually found housing and land on an unoccupied coffee plantation recently bought by a Chagga woman and her British husband. We arranged to renovate the buildings in exchange for rent and invited acquaintances from Lucere, a neighboring community, to join the cooperative. Our first coresidents were Petro Kasulu, his wife, Ruth, and their three children. They had been managing the farm and living in the servants' quarters. They brought with them two boys, Salum and Pazi, who were fourteen and eleven years old and had been abandoned during a family conflict.

It seemed ideal to start a family while we lived in a farming community far from the tumult of the United States in the late 1960s. Our first son, Matthew, was born on Mt. Kilimanjaro two years after we arrived, and Christopher was born two and a half years later. Petro and Ruth became Matthew's godparents and later had two more children of their own. Another couple who moved in, Fatima and Mohammed Ruaha, were childless. Four teenage boys from distant villages also moved to the cooperative; we lived close to their school, allowing them to save time and bus fare. Over the years, ten more people moved to the farm, some for only a few months, others permanently. My family and I occupied the three-room guest house, and most of the others moved into the main house, which had been built during the German colonial period.

My experience had prepared me in some ways for the absence of privacy in cooperative life, but I lacked two essentials for working on Kilimanjaro: language and culture. Two languages were of major importance: Swahili and Chagga.[1] Swahili, having developed as an East African coastal and trade language, was becoming the dominant means of communication on Mt. Kilimanajaro, along with some other inland communities in Tanzania. On Kilimanjaro, Chagga was widely used; it was the only language of a few elders, but most of the younger people preferred to speak Swahili. Nowadays, many people throughout the region speak several languages as a result of formal schooling, migration, and intermarriage. I had studied Swahili at Michigan State University, and in fieldwork on Mt. Kilimanjaro I relied primarily on Swahili because most young people preferred it over Chagga. I learned a few words and phrases of greeting in Chagga but not enough to converse for long.[2]

My first year on the mountain, I taught in the International School, a private day school with classes in English for the children of foreign professionals who worked in local churches, hospitals, and economic development agencies. The job provided income to add to my husband's fellowships, given to support only one person. Teaching also gave me the opportunity to engage Chagga elders to visit some of my classes to teach about important aspects of their lives, but it removed me from developments in our cooperative to some degree and put me in the more familiar world of school and English for much of the week.

Strangely, my own ethnocentric biases were reinforced by many of my better-educated Chagga friends. When I arrived in Kilimanjaro, I was initially surprised by the many European and U.S. influences in Chagga dress, music, and religious orientation. It was quite a contrast with the image I had developed from old ethnographies. At first glance, the wealthy and educated seemed to be almost totally integrated into an urban mode of life. Both poorer people and well-to-do professionals chastised me for my tendency to take up the customs of Chagga farmers. "Are you trying to mock African culture?" a friend once asked when she found me working on our farm dressed in a *kanga* cloth. "Why don't you have servants when you can afford them?" I could walk a mile down the mountain to Shanty-Town, as the wealthy suburb of European, Asian, and African professionals and businessmen was called, and request a dry martini and my choice of stereophonic music at a number of well-furnished Chagga homes—a stark contrast to life in most mountain households, where socializing took place outside the simple adobe-and-grass abodes used for sleeping and housing cattle.

It was in the wealthier homes, though, that I was initially taught Chagga manners. For example, I learned that it was rude to ask people how many children they had and that one does not usually speak during meals (although many wealthy people did). Friends took pride in teaching me how to prepare Chagga cuisine and in displaying their hand-carved wooden Chagga bowls for serving food onto plates of fine china. After-dinner conversations ranged over Kilimanjaro history and critical reflections on local events. Although highly educated people insisted that what they called "superstitions" had disappeared, some probably spoke out of sensitivity to their *wazungu* (European, white) guests.

It would take a long time for me to understand how remnants of older knowledge continued to shape the present. Furthermore, I naively expected people to follow their own rules. I thought that customs would assure predictability, and I became frustrated when someone would tell me what was expected and then turn around and do the opposite. Even though I was fully aware of my own society's contradictions and ambiguity, the challenge of learning and following new sets of rules diverted my attention from cultural variation on Kilimanjaro. Life, however, would soon become even more complex. My first shattering lesson came with Roberto's death.

A Child Dies

Living in the cooperative, I was in daily contact with poor people, and they brought all the problems of poverty with them. Child malnutrition and death became a personal experience, collapsing the boundary between me and my research. Roberto was a child born at our cooperative at an unfortunate time and under difficult circumstances. His story begins with his aunt, Fatima.

Roberto's story, 1970

∼ Fatima Ruaha was a husky, outgoing woman with a deep, authoritative voice and a great deal of self-assurance. She and her husband, Mohammed, had been working on a *shamba* (field) belonging to her cousin, who lived a mile away in Shanty-Town. Mohammed, a poor Muslim immigrant from Dodoma, had no farmland of his own. Perhaps simply because of her friendly, vibrant nature or perhaps to gain some future advantage, Fatima decided to be my teacher.

Initially I enjoyed her generous spirit and vitality, as I had become lonely and had few women friends in the local community. Fatima spent hours working on my Swahili and teaching me gardening methods suitable to the hilly terrain and soil. In the local markets, Fatima taught me how to bargain and how to become a favored client of certain vendors. As friends do, we shared many intimate details of each other's lives and tended to support each other, sometimes in opposition to our husbands, during our cooperative's judicial meetings. Fatima had an infectious laugh and an ability to get me to see humor in my own failings. An outsider to her own community, she somehow had come to identify with me, and I with her, but our friendship was short-lived.

"*Ayee!* Why are you throwing this away?" Fatima demanded one day as she sorted through a burning trash pile while I hung laundry out to dry. She had just retrieved a couple of glass jars and some tin cans. The jars would be valuable for storage and the cans could be fashioned into little lanterns.

"You mustn't be so wasteful, *Mama* Maria![3] What else do you have that you want to pitch out? Oh, that reminds me, Mohammed and I want to use your radio—only when you're not listening, of course. We'll take good care of it. Give it to me; please, give me your radio."

Her requests became incessant. I had imagined myself to be poor, and according to the standards of my own society, I was. On the other hand, Tom and I wore watches and had a motor scooter, a radio, and other material belongings that made us seem well-off on Kilimanjaro. I was not as thrifty as other better-off people on the mountain, and Fatima may have thought me loosely attached to all my property. She started helping herself to food from our cupboard and even clothes from my closet. I had little understanding of rules governing exchanges on Kilimanjaro and gave in to her requests until they became too much. Her demands grew, and our relationship began to deteriorate. Then she brought her pregnant sister, Anna, to stay at the farm.

Fatima and Anna both had suffered the deaths of many children. Fatima was childless after eight pregnancies, some having reached term only to be followed by early deaths. Anna had a five-year-old daughter, Rosa, but had lost five other children. Both women had unstable relationships with men. The man involved with Anna, who was not Rosa's father, came to visit Anna at the cooperative a few times but disappeared late in her pregnancy.

Anna gave birth to Roberto, and she soon complained of having no breast milk. As she was not to breastfeed Roberto, Fatima came forward to care for him. Meanwhile, Anna made frequent trips to town to tend to her business of making and selling *pombe* (beer made from bananas and millet; *mbege*).

Fatima seemed delighted to take responsibility for Roberto, but her attention wandered. When she was with him, she focused on him intensely and affectionately and even took the trouble to teach Rosa how to handle her baby brother. Roberto often ended up on my living room couch, however, with only Rosa and me to look after him. Other responsibilities competed for Fatima's time, leaving Roberto with no consistent caretaker. After a while, I noticed that Roberto had a foul odor, in part because his clothing always needed changing, but also because he had chronic diarrhea, which was beginning to alarm me.

"What are you doing?" I asked Fatima as she helped herself to the milk in my refrigerator. I had become accustomed to sharing much of the food in my house and making sure there was enough milk for the baby.

"The baby's hungry, can't you see? Now, I'll pour a little milk, like so. Uh-huh. And then I add a little water, like so. Good. I'm ready."

"But you can't do that! We have to boil the water first and then sterilize the bottle. That water comes straight from the irrigation ditch. I get sick even if a little bit gets in my mouth while I'm showering!"

"Oh, you *wazungu* have such soft stomachs!"

I was becoming distressed with Fatima's way of preparing the baby bottle. It was exactly as I had read in the library—whole cow's milk poured into a dirty bottle and diluted with unboiled water. But Fatima was not persuaded.

"What do you know of our ways? Didn't the rains flood your garden, just as I predicted? What do you know about children, anyway?" she asked while eyeing the little bulge of my early pregnancy. Fatima then confidently placed the nipple on the bottle and began to ease away from our crowded kitchen to avoid any further exchange. It was clear that she resented my intrusion and the implication that she lacked competence.

I was growing impatient, and finally, in exasperation, I said, "*Fatima, utaona. Mtoto ata kufa usipochemsha maji na chupa* [Fatima, you will see.

The baby will die if you don't boil the water and the bottle]!" Her eyes widened. She stood stunned in momentary silence. Then, looking right through me, she picked up Roberto and left the house.

Unknowingly I had spoken a powerful Chagga curse. I learned later that merely saying the words "you will see" is enough to put a curse on a person, inviting some future, unnamed misfortune. Unfortunately, I had also made the curse specific and, from a Chagga point of view, I had threatened Roberto with death.

It was questionable whether most people believed that I had put a curse on Roberto; they were aware that *wazungu* lacked understanding of Chagga ways. The intensity of the conflict growing between Fatima and me was, nevertheless, typical of situations that escalated toward accusations of curse, evil eye, witchcraft, and sorcery. The conflict eventually weakened Roberto's makeshift family—Anna, Fatima, and me—as he became sicker.

We could not ease his crying, and the tension it produced was visible on our faces. Anna took him to the hospital, but his condition only worsened. He seemed to withdraw from us because carrying him only caused him pain; his body was swollen and tender from malnutrition. With a sense of his approaching death, we also began to pull away from him. There was no pleasure in trying to cuddle a sick and unhappy infant.

Anna finally took him to her *pombe* shop in Moshi. The next day, Katrina, Anna's and Fatima's cousin and the owner of our farm, visited me early in the morning. "I'm so sorry to tell you, Mary," she said while softly weeping, "but the baby just died. I've come to fetch you for his burial."

I felt numb. In a short while, we were on our way to the southern end of Moshi town. We entered a tiny house where Anna had been struggling to manage a *pombe* shop financed by Katrina. Roberto's body was wrapped in his blanket on top of the kitchen table. Katrina had brought some fine white cloth used for binding the dead, and as we uncovered the corpse she gasped at his changed appearance.

"What a horrible, horrible tragedy that we bury this little one without the benefit of baptism. This didn't need to happen," she said to me in English while wiping away her tears.

With these words, I began to weep openly with the others and kept repeating to Katrina, "I'm sorry. I'm so sorry."

"But it's not your fault, my dear. *Hi ni shauri ya Mungu* [these are the affairs of God]." Without saying anything else, Katrina glanced knowingly in Anna's direction, suggesting her complicity as well.

At the burial, Fatima wailed over Roberto's grave, and we could not pull her away. We left her there to spend the day in grief. Somehow Fatima absorbed responsibility for Roberto's death, while Anna, his biological mother, was saddened but seemed resigned and shed few tears. As an unwed mother, aware of the stigma of giving birth to an illegitimate son, she had formed only a loose tie to her infant.

Katrina had assisted Fatima in taking Roberto to the clinic and had helped Anna get established in a business, yet Katrina and I both felt a nagging sense that we could have done something more. Neither of us had an adequate explanation for our reluctance to take extraordinary measures to save Roberto. Perhaps we projected our anger toward Anna and Fatima to mask our own sense of failure.

Over the following months, my relationship with Fatima continued to deteriorate until we no longer spoke. Fatima became hostile toward our cooperative. She stopped cleaning up after herself in the common rooms, and she harvested and sold some of our crops and pocketed the money. She even went so far as to steal eggs from the schoolboys' hens. She upset everyone in the cooperative, especially me.

I could no longer tolerate it and called for a *baraza* (judicial meeting) of our community. The father of one of the schoolboys was visiting, and I requested that he moderate the meeting, partly because he was a *balozi* (neighborhood leader). The evening before the *baraza*, I was snacking on roasted maize while discussing the day to come with Aloisi, the *balozi*'s son, and another boy.

"I've really had it with Fatima! I'm going to confront her tomorrow in the *baraza*."

"No, no, *Mama* Mary," they responded excitedly.

"Why not? Maybe she'll mend her ways."

"Oh, but *Mama* Mary," Aloisi said, glancing about to make sure no one could hear, "Fatima is a witch! You see, some people can do bad things. I've seen others get hurt. Speaking at the *baraza* like that would not be wise, if you don't mind my saying so."

"I'm not going to be intimidated," I thought.

The next day, with the whole community present, a round of introductions was made and Aloisi's father began the proceedings. The first half hour was filled with the usual business about the community's needs while I daydreamed about my wishes to be more assertive. Suddenly I raised my hand and blurted out with growing force, "Fatima has been my friend. Yet lately she has been causing problems, including theft from our farm. This is no way to show friendship!" I felt great relief after my remarks and glanced about to see how everyone else was reacting. They all sat with eyes cast downward while the room grew silent.

Mohammed, Fatima's husband, patiently tried to mediate. "Perhaps *Mama* Maria is having these strong feelings because of her condition [pregnancy]. As we all know, such women are *kali* [strict, sharp, powerful, mean] beyond their control. Surely things are not quite so bad." After

Mohammed broke the silence, much discussion ensued in which others began to support my claims. Eventually, Fatima broke down and admitted to the thefts.

It was decided that she would have to leave the community and stay away for four months, the two months before my baby's birth and two months after. She was deeply distressed by the decision, and the members of the farming cooperative agreed to help her and Mohammed make a temporary home not far away. A few days later, Fatima had a violent argument with her husband and went into a trance, chanting as if possessed by spirits. They finally moved on Christmas Day, and Fatima joined others in drinking *pombe* in Lucere. ⌒

At the time, I had a defensive response to Roberto's death, partly as an effort to project the blame onto someone else. I blamed Anna and Fatima. As I had originally hypothesized for my research, a dirty baby bottle was involved; few precautions had been taken to keep Roberto's bottle from becoming a source of infection. His death, however, also brought me to confront poverty, social instability, emotional conflict, sorcery, and ideas about the power of a Chagga curse.

Anna had been unable to care for Roberto herself; her involvement in the *pombe* trade in Moshi town took all her time and attention. Selling *pombe* was her way of making a living; as a single mother, she had little choice. Anna had no access to farmland because she had no husband, and farmland usually passes through male lines. New mothers usually receive assistance from their mothers- and sisters-in-law; lack of a husband left Anna without this form of support as well.

Fatima's attempt to help her sister by giving her a home in the last months of pregnancy and taking responsibility for Roberto were generous, but she was severely handicapped by her approach to bottle feeding, which became the source of Roberto's life-threatening infection. Her disdain for my advice should not have been so surprising to me. I had chastised her on the basis of my approach to child health which came from the biomedical paradigm and conflicted with local Chagga knowledge (and with most other cultures around the world). It is doubtful whether Fatima could have taken advice on an issue as serious as Roberto's illness from someone in my situation, with no official medical position, no experience as a mother, and seeming incompetence because of my immature knowledge of Swahili and of Chagga culture. Anna had taken Roberto to the hospital, but it had failed her. I eventually realized that the cause of Roberto's death was far more complex than bottle feeding.

An intense drama had begun around Roberto's illness, when Fatima began to fight with us and victimize our community. Her actions only caused her more trouble, though, as the community blamed her for Roberto's death and required that she leave because of ongoing conflicts. She was surrounded by an atmosphere of stigma, failure, and hostility.

Fatima's Revenge

〜 The day after Christmas, I met Christina, a woman who came to visit our household for the first time. She had been drinking *pombe* the night before with Fatima, who had just moved from the cooperative. At the time, I did not suspect that Fatima might be using Christina for revenge. On her visit, Christina acted *kichaa* (crazy), and Katrina and I took her to the hospital, where she was admitted with the diagnosis of acute alcoholic psychosis. She seemed to have a special affinity for me, as she frequently touched me while she spoke nonsensically in German, English, Chagga, and Swahili. In the hospital, she shadowed my every step, bumping into me whenever I stopped walking. At the time, I was not particularly worried, as I had worked with many people with psychiatric disturbances in the United States. I took Christina's affinity as confirmation that my talent for dealing with mental illness transcended cultural barriers.

We left her at the hospital, but that evening she showed up on my doorstep. She was speaking in tongues one moment and catatonically rigid the next. We persuaded her to stay in a nearby house for the night, and the next day her husband joined a group of us to take her home, eight miles up the mountain. We talked her into the trip by telling her that the visit would be brief. Some time after our arrival, the others sneaked into the car with me while Christina was behind the house with her father. When she heard the motor start, she ran toward us and with a final burst of speed lunged against the window with a vicious look on her face. With relief, we left her behind.

Later that night, I awoke to the sound of something hitting the tin roof. It went *ping, ping,* in an odd pattern. My husband got up to investigate whether someone was throwing pebbles onto our roof. He slowly opened the porch curtains and peered into the darkness. Suddenly, he found himself face-to-face with Christina. They both screamed and ran in opposite directions. Tom and I shouted, "We'll call the police if you don't leave us alone!" After a sleepless night, I found my doorstep littered with objects that Christina must have left: flower petals, charcoal, coffee beans, and stones. Someone had already taken her home again.

A week later, as I was picking lilies by the irrigation ditch, Christina appeared in the distance, coming toward me. She carried an iron pipe in one hand and a rag bundle in the other.

"What do you want now?" I asked her without any greeting. I felt especially vulnerable, as I was in my ninth month of pregnancy.

She kept approaching without saying a word. Suddenly she raised the pipe as if to strike me; I screamed, and Christina abruptly fell to her back on the ground with her legs sticking straight up in the air. Thinking that perhaps I had misinterpreted her gesture, I walked toward her. As I approached she jumped up, opened her bundle, and thrust it toward my face. Again I screamed, and everyone at the farm came running. In later discussions, community members explained that Christina attempted to cast a spell on me because she had been bewitched by Fatima. ⌒

Fatima seemed to be the center of a cyclone of threat and tragedy striking Roberto, me, the rest of the cooperative, and now Christina. The relentless swirl of months of bad fortune, despite Fatima's early efforts to be a generous teacher, sister, and aunt, began to shock me into a different way of seeing child malnutrition.

Reflections

Unlike most Chagga children, who are born to a mother and father bound in marriage in a household with a stable livelihood and a large kin network ready to welcome a young relative, Roberto was born at a disadvantage. He was, however, more typical of malnourished children, with his birth into poverty, the chaotic life of his mother, his inadequate care, and the caretakers' actions that inadvertently exposed him to infection. It was also typical that his relatives' attempt to use biomedicine was unsuccessful because of inappropriate services and insufficient understanding. Mothers often resisted advice from relatives, and relatives were reluctant to intercede. Talk of curse and sorcery was frequent, as was blaming parents, especially the mother, for a child's illness.

Memories of Roberto, 1996

⌒ Many aspects of Roberto's story perplex me to this day. I have tried to assuage my Irish Catholic guilt over his death by reminding myself that at the time, I was a full-time teacher and had many responsibilities on the farm. I knew all along, however, that I resented Anna's presence. I suspected that Fatima, taking my husband's jokingly stated appreciation for women seriously, might have brought her sister to the cooperative with the hope that Anna would establish a liaison and gain financial support. It never grew beyond a flirtation but nevertheless, I felt threatened and resentful, and I saw later that my feelings had affected my relationship with Roberto.

I took his death as confirmation of the danger posed by the baby bottle, and I dwelt on it out of a need to impose clarity on an emotionally confusing situation. I developed a missionary fervor about cleanliness and the importance of breastfeeding. My zeal continued through 1972, as my firstborn son, Matthew, began to crawl and get his first teeth; he was putting all he could find into his mouth.

I made every effort to ensure an aseptic floor for my son to explore, and I washed the house's cement floor and the walk outside daily. People sometimes jokingly referred to me as *Mama Fagia* (Mama Sweeper). I would often sit outside and admire the view of Mt. Kilimanjaro while Matthew played, and on one of our outings, my son reached down and picked something up from the gravel drive. Before I could stop him, he put it in his mouth. I rushed to retrieve what I assumed would be a stone and was shocked to find instead a large lump of goat dung. ∽

These events, ranging from the tragic to the ludicrous, began to undercut my firm conviction that children had to be isolated from all sources of infection. I found myself pondering the tendency to blame mothers when that effort failed. More importantly, I began to appreciate that malnutrition could not be explained simply by one factor alone. A multitude of causes embedded in world events, local culture, and the economic and emotional stability of the family would come to shape my view of child malnutrition.

Child Malnutrition

Scientific understanding of child malnutrition has developed largely over the last sixty years. In earlier times in Europe, the death rate of children was high, and most people saw it as natural. Some viewed rates as high as 50 percent during the Industrial Revolution as a form of population control that operated mostly on the lower class in a Malthusian fashion (Scheper-Hughes 1987:1).

In 1855 the British Registrar General spoke of high urban levels of child sickness and death as "wasting" (Scheper-Hughes 1987:1). Early scientific descriptions of kwashiorkor, the most common form of severe malnutrition on Mt. Kilimanjaro, include the work of Patron Correa in Mexico in 1908 (Torun and Viteri 1988:746–747) and of Procter in Kenya in 1926, when he described a "nutritional edema of unknown cause":

> The disease occurs only in quite young children; the child is nearly always of an extraordinary light color and is usually brought up on account of swelling of the feet. The only history obtainable appears to be that in a number of cases there has been slimy motions [bowel movements] for some time. As the disease progresses, the child becomes pale in color and the pigment seems to be concentrated into a curious black desquamation which is often noticeable on the arms and legs. The child, as far as my information goes, nearly always dies. (Procter 1926:284)

Early descriptions of the signs and symptoms of kwashiorkor were fairly accurate. In their struggle to understand the condition, physicians postulated a variety of causes of kwashiorkor: tropical parasites, congenital syphilis, "edema disease" (McConnel 1918), "fatty liver disease" (Waterlow 1948), and pellagra (a disease from deficiency of B vitamins and other nutrients) (Torun and Viteri 1988). In 1935, Williams, a physician working with the Ga people of what is now Ghana, adopted their term, kwashiorkor, meaning "the sickness the older child gets when the next baby is born" (Williams 1935; see also Torun and Viteri 1988). The Ga people and Williams thus characterized the disease as related to weaning or late infancy. Noting the variation in symptoms, she later wrote:

> It is, in fact, rarely possible to see a clear cut case of one specific nutritional deficiency. Most cases that one sees are of non-specific conditions usually mixed in manifestations and in etiology, often mild or marginal and differ greatly according to the stage that the disease has reached when observations are first made. (Williams 1973:335)

In the past, scientists thought that protein deficiency caused the puffy skin, oozing sores, and swollen bellies of children with kwashiorkor. They thought that caloric deficiency caused marasmus, giving children the wasted, skin-and-bones appearance familiar in images of widespread, devastating famine. These theories were too simplistic, however (Torun and Chew 1994); presently, kwashiorkor and marasmus are seen as different syndromes of protein-calorie malnutrition (Torun and Viteri 1988), because deficits of protein and calories occur together, not in isolation. Furthermore, marasmus can turn into kwashiorkor or the reverse, and both syndromes also can occur together. On Mt. Kilimanjaro, kwashiorkor is the most common syndrome. Nowadays, it is technically known as "edematous protein-calorie malnutrition" (Torun and Viteri 1988), but we refer to it as kwashiorkor in conformity with widespread usage on the mountain.

Kwashiorkor is a deceptive form of malnutrition; it often has a slow onset, and most of its symptoms can also occur in other diseases. Its main symptom is edema, causing the puffy skin on the child's arms, legs, and face that can give a child the appearance of being plump (Golden 1985; Viteri and Torun 1980).[4] A thumb pressed down on the skin, however, will leave a visible dent; the skin does not spring back as on a healthy person, and the child may have wasted muscles underneath the appearance of plumpness. The fluid retained in the puffy skin raises a child's weight, often to a point misleadingly close to the weight of a healthy child (Torun and Viteri 1988). A swollen belly, partly from an enlarged liver, is another deceptive symptom implying that the child does not lack food.

In kwashiorkor, a child's skin often breaks out in sores that do not heal quickly, and it peels off "in large scales, exposing underlying tissues that are easily infected" (Torun and Viteri 1988:758). A sign of severe kwashiorkor is a "moon face," caused by edema. The child's hair becomes dry and brittle and pulls out easily without pain; the hair lightens, sometimes developing a blond stripe called a "flag sign," from depigmentation (Torun and Viteri 1988:759). A child with kwashiorkor is often quiet and passive, becoming irritable when approached.

In cases of protein-calorie malnutrition, the food given to children is insufficient for both health and growth. Under these circumstances, growth is the first sacrifice made by a child's body. Loss of muscle tone and strength make a child apathetic. In kwashiorkor, these problems are compounded by a child's loss of appetite and tendency to vomit after eating (Torun and Viteri 1988:758). Gastrointestinal infection is often a complicating factor that interferes with normal physiology and, in many cases, causes diarrhea, worsening malnutrition. For all of these reasons, once kwashiorkor develops, it tends to get worse.

Moderate malnutrition can rapidly change into a state of severe malnutrition, threatening children's lives; they may continue in that state for months or die quickly from a disease that tips the balance. In children with severe protein-calorie malnutrition, mortality rates can reach 40 percent, decreasing to 10 percent or less with adequate treatment (Torun and Viteri 1988:761). If a child survives a long period of malnutrition, its growth will be permanently stunted (Eveleth and Tanner 1990:195).

Each year in less developed countries, 12.7 million children die before reaching their fifth birthday (Grant 1993:i), and malnutrition is implicated in 68 percent of those deaths (Hull and Rohde 1978).[5] When a child is malnourished, ordinary childhood diseases become killers; for example, measles kills 880,000 children annually in less developed countries (Grant 1993:7).

In more developed countries, improved living conditions, public health measures, and biomedicine have eliminated many diseases. The result is that "tropical diseases," which have only recently been limited to less developed countries, are assumed to be a "natural" part of life there (see Turshen 1984; also Feierman and Janzen 1992; Franke and Chasin 1992).[6]

It is not "tropical diseases," however, that make life dangerous for young children. In less developed countries, measles, which is a worldwide disease, kills more children than does malaria (Grant 1993), now limited to the tropics.

Though a mundane measure compared with high-technology vaccination, providing adequate nutrition would dramatically improve child survival in nearly every less developed country. The tropics thus are only the stage for the massive tragedy of death in early life, not the cause of it. The inequitable distribution of food is the main cause of high rates of child death in the tropics, not disease ecology.

Protein-calorie malnutrition annually affects an estimated 30 percent of children in Africa under the age of five years (Grant 1993). It is most common among young children and infants because they have relatively high requirements for protein and energy, "cannot obtain food by their own means and, when living under poor hygienic conditions, they frequently become ill with diarrhea and other infections" (Torun and Viteri 1988:748). Severe protein-calorie malnutrition, which is life-threatening, affects approximately 3 percent of young children in Asia, Africa, and Latin America (Torun and Viteri 1988:748), approximately one tenth of the percentage of those with "moderate malnutrition." Malnutrition in general threatens the lives of many children in less developed countries as a result of global, regional, and local inequality in food distribution.

Malnutrition on Mt. Kilimanjaro

Over the past twenty-five years, surveys of young children have shown rates of malnutrition on Mt. Kilimanjaro to be among the highest in Tanzania. The contrast between Kilimanjaro's high rates of malnutrition and the Chagga people's success in education and commerce is striking. The argument that we present in this book is that during the latter half of this century, high rates of malnutrition have plagued the poorest segment of the Kilimanjaro population, reflecting the widening gap between wealthy and poor on the mountain.

The backdrop of this argument is the economic situation of Tanzania, which has faced considerable financial difficulties over recent decades, along with other East African countries (see Appendix A for comparisons of Tanzania, Kenya, Malawi, the United Kingdom, and the United States, nos. 4, 6–10). In 1990, Tanzania was one of the poorest countries in East Africa in gross national product per capita. In 1989, only 1 in 1,000 people in Tanzania had a television, an eloquent contrast with the United Kingdom (434 televisions) and the United States (814). Tanzanian

Table 1 *Nutritional Status of Children Less than Five Years Old in the Kilimanjaro Region, 1964–1988*

Year measurements were taken and location	description	MALNUTRITION severe	total
1988[a]			
Kilimanjaro Region	221,736 children	5.9%	32.2%
1987[b]			
Kilimanjaro Region	4,105 children	8.4%	26.0%
Hai District[c]		3.5%	34.0%
1985[d]			
Kilimanjaro Region	327 children		
Hai District	(see d below)	11.1%	25.4%
Moshi Rural District		7.5%	26.6%
Rombo District		12.0%	38.4%
1981[e]			
Kilimanjaro Region	502 children (see e below)		47.2%
1972[f]			
Under-five clinics, Kilimanjaro Region	418 children	2.0%	22.0%
1967[g]			
Bukoba District		3.0%	12.0%
Dodoma District		4.0%	22.0%
Kilimanjaro District		5.0%	26.0%
Tabora District		1.0%	8.0%
1964[h]			
Kilimanjaro Region	211 children	2.0%	64.0%

Weights for age standards are not always specified in these studies, but generally Tanzanian researchers used the Harvard School of Public Health standard.

[a] Source: Kilimanjaro Regional Development Director's Office, 1991, citing Regional MCH Report.

[b] Source: Hai Nutrition Campaign 1987.

[c] Source: Women and Children in Tanzania 1990.

[d] Source: District Executive Director's Office, Rombo and Tanzania Food and Nutrition Center, 1986. "Severe malnutrition" is explicitly defined as <2 standard deviations below the median weight for age in the standard; total includes all children ≤2 standard deviations below the median.

[e] Source: Shayo 1981; malnutrition was ≤ 80% of the standard weight for age.

[f] Source: Lindner 1972; see also Appendix B. In this case, severe malnutrition means that the child has symptoms of kwashiorkor.

[g] Source: Kreysler 1973:21, from surveys between 1965 and 1968.

[h] Source: Women and Children in Tanzania 1990.

maternal and child health has improved greatly since independence, although it is still quite poor compared with more developed countries.

Table 1 shows rates of child malnutrition on Mt. Kilimanjaro between 1964 and 1988. Variation among rates reflects fluctuations over time, regional differences on the mountain, and different definitions of malnutrition in different studies. The 1988 study gives a rate of malnutrition of 32.3 percent in a sample of 221,736 children, large enough to dismiss problems of sampling bias.

Over the two decades shown in Table 1, 2 percent to 12 percent of children less than five years of age were severely malnourished.[7] These rates are high enough to be considered cause for alarm and intervention. Severe malnutrition is a life-threatening state, whereas moderate malnutrition usually means that children weigh considerably less than healthy children of their age but are not yet moribund. From 1964 to 1988, the rate of severe and moderate malnutrition combined ranged from 26 percent to 64 percent of children less than five years of age—about one quarter to two thirds of young children on Mt. Kilimanjaro.

Malnutrition usually strikes hardest after weaning. Breastfeeding provides the ideal nutrition for an infant for the first six to eight months of life; it also conveys maternal antibodies that enhance infant resistance to infection (Jelliffe and Jelliffe 1978; Van Esterik 1989). In the 1970s, most women on Kilimanjaro weaned their children in the second year of life or later (see Appendix B). In many households, infants would have experienced mixed feeding—breast milk and other foods—for some period of time; their mothers usually left them at home in someone else's care while they worked through the day in the fields. Weaning often marks a transition to a more precarious health status. The problems can be serious in the poorest households, where there is neither enough food nor enough time to feed a young child adequately.

At first glance, Kilimanjaro's record in child malnutrition contrasts with the strong record of the Chagga in education, agriculture, commerce, and government service. For example, in 1967, although the Chagga people comprised only 3.6 percent of the national population, 12.4 percent of the secondary school students were Chagga. Of students attending the University of Dar es Salaam in 1972, 33 percent were from the Kilimanjaro region (Samoff 1974; see also Ishumi 1980). In the 1970s, the area received 60 percent of the dairy cattle that were imported into Tanzania and produced about 30 percent of Tanzania's coffee, a principal export (Zalla 1982).

This successful record obscures the problems of impoverished Chagga households. Although Chagga students have impressive achievements, many of Kilimanjaro's children do not go far in school (less than 10 percent stayed in school for more than eight years in 1972; see Appendix B, nos. 3, 7,

9, and 13). Many grow up to live in poverty. (Although 68 percent of men were full-time farmers in 1972, 62 percent of those living in the middle belt of Mt. Kilimanjaro had one acre of farmland or less.) Chagga farmers clearly are vulnerable to hunger, as evident in the 1972–74 economic and environmental crises in East Africa, when a drop in coffee prices, rapid world inflation, and coffee berry disease hit the Kilimanjaro area.

The drought on Kilimanjaro began in 1972 and led to the famine of 1973 through 1975, when severe malnutrition rose to affect 40 percent of children under five years of age. Food relief was sought by fifty thousand households, estimated to be about one fourth of the Mt. Kilimanjaro population. It was the most severe food crisis in past decades and was not surpassed by subsequent crises that occurred in 1984 and 1994. According to numerous studies, child malnutrition on Mt. Kilimanjaro has varied from substantial rates to crisis levels over the past two decades; while various programs and government efforts have saved lives, they have not succeeded in eliminating the problem.

Involvement with Research and Medical Treatment of Malnutrition on the Mountain

After Roberto's death, I was driven to try to make sense of it and other aspects of a confusing first year on Kilimanjaro. I renewed my aim of improving child health and initiated discussions with health experts and Chagga friends about the causes of Roberto's death. I got a position as a consultant in the Community Health and Pediatric Departments of a large regional hospital, Kilimanjaro Christian Medical Center. Through this affiliation, I joined a research team and took the first step toward government clearance for my own Ph.D. research. Life on the farm continued to give me valuable insights that helped to inform team investigations.

I started consulting for the Medical Center just as innovations were being devised to end child malnutrition. Later, I realized that this effort helped to set the world standard for decades to come and still remains an ideal for many health planners. Those who made the innovations at the Medical Center were physicians from Scandinavia and Germany. The major innovations of the hospital were mobile child health clinics to improve access, a nutrition center (NURU) to treat and prevent child malnutrition, and ongoing research to provide a basis for improving these programs. These endeavors were based partly on successful projects in other countries and partly on several assumptions that we soon had to question.

NURU aimed to prevent and cure child malnutrition through several programs. Children who were on the verge of death were hospitalized and given intravenous treatment. Children who were seriously malnourished but not moribund were to be housed at NURU until they had returned to good health. Treatment at NURU avoided medicines and medical technology, instead emphasizing the importance of food in healing the child. Staff members thought it important to counter the notion that the symptoms came from a disease that could be stopped by medicines or more dramatic biomedical treatment.

Mothers of children in NURU were required to live there to learn to how to prevent child malnutrition. Two large, whitewashed concrete buildings were erected, one to house mothers and children, the other for teaching and offices. Each mother-child pair would stay at NURU until the child's full recovery, in about three to six weeks. In a typical day, a woman would carry out the domestic activities necessary for herself and her child, including cooking, washing clothes, and cleaning the premises. The main focus of the program for the women, however, was on cooking demonstrations, nutrition, and preventing sickness. NURU also had gardens and rabbit and poultry houses, where women were required to work to learn new farming techniques and to assist in supporting the center. Agricultural experts came regularly to give women advice and to monitor their work, and volunteers from the community taught sewing. The women also occasionally sat about and shared their life stories with one another and the staff.

NURU's planners intended the program to approximate normal Chagga life and to present concepts of health, nutrition, and gardening in ways as compatible as possible with local traditions. The effort at prevention was a forward-thinking aspect of NURU; however, two underlying assumptions were flawed. The primary cause of child malnutrition was assumed to be mothers' lack of knowledge of child care, nutrition, and vegetable gardening. Women were even awarded a certificate at the end of their stay to emphasize the triumph of education over adversity. The assumption that maternal ignorance was primary was not questioned at NURU; the value of the education seemed too obvious at the time.

The planners also assumed that women's work was largely at home in their compounds and ignored the central role of women in staple food production, animal husbandry, and coffee farming. These assumptions underlay all NURU's efforts at prevention, and similar approaches continue in many programs worldwide. Although NURU was designed to incorporate public participation and cultural sensitivity, assumptions underlying the planning were so fundamental that these ideals could not be fully realized. In his wide-ranging discussion of the failures of programs to end malnutrition in less developed countries, Escobar notes that in Colombia in the 1960s and 1970s, various organizations used the concept of participation differently, often assuming that they could incorporate it with standard management techniques to make programs successful rather than to empower local communities (1995:141). Similarly, NURU was planned and implemented in a way that maintained local power relations and gave little voice to clients and their families. NURU provided a state-of-the-art example of medical efforts against malnutrition in the 1970s, and it remained a model for decades to come, despite its inadequacies. Redirection of many of its programs in the 1980s made it more effective but put it at odds with the founding assumptions.

Team Research Begins

My research efforts started in 1971 with the clinic survey, designed to gather information to provide a basis for NURU's staff to make their instruction culturally appropriate. In the survey, a Medical Center team inventoried health concepts and practices of people (usually mothers) who brought children to clinics in a region of Mt. Kilimanjaro (see Appendix C; see also Lindner 1972). Our research, the mobile clinics, and NURU were funded by a private donor from the United States. Data included one-hour interviews with 418 people who brought children to the clinic, primarily mothers, and clinical assessments of the children's health. The study was supposed to provide a rationale for the mobile clinics and NURU; however, they began before the data had been analyzed. This did not trouble me at the time because, like so many other foreigners involved in solving health problems in a developing country, I thought I could make a contribution by helping to build an institution, in this case, NURU.

Three months later, I began participating in a UNICEF study that evaluated NURU, addressing maternal and child health issues in a broad social, cultural, and economic context (see Appendix C; see also Von Freyhold et al. 1973). The study was funded jointly by UNICEF and the Tanzanian National Scientific Research Council. The aim of this project was to investigate maternal and child health in Moshi District, a large area in the Kilimanjaro region. We collected data on child care, division of labor, land tenure, Kilimanjaro's economy, population trends, food consumption patterns, and infant and child morbidity and mortality rates. Part of my work assessed NURU, and I noted the energy and dedication of the nursing staff, in contrast with the tenor of other health programs in the area. It was immensely satisfying to me to know that something I had a hand in designing was saving children's lives.

No one, however, predicted an environmental and economic crisis. A severe drought that would last for two years began in 1972. Coffee berry disease was slowly infecting farmers' crops and became so threatening to their livelihood that people were severely fined, even jailed, for not properly spraying their crops. This was doubly frustrating because world inflation at the time was putting the spray and supplies out of the reach of some farmers. The number of sick children was increasing with the cumulative effects of the drought, coffee berry disease, and inflation. The crisis peaked in 1974 and continued to wreak havoc until sometime in 1975.

A year after NURU's opening, however, mothers were withdrawing their children from treatment prematurely and leaving NURU, and other children who had been cured of malnutrition were returning, again malnourished. These developments provoked those responsible for NURU to call for a more thorough evaluation. They contacted Marja-Liisa Swantz, a professor of anthropology at the University of Dar es Salaam. She designed and secured funding for the NURU study, a comparison of households with a child who had been in NURU to neighboring households with healthy children. The general goal was to find causes of child malnutrition and reasons for NURU's failures (Swantz et al. 1975).

The bulk of the fieldwork was carried out by five female university students from Kilimanjaro and me. We investigated 111 families altogether, 42 of whom had malnourished children at NURU. For the three months of university vacation, each student interviewed and observed families who lived near her own home. I studied thirty families (ten of whom had had a child in NURU) who lived near the mission clinic, where I stayed for one and a half months, and I continued with less frequent visits for a few more months.

In addition to each household in the study with a child who had been in NURU, we interviewed an adult at two neighboring households for comparative purposes. We asked similar questions in all households, and we also asked neighbors about the causes of the illnesses of the children who had been in NURU. We visited sixty-nine neighbor households; some participated as neighbors of more than one hospitalized child.

We aimed to solve community problems as well as collect data. Our activism received an ambivalent response, however, and forced us to confront social, cultural, and economic aspects of life on Kilimanjaro and the frustrations of the neighbors and families of hospitalized children as they attempted to cope with poverty, food crisis, and shame. We wrote daily in our journals about our visits and other observations, conversations, and personal impressions. We also collected information on a variety of socioeconomic, demographic, and environmental factors identified on a questionnaire.

After many years of reflection, writing a Ph.D. thesis, returning to Kilimanjaro, and reading the growing body of literature on famine, I see that people on the mountain used a plurality of ideas to construct explanations of child malnutrition. Many included some combination of disease and human culpability in their explanations. Some claimed economic and environmental catastrophes as causes. Some cited supernatural factors as having played at least a partial role in a child's illness, while still others seemed to rely entirely on the supernatural realm to explain malnutrition. Some better-off people drew from these ideas to justify not helping their impoverished kin with starving children. Instead, they blamed the child's parents for their poverty. If parents failed to adhere to local customs, they also were blamed, leading to their marginalization.

I buried the impact of Roberto's death and my conflict with Fatima as I joined research teams to carry out three year-long projects. Roberto and Fatima's story never entered any of the final reports and appeared only in a footnote in my Ph.D. thesis. While each of the three research projects brought some understanding of child illness, my own experiences forced me to try to look at the problem of child malnutrition from the perspective of those who live through it. Most outsiders ignore local conditions, just as I once did, and see little logic in the ways local people cope with hardship. The clash between my experience with the people of Mt. Kilimanjaro and ongoing efforts to prevent malnutrition led me to develop a more critical eye toward outside solutions for local health problems.

Chapter Three

Poverty Amidst Plenty

⌒ *The story of Francis and Bibiana Lema and their children is an account of the creation of poverty and the struggle against it. The family's suffering through crop failure, the erosion of mutual aid, and shame dramatizes the predicament of the poor on Mt. Kilimanjaro. Francis and Bibiana had relied on the coffee harvest for the bulk of their income, and an institution far beyond their control, the international market, had experienced a serious downturn before my visit.* ⌒

My First Encounter with Francis and Bibiana Lema, 1974

⌒ The local government office was surprisingly unpretentious. Standing beside a main road in the upper reaches of Mt. Kilimanjaro's middle belt, it was a small concrete building painted blue and flanked by a beer shop on one side and a tiny dry goods store on the other. Inside, pictures of President Julius Nyerere hung in the two rooms, which were furnished simply with a large wooden desk, benches, and chairs. The secretary sat at a small table with a typewriter, and he tried to shoo away the people who were looking in the window to see what I would do.

I had come to introduce myself to the local chairman of TANU (Tanganyika African National Union, the only political party) before starting research in the mission area. He was friendly and expressed gratitude that I would be continuing the work of Mrs. Kimario, the researcher I was replacing. His manner immediately put me at ease, and I ventured to ask where I could find the Lema family, as I was planning to visit them the next day.

"Oh, that family! Yes. They truly have had *bahati mbaya* [bad luck]," the chairman stated emphatically. "They don't live too far from here. Come. I'll take you there."

Before I could prepare myself, we were on our way, in the company of most of the officials and visitors from the TANU office as well as many of the onlookers who had gathered outside. I was a bit anxious about the large entourage because I hoped to develop trusting, private relationships with the families in my study. "Then again," I thought, "perhaps the troubled family might be cheered by the community's interest."

Along the way, we came upon an odd-looking man. He was dressed in tattered burlap sacking, and his gray hair was uncombed. My first reaction was that he might be *kichaa* (crazy), as were other unkempt people I had seen in the region.

The TANU chairman chided him, "Look at your hair, *bwana* [mister]!" He grabbed a handful of the startled man's hair and said, "You must cut it. You're going to have visitors, so go home and change your clothing! It's a filthy disgrace."

"Yes, yes, *mzee* [my elder]! This is disgraceful clothing. I was spraying coffee trees at the mission," the man said, his eyes cast downward. He abruptly rushed off, and as he turned I noticed his roughly woven shirt was made from a burlap sack for shipping coffee; on his back was "KNCU" (for Kilimanjaro Native Cooperative Union, the coffee growers' cooperative headquartered in nearby Moshi).

I was surprised to learn that the man was Francis Lema, the father in the household we were going to visit. Usually the Chagga give long, courteous introductions, but none of the normal forms of address had been used by my companions. Instead, they seemed ashamed of Francis. A litany of his failures filled their conversation as we proceeded.

The road we took was broad and muddy. We saw few houses because most were set back in privacy behind a dense, glossy, green barrier of coffee trees interplanted with bananas and bushes, neatly bordered by decorative shrubs edging the roads and paths. I had the impression of walking through a sparsely settled tropical forest rather than densely populated farms.

We followed a neatly swept path of bare earth bordered by a hedge of dracaena bushes and arrived at an impressive housing compound. It belonged to Edwardi Lema, an executive in the coffee cooperative, owner of a large wholesale meat business, and Francis's first cousin.

The main building was a sprawling ranch house of cement block that was furnished luxuriously by local standards with a refrigerator, other appliances, upholstered chairs, and store-bought furniture. A motorcycle and a small new car, additional signs of affluence, stood by the house. The next building housed four imported Jersey cows. Its glass windows, cement block walls, and electricity made the barn a considerable improvement over the home of the closest neighbors, who were also Edwardi's cousins.

Well beyond the compound, we found Francis's tiny house. It was clearly visible from the road, lacking the hedges, trees, and plants that would normally have created privacy. Under a disheveled thatched roof, mud walls bore patches of flattened tin cans to keep the rain out.

When we approached the house, Francis's wife, Bibiana, quickly ran inside to change clothes. She finally emerged, still dressed in rags, as were her four listless children. She kept exclaiming, "*Yesu* [Jesus]!" while holding her hand over her mouth to muffle her giggles. I had no idea how to respond, but she soon calmed down.

After a few moments, Francis himself stepped outside, holding their infant daughter. His best clothes were as tattered as his wife's, but he brought with him an air of calm, dignity, and wisdom. His composure was remarkable, a contrast to our earlier meeting and his wife's frantic manner. Francis was fifty-two years of age, nearly twenty years older than Bibiana, and clearly older than the TANU chairman, whom he had addressed respectfully as *mzee*. With gray hair, large, liquid brown eyes, and a tiny frame, he appeared frail.

"*Mama* and *mzee*," I began as we sat on the ground, "I'm working with the hospital where your children stayed. We've come to get a better understanding of the difficulties people are facing these days. With your information, we will teach the hospital and the government so that they can improve."

I was expecting a reply from either Francis or Bibiana, but a neighbor interrupted. "As you know, the government promotes *kujitegemea* [self-reliance]. People must take responsibility for their own conditions if they wish to improve."

"That is true," Francis said, "but it is also true that the government is our father and our mother. We can expect help in times of crisis. Like many others around me, I am having difficulties providing food for my children. That's why they became ill."

I asked if I could meet his children, and Francis led me up to his house, where four of them had gathered. The older two children remained outside while the younger ones scurried into the house to hide from the *mzungu* (white person). From what I saw, all four still had signs of kwashiorkor—hair loss, bloated bellies, petulant expressions.

〜 Figure 10 *Francis and Bibiana Lema's children in 1974. Adija, age five (upper left), died, and her brother Justin, age three (on the right) was left severely stunted. The baby (at bottom) was still breastfeeding and survived in good health.*

I entered their home. A dark, poorly ventilated room formed the main section of the house, where the seven family members slept. Two beds made of sacks and leaves lay in the far corner and reeked of urine from the small children, who didn't wear diapers. A couple of rickety stools and a few cooking pots were the only other belongings. An additional section had recently been added to the house for a milk cow or goats that Francis hoped to borrow from a relative. As Francis later explained, though, "Who would be foolish enough to lend me a cow when I can't afford a stall door to keep thieves away?"

I opened a discussion about how all the children in a family could become ill. Everyone said it was because food was too expensive. One person said, "One pint of milk these days costs one shilling and twenty cents [U.S. $0.25]. What do you do if you have no money?"

Instead of further discussing the stark insight that you can't purchase food if you don't have the money, I started to interview Bibiana according to the research protocol. "The hospital wants to know, *Mama* Bibiana, what foods are considered good for children to eat," I said as I rustled through my purse to find my pen and pad.

She answered, "Bananas, vegetables, meat, fruit," and her husband added, "Milk, eggs, and beans." Everyone who was there agreed, though, that the family simply couldn't afford those foods. 〜

The predicament of Francis's family grew out of the larger story of the Chagga people. The history of wealth, poverty, and food crisis in their society began well before the colonial period; traditions of aiding the poor also can be traced back to early times, when responsibility lay in the hands of relatives and the chief.

During the era of European domination, the situation of the poor changed drastically, often for the worse, as colonial governments weakened Chagga political leadership. With national independence, Chagga coffee farmers have increasingly embraced the global coffee market, and the gap between rich and poor has widened considerably. Local assistance to destitute families has continued to erode over the century.

The Chiefdom and the Poor

Chagga chiefdoms probably began in the late eighteenth and early nineteenth centuries, with inequality an early feature. The chiefdom was the largest political unit on Mt. Kilimanjaro in precolonial times (Stahl 1964). The Chagga chief was ruler, head priest, supreme judge, and personal advisor. He came from a specific lineage, distinct from commoner lineages,[1] and oversaw taxation, land distribution, the irrigation system, the military, and aid to the needy. A chief's heir in the early twentieth century learned:

> The poor should be received at the court with kindness, for not only do they produce more offspring than the rich, but they are also more faithful: they would rather starve themselves than have their chief want anything. The rich are a moral danger for they rely on their wealth to excuse or if necessary redress wrongs which they have perpetuated. Widows, orphans and expectant mothers are specially recommended to the chief's consideration. (Gutmann 1926: 379)

These teachings imparted aspects of inequality in Chagga society.[2] The chief presided over a court, but he was supposed to avoid being arrogant and to work to ensure political support. He was supposed to take considerable responsibility for the poor and to be able to depend on their loyalty.

The central authority of the chiefs drew support from the belief that the spirit realm mirrored the everyday Chagga world and that ancestral spirits of chiefs dominated those of commoners (Moore 1986). Ancestors' spirits were thought to cause misfortune, which called for sacrifice, and commoners met the usual afflictions with sacrifices to their lineage spirits. When misfortune affected an entire chiefdom, the trouble was thought to come from a spirit connected to the people as a whole, such as an ancestral spirit of the chief or Ruwa, the supreme god, believed to inhabit Kibo, the snow-capped peak of

Mt. Kilimanjaro. Major affliction required sacrifice on a large scale (Raum 1940). Afflictions and misfortune addressed in these ways included famine and some instances of kwashiorkor.

Rites of petition to the ancestors or to Ruwa often called for animal sacrifice. After the offering had been made, the animals were butchered and the meat divided. Meat distribution reflected the social order, with preferred cuts going to people of high status, who then divided the meat among their kin (Moore 1986). The division of food thus enacted principles of inequality, commensality, and aid to the less fortunate and formed the basis for an economy based on redistribution.

A chiefdom usually occupied a ridge extending down the mountain, bounded by rapidly flowing rivers. Related households occupied neighboring farms, raising bananas, millet, vegetables, fruit, cattle, and goats (Stahl 1964). Although the soil was volcanic and quite fertile, rainfall was unpredictable and the region suffered periodic droughts. Irrigation thus was necessary for steady annual yields, and the chief also stockpiled grain taken in taxes for use in times of crop failure (Stahl 1964).

The material basis of the chief's authority lay in his responsibility to oversee an elaborate irrigation system that diverted rivers and streams through canals and tunnels. With his central authority, the chief had to recruit and coordinate laborers to maintain the system, and centralized decision making was necessary to apportion water (Stahl 1964). This and other labor requirements made every able-bodied person, including poor people, valuable to the chiefdom.[3]

In the nineteenth century, Mt. Kilimanjaro had as many as seven hundred chiefdoms.[4] Each chiefdom included a collection of patrilineages, groups of relatives defined by descent through males. The chiefdom probably developed from the age-grade system in which power was more or less equitably distributed among lineage elders (Moore 1986:339). A chief who was deemed unworthy could be deposed by the warrior age grade, giving commoners some political power and providing the chief with a practical reason to fulfill his official obligations.

Each chiefdom was subdivided into geographical areas known as *mitaa* (districts or parishes; Moore 1986:19). Each parish had a district head, appointed by the chief, who wielded more authority than lineage heads (Moore 1986). The district heads often took advantage of their position to amass wealth in cattle.

Cattle played a central role in the economy and culture as a primary form of wealth and exchange. Goats were also important but had a lesser value, several goats being considered equivalent to one cow. Cattle produced milk, meat, and blood to eat; hides to wear; and manure to spread in the garden for fertilizer. Celebrations and rituals to ward off misfortune required the sacrifice of cattle, which were also used as gifts to legitimate marriages and to further other ties in the lineage. Complex rules specified the distribution of meat to lineage members when a cow was butchered. Certain parts went to specific persons. Failure to follow the specifications caused great insult and could result in resentments and long-term disputes.

Cattle were the main form of wealth, passed on in a complex inheritance system, and they were also used to pay restitution in legal cases and as a form of tribute to chiefs (Moore 1986). Cattle raids between chiefdoms and by Maasai warriors led Chagga farmers to keep their livestock in stalls rather than taking them to pastures to graze. The stalls were usually at one end of a house, next to a room where people slept, and the animals provided "central heating" during the cold rainy season (Moore 1986:64).

The chief was responsible for enforcing people's rights to farmland. The most desirable type of land (*kihamba*), with fertile soil and irrigation, lay in the middle belt of Mt. Kilimanjaro. It accommodated permanent crops such as cooking bananas, taro, yams, and fruit trees. Large vegetable gardens were planted close to the homesteads. The *kihamba* passed from father to son under permanent freehold rights (Dundas 1924). A man who had land usually provided *kihamba* land to each wife for cultivation. The process of inheritance was complex, with the youngest son receiving the family homestead and the largest plot of *kihamba*, the oldest son receiving another *kihamba* plot if land was sufficient, and middle sons receiving plots only in families with abundant land. Normally ownership of land did not formally transfer from father to son until the father's death, but sons who were to inherit land would usually begin living there and their wives would begin farming it in the early years of their marriage. Middle sons without land could petition the chief, who could grant them land that was not under cultivation.

Shamba land lay on the lower slopes of the mountain, lacked irrigation, and could produce only drought-resistant crops, such as bananas and grass for the cattle. Traditionally it was held on a year-to-year basis at the discretion of the chief, but he could also give a landless man a plot of the land, to be incorporated into *kihamba* tenure system. Daughters almost never inherited land, although if there were no sons, a daughter's husband would be a likely heir.

Unequal inheritance placed middle sons and women in structurally weak positions and contributed to economic inequality (Moore 1986). Men who had land could accumulate wealth through increasing crop production, acquiring more cattle, and marrying more wives, who then joined the farm labor force.[5] During the twentieth century, inequality of inheritance, coupled with an increasing population and consolidation of land into plantations, resulted in large numbers of people being deprived of land and ultimately becoming poor.

Inequality in various forms encouraged exchange among relatives, and the reciprocity usually benefited both sides. Obligations among kin were complex and involved various mutual exchanges. For example, grandmothers provided child care for their grandchildren while their daughters-in-law worked in the fields, and women provided meals for their parents-in-law as a sign of respect (Raum 1940).

The loan of livestock to poor kin was widespread. It allowed better-off men to acquire more cattle and goats than their own wives could tend and also provided a way to hide assets. The poor would care for a milk cow and receive specific benefits, for example, the milk, manure for fertilizer, and a calf. The caretakers could make repayment through work, return of the cow, or part of a harvest (Moore 1986). Aid to poor people was part of a long-term patron-client relationship that brought returns to both rich and poor while fostering dependency. In this manner, wealthy people who assisted their poorer kin and neighbors through loans of cattle often received in return material resources in the form of some of the calves and some cattle products, as well as continued obligations from the indebted.

Prior to the advent of a cash economy, there were limits on the extent of wealth accumulation by commoners and, to a lesser extent, by chiefs. Massive accumulation was partly constrained by the forms of wealth—food, cattle, and in a sense, the family labor force. Although the Chagga lacked cash, they did have other portable forms of wealth, including cloth, beads, and iron blades for hoes (Iliffe 1979), but stockpiling them in large quantities was not desirable. Even the chief faced limits on his wealth, because his authority rested partly on continuing benefits to the people in his chiefdom. Social relations and the economy both enforced inequality and limited the severity of poverty.

The economic system was characterized by its emphasis on food production for the home and for tribute and by redistribution of land, cattle, and other tribute by the chief. The society had features that encouraged centralized political control: a complex irrigation system that required central authority for construction and maintenance; the need for a military force to protect a settled population; and a theocratic government with the chief as political and religious head. The system of taxation and redistribution reinforced the central authority of the chief. The heavy demand for labor to maintain both irrigation and military defense made the able-bodied poor valuable to the chiefdom.

The emphasis on subsistence and redistribution contrasted with accumulation in capitalism, which was to arrive in Kilimanjaro late in the nineteenth century. In the precolonial system, wealthy and poor Chagga were directly and materially interdependent. A better-off man needed his poorer relatives to care for some of his numerous cattle. Poor relatives needed the cattle to provide milk, blood, and fertilizer, and they also had ownership of specific calves to found their own herds. A poor family could work their way out of poverty with good fortune and steady labor. Thus, dependence on the largess of wealthier kin was not necessarily permanent. In this redistributive economy, a poor man such as Francis had a dignity connected to his economic role and was not simply an object of charity and blame.

Chiefs sought to expand their control over cattle, labor, and trade throughout the nineteenth century. In the first half of the century, long-distance trade reached the Kilimanjaro region from the coast and brought a demand for local ivory, slaves, and provisions for the enormous caravans passing on the way to Lake Victoria (Iliffe 1979). The Chagga engaged the Arab traders as middlemen in small-scale ivory trading, and they exchanged captives obtained in war for goods.

In explaining his role in the slave trade, one chief retorted to a reproachful European traveler:

> What am I to do? To kill captives would be wrong. If I return them to my enemies, they would just fight me. If I kept them in my own land my people would say, "If strangers are to occupy the soil, where is the room for our children to cultivate?" Then what can I do but sell them to the Arabs? (Moore 1986:61, paraphrasing Johnston 1886:180)

In earlier times, there was no slavery among the Chagga as it is commonly conceptualized (Moore 1986), although there was a form of personal dependency of a few captives and the destitute on the chief, and children of commoners worked for him as servants (Iliffe 1979; Moore 1986).[6] During the nineteenth century, the demand for slaves grew, bringing slavers inland from the coast and resulting in shockingly brutal practices previously unknown in most of the region. Through the slave trade, some Chagga chiefs acquired guns for protection and further conquest.

Provisioning the caravans proved highly profitable for households and chiefdoms, which sold meat, vegetables, and beer. Trade with the caravans encouraged more food production and continued military development (Moore 1986:37). Local production of vegetables was expanded in part through the chiefs' use of corvée labor (work paid as tribute by commoners). The production of cooking bananas, Kilimanjaro's staple crop, was not labor-intensive, and it allowed women to expand their already well developed market system to trade with outsiders. Production for profit thus began before colonial domination and the development of coffee plantations in the latter part of the nineteenth century (Moore 1986:32).

A military force developed out of the age-grade system, which ranked men and women in age-defined groups with complementary duties under the direction of lineage elders. Each chiefdom maintained its own corps of warriors, built high fences for protection, and dug large tunnels to hide women, children, and cattle (Dundas 1924). During much of the nineteenth century intermittent warfare between chiefdoms was common. Some Chagga chiefs consolidated power through military action and clever alliances with neighboring chiefdoms. The growing nineteenth-century slave trade provided a ready market for war captives, giving chiefs further incentive for raids and military defense.

Chiefs collected taxes in the form of food crops, cattle, and labor. In addition, each family with at least three children owed a child as a "bonded serf" to the chief (Moore 1986). Boy serfs were used to herd goats, and girl serfs were used as servants for the chief's wives. Earlier ethnographers considered this form of taxation a system of slavery, although it was compatible with the custom of sending children to live in other households in the lineage. Nevertheless, the ethnographers reported, the chief's requirement was deeply resented by the commoners (Moore 1986:100). The chief was ideally to give food to the needy and, during famines, to the general population as well. The widowed, the crippled, and the destitute were to rely on the chief for support. Poor men with little land or no cattle could usually earn a living by working for wealthier kin or the chief.

Expectations surrounding reciprocal exchanges were subject to various contingencies. Some chiefs abused their powers, and some commoners refused to repay debts. A history of conflict and ill will could invalidate customary expectations. Individuals might develop bad reputations from immoral actions and become marginalized or formally excluded from their patrilineage. These instances would throw ordinary expectations open to negotiation and possibly result in an individual's economic failure. Even though earlier ethnographic accounts somewhat exaggerate the harmonious relations between chief and commoner and between rich and poor during the precolonial era, Moore suggests that there was some basis to these claims (Moore 1986:97). In general, the precolonial economic system prevented extreme poverty.

Confrontation with Europeans: The Chiefdom Weakens

The encounter of Chagga and Europeans began with tolerance and religious conversion and eventually led to the cessation of warfare between chiefdoms. It also ushered in new forms of repression, bloodshed, and brutality, as well as new economic opportunities leading eventually to an expanded involvement in the international market. A host of contradictory forces struck at the heart of the chiefdom and eroded its authority, wealth, and unity. The gap between wealthy and poor widened, and aid to the less fortunate eroded with the shift to a cash economy based on coffee production and the availability of new forms of wealth. The increasing isolation of poor people deepened their poverty, as is evident in Francis's story.

Francis's family history, told in 1974

⌒ As a young man, Francis's father had been forced by the British to leave Kilimanjaro to work on the sisal plantations on the coast. Under the Muslim influence on the coast, he converted to Islam and married a local woman. Shortly after his wedding, he returned with his wife to the Kilimanjaro region.

As a middle son, he had inherited only a small *kihamba* field from his father. Upon his return to Kilimanjaro, he obtained a *shamba* on the lower slope near the plains, where there are Muslim settlements, and lived there the rest of his life. The couple had four children, a girl and three boys, with Francis the youngest.

Francis told me that when he was only four, his mother died, and it gave him a "bad start." His sister, the oldest child, cared for him and his brothers. Francis lived most of his life on the lower slope, although he did help his father plant coffee trees in the upper *kihamba*, as young sons do.

Francis's father refused to partition land among his sons when they reached adulthood. In Francis's view, this was because his father was *kali* (mean). When his father died, Francis was forty-eight years old and, for lack of land, not yet married. His sister received the lower *shamba*, a rarity among Chagga, and Francis inherited the upper *kihamba*, next to the farms of his cousins. It took courage for a lone Muslim to move into a community of Roman Catholics only a few minutes' walk from their church. He finally married, built a house, and began fatherhood and coffee farming at an age when most men were already grandfathers. ⌒

The journey of Francis's father to the coast was part of widespread labor migration throughout the region in colonial times. Migration detracted from the unity of the chiefdom, which also lost power because of the major disruption of the local economy beginning in the 1890s (Iliffe 1979; Moore 1986). Europeans brought several key institutions to Mt. Kilimanjaro that changed Chagga life: the cash economy, connection to a world market, Christianity, and formal education. European exploitation built on existing Chagga inequality and the quest for power and achievement.

In the mid-1800s, European missionaries and settlers had come to Mt. Kilimanjaro (see Table 2). They found that the Chagga already knew out-

Table 2   *An Overview of Chagga History*

Precolonial period[a] ————————————	*Before 1850*

Chagga forebears arrive in
Mt. Kilimanjaro region
at least 500 to 600 years ago;
perhaps much earlier

Continuing contact with other societies:
trade, war

East African trade: iron, salt, cereals

Trade outside Africa under Arab and
Portuguese domination: ivory, slaves
began by 1700

Long-distance trade reaches Kilimanjaro,
first for ivory, then slaves
about 1800 to 1850

Major famine, Mt. Kilimanjaro
mid-1800s

Colonial period ————————————	*1850 to 1961*

European missionaries, settlers, planters
1850s to 1870s

Tanganyika[b]

    German wars of conquest,
        local wars of resistance,
        famine, epidemics,
        Chagga rebellion, 14 chiefs executed
1880s to about 1911

    German rule
1886 to 1916

    British rule
1916 to 1961

        League of Nations mandate
1916 to 1945

        Abolition of slavery
1919

        U.N. Trust Territory
1946 to 1961

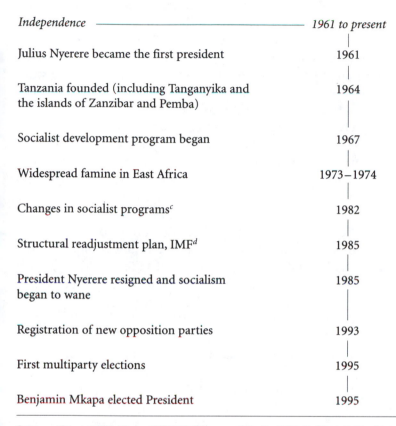

Independence ———————————————— 1961 to present	
Julius Nyerere became the first president	1961
Tanzania founded (including Tanganyika and the islands of Zanzibar and Pemba)	1964
Socialist development program began	1967
Widespread famine in East Africa	1973–1974
Changes in socialist programs[c]	1982
Structural readjustment plan, IMF[d]	1985
President Nyerere resigned and socialism began to wane	1985
Registration of new opposition parties	1993
First multiparty elections	1995
Benjamin Mkapa elected President	1995

Sources: Kerner 1988; Moore 1986:11; Moore and Puritt 1977; Stahl 1964; Turshen 1984.

[a] Little attention is given in this account to the dynamic precolonial history of the Chagga because of our focus on changes over the last century.

[b] Tanganyika was the colonial designation including the part of Mt. Kilimanjaro where the present study took place. Tanzania combines the former Tanganyika, Zanzibar, and Pemba.

[c] These changes were coupled with structural readjustment and resulted in "limited encouragement of private estate development," a lessening of regulations on internal and external trade, "reinstatement of producer cooperatives, reinstatement of local district councils which manage their own budgets from tax revenues, and a devaluation of the currency" (Kerner 1988:64).

[d] IMF: International Monetary Fund.

siders through providing cattle, other food, and captives to caravans traveling between the coast and the interior (Iliffe 1979). Nonetheless, when offered jobs by early missionaries and settlers, local people refused because they were not interested in earning money.

German commercial interests began to recognize the agricultural potential of the region, and the German government moved to consolidate power
in East Africa. Between 1885 and 1890, through treaties with Britain,
Portugal, and Zanzibar, Germany obtained control of what became known
as Tanganyika (the mainland portion of what is now Tanzania), Rwanda,
and Burundi (Iliffe 1979). It was not until 1891, however, following a series
of battles with local inhabitants, that Germany was able to take over administration of the territory. During the 1890s, the efforts of the German
administration to restructure the economy of Tanganyika were hampered
by diseases devastating to cattle and people, by widespread famine in many
parts of the country, and by continuing armed resistance. According to Iliffe,
there is evidence that the Tanganyikan population declined seriously in this
decade—losing 750,000 people to famine, according to one observer—and
the decline probably continued until 1925 (Iliffe 1979:165).

In 1898, to force people "to use money, sell surplus crops, work for
Europeans, and obey a distant government," the colonial administration
imposed a "hut tax," an annual property tax of one to four shillings on each
house (Iliffe 1979:133). The tax compelled people to participate in the cash
economy. Money had already become a medium of exchange at the Machame
market on Kilimanjaro by that time, but most Chagga did not pay the first
annual tax in cash (Iliffe 1979:132). The Chagga refused to become the docile
plantation workers the colonialists had hoped for; in 1908, the government
stationed troops on Kilimanjaro and conscripted men as laborers on public
works if they refused work on plantations (Iliffe 1979:153). By 1910, the district officer had implemented a labor tax that required each man to work for
a European for specified periods, for example, thirty days every four months.
By 1912, the system was applied throughout the colony (ibid.).

In many parts of Africa, European colonials used whole communities,
such as the Chagga, as sources of labor, raw materials, and agricultural production, sometimes with little concern for the human suffering that
resulted. Some humane policies were instituted, but there was so little con-
sistency that benefits generally did not accrue for long to local people.
Colonial labor policies sparked rebellion.[7] Armed resistance to German rule
continued in various areas, and at the turn of the century, a German captain
hanged two Chagga chiefs and "seventeen other notables," perhaps with the
complicity of Chief Marealle, who as a result became "the most powerful
ruler Kilimanjaro had ever known" (Iliffe 1979:102). In southern Tanzania
from 1905 to 1907, the Maji-Maji rebellion broke out, causing at least
120,000 southern Tanganyikans to die. With its end, active resistance to
European political domination was more or less crushed.

The German government had promoted coffee production in the early
1890s, but a major downturn in the international market was beginning,

and before 1902, none of the plantation companies in Tanganyika showed a profit (Iliffe 1979:126). The Chagga deeply resented hut taxes and forced labor, but they began to take advantage of opportunities to gain wealth through cash crops such as coffee. In fact, in the first two decades of this century, they struggled with European settlers for the right to compete in coffee production. By the 1920s, the international market had made coffee production profitable again, and areas in Tanganyika favorable for cash crops quickly developed an economic lead over less favored areas, accentuating existing differences (see Fuggles-Couchman 1964:19).

Some chiefs allied with German administrators to gain legitimacy and consolidate power against other chiefs. Although war and raiding were no longer ways to gain wealth, chiefs still levied taxes and fees, and they also taxed and recruited labor for the state. Taxes paid to chiefs were estimated at seven times those paid to the colonial government, and chiefs tended to accumulate more wealth than in precolonial times (Gutmann 1926:390–95; HRAF:350–54 cited by Moore 1986:97–99). Chiefs no longer redistributed cattle on a large scale because members of chiefdoms were no longer the sole basis of power and redistribution no longer provided chiefs with a major route of gaining political support.

Some chiefs were willing to sell land to settlers, and despite the efforts of Governor Rechenberg to protect Chagga holdings, including banning new settlement for a period in 1911, settlers made considerable inroads. By 1913 the settlers and missions held about fifty thousand acres of arable land on Kilimanjaro and as much as 30 percent of the land in the *kihamba* belt. In that year there were about 110,000 Chagga living on the mountain and only 882 European men who were agriculturalists in the entire colony of Tanganyika (Iliffe 1979:141, 144). Some chiefdoms were so short of *kihamba* land that members had to seek it elsewhere, and "scores of landless people squatted on Roman Catholic mission land at Kilema" (Iliffe 1979:144). Although land on Kilimanjaro was not alienated to the extent that it was elsewhere, external commercial interests increased the pressure on land. During the British era (1916 to 1961), the smaller local chiefdoms disintegrated, and more-powerful chiefs gained control of larger areas. Respect for wealth increased the social standing of Chagga coffee farmers who were successful in the international market.

Chagga entry into the cash economy blew the lid off the precolonial system on Kilimanjaro, widening the gap between rich and poor. Some Chagga, often from chiefly lineages, were able to amass vastly more wealth than was possible in precolonial times. The introduction of cash cropping and contact with the European market provided the commercial means to accumulate wealth, particularly through growing coffee, the cash crop most important to Chagga farmers. Some Chagga commoners quickly put their profits into large numbers of cattle, rocking the value of cattle in the local economy, in which cattle were a major form of wealth.

Christianity and capitalism brought new systems of values, including a different morality that allowed new ways of justifying everyday decisions. Capitalism and individualism allowed people to reduce aid to poor kin without necessarily being branded immoral. Better-off people felt more pressure to hoard their riches, and the chiefdom lost political authority and economic power, reducing the chief's ability to assist the poor. Poor people who had counted on the chief and on relatives had far less assurance of assistance. The precolonial system, in which chiefdoms were responsible for providing food for the needy, had eroded under the force of colonial wars, laws, and economic shifts. Poverty intensified in households with little land and few other means of support, isolated the inhabitants, and left children without adequate food.

Independence

The gap between better-off and poor Chagga continues to grow today. Neighbors and close kin, including fathers and sons, often have extreme differences in yearly income. Although the Chagga are more affluent than most Tanzanians, desperate want continues.[8] During the early to mid-1970s, a long drought precipitated a food crisis even for farmers with irrigated land, increasing the ranks of the poor.

1974

∼ "Isn't there anyone in the neighborhood who can help your relatives, as people used to in earlier days?" I asked Philippe Lema one day in a discussion about her husband's poorer relatives. We were sitting on her veranda, enjoying a cup of tea with Lourdes, my research assistant. Our table was covered with embroidered linen and set with fine cutlery. I had come to appreciate Philippe's concern for Francis's family in particular and felt comfortable speaking frankly.

"People do help when there's a crisis, for example, when someone's house burns down. You can expect help in building anew. But when a family is always in need, they can get help from the Church," Philippe said.

I wondered whether there was any chance that help would reach Francis, a Muslim. "What do you think caused Francis and Bibiana's children's illnesses?" I asked, expecting Philippe to respond.

Instead Lourdes answered. "They should be very grateful for NURU. Without the help, their children would be dead. Bibiana is too busy in the *shamba* and doesn't look after the children properly. In fact, Francis brought them to the mission clinic and when Sister suggested that Bibiana take them to NURU, Bibiana refused. It was Francis who took them to NURU, and he stayed for a month. Then the TANU chairman forced Bibiana to go."

"How long did she stay?" I asked, surprised at Lourdes's knowledge of their story.

"From June ninth to September tenth," she replied, "and she left before the children had fully recovered." Lourdes had grown up in the neighborhood, and she had worked with Mrs. Kimario, the previous researcher; as a result, she had a great deal of information about the families. They were also her neighbors.

In defense of Bibiana, her sister-in-law, Philippe, stated, "But she had good reason not to go to NURU. She was *mwandani* [observing the tradition of seclusion and rest at home required of mothers after a birth]. Then again, the children are sick because Bibiana had them so rapidly without a rest in between." Philippe herself had borne nine healthy children in twelve years but apparently saw no contradiction in her criticism of Bibiana.

In discussing ailing children, neighbors such as Philippe vacillated between blaming the parents and lamenting their misfortune of being so poor during a time of widespread hardship.

As I continued asking people about aid from relatives, I frequently received the reply "You can ask for help once, but the second or third time, it will be denied." Perhaps demands from the growing number of needy kin led to the grudging offers of aid. Edwardi, Francis's wealthy cousin, had three destitute households as neighbors, all of them kin, including Francis's family. The three fathers were working as laborers during the coffee harvest at the nearby mission—poorly paid work usually left to schoolgirls.

Later, Francis declared his own responsibility for the children's poor health and related that for working at the mission eight to ten hours a day, he earned only five shillings, not enough to buy basic daily necessities such as beans, milk, eggs, cooking oil, and lamp oil.

I was surprised to learn that Francis's coffee farm was about average in size, with 1,500 coffee trees. To me there seemed to be no clear reason for his family's poverty, as his farm normally would have been big enough to provide adequate income.

Francis had tried to obtain a loan for farm supplies from the coffee cooperative, which had accepted his dues and had taxed him, along with everyone else, for processing his harvest. With the drought, coffee berry disease, a drop in coffee prices, and rising pesticide and fertilizer prices, though, he appeared to be a poor risk and the loan was denied. On the other hand, Edwardi and other wealthy men classified as creditworthy kept borrowing from the cooperative's coffers in spite of regular defaults on their loans. The poor, in effect, were subsidizing the better-off members of the cooperative. ⌒

Francis's story presents, in human terms, the basic paradox of poverty amidst plenty. Here was a family, obviously destitute, living in a relatively wealthy society. They existed in squalor only yards away from wealthier people who were, in fact, their close relatives. Their predicament collided with my idealistic picture of Chagga family and community cooperation. The poorest people had been marginalized and had become scapegoats, objects of blame and derision in the community.

Unlike many of the poor, Francis and Bibiana had a coffee farm of average size; however, they could not afford the agricultural supplies necessary to maintain good harvests. They were dependent on cash income for buying food and could not purchase enough to feed their children. The problem became acute when the price for coffee dropped on the international market. Bibiana became pregnant in the midst of the food crisis and had to stop working in the *shamba*. Edwardi, Francis's cousin, had a relatively large coffee farm, but his income had dropped, and he was unwilling to help Francis and Bibiana and several other impoverished close relatives. Francis went to work as a day laborer at the mission but could not support his family on that income either. He was reduced to going to work in clothes made of burlap coffee sacks; his clothing was a source of shame to him and also to local officials. Despite his embarrassment, however, Francis could still speak with dignity, insist on the importance of his own children, and call for help for his needy neighbors.

The poverty of Francis and Bibiana was clearly tied to the coffee crop, although the origins of poverty on Kilimanjaro lay in the precolonial era. Coffee production provided a vehicle for fortunate people to accumulate greater riches, and various other changes caused the marginalization of the poor. As Chagga farmers entered coffee production, the cooperative movement began, and in 1925, they formed the Kilimanjaro Native Planters Association which later became the Kilimanjaro Native Cooperative Union. Cash crop production by the Chagga was firmly established by the late 1920s and rivaled the plantation sector in economic power and significance.

In the same period in many regions of Africa, better-off farmers were emerging from local farming populations to gain large land holdings that they farmed with hired labor. A similar process occurred on Kilimanjaro, although land holdings were generally smaller there.[9] The farmers who were commercially successful and had large land holdings led the cooperative movement, which grew rapidly throughout Tanganyika. Frequently the cooperatives became a tool used by better-off farmers for their own commercial advancement, often at the expense of less-educated, less-knowledgeable members such as Francis Lema. To this day, the coffee cooperative on Kilimanjaro is dominated by wealthier farmers.

In the 1970s, some households were wealthy according to local and national standards, but they were not economically secure.

> An outsider's first sympathy is with the weak members of the lineage, and their wives and children, the victims of this harsh system. . . . But those on top are precariously placed, too. Their resources are not sufficient to carry the poor relatives along without serious risk to themselves. And they know there is not enough land for their own sons. Compared with Western industrial workers, many Chagga "rich" are poor. (Moore 1986:308)

By the 1980s, a few wealthier households had reached incomes equal to those of the best-paid industrial workers in more developed countries, and a handful had even higher incomes. Some of the wealthier people were probably being supported by highly educated children who were sending remittances from outside Tanzania. Most people, however, were prosperous in local terms but could not afford cars, glass windows for their houses, or large household appliances such as refrigerators.

In the first two decades of independence, Julius Nyerere, the first president of Tanzania, implemented what he called "African socialism." In the rural areas, it was to involve *ujamaa* villages, where people were to live and farm in cooperatives. Under the *ujamaa* villagization policies, instituted in 1976, scattered farming households were supposed to come together to form centralized villages, providing better access to sanitation, health services, and education. On Kilimanjaro, however, nearly all the land in the *kihamba* belt was already divided among contiguous farms, allowing no room for new villages; hence, the old districts were renamed villages and new political structures were added (Moore 1986:139). Local people, seeking to gain power, land, scarce commodities, and access to primary and secondary education for their children would often take positions in TANU (Tanganyika African National Union, the governing political party). Better-educated, better-off people were often able to take advantage of government programs that aimed to improve the situations of poor people. (See Samhoff 1979:19 on education as an important cause of social differentiation on Mt. Kilimanjaro.)

The government also emphasized continuing coffee production in the Kilimanjaro region because of the national economy's great need for exports. It was against the law to uproot coffee trees, even though some people wanted to replace small numbers of them with food crops. This law was part of the reason for Francis and Bibiana Lema's difficulties; they had coffee trees, but when the harvest was poor, they had no income to buy food. Some Chagga converted parts of their coffee groves to vegetable gardens anyway and chanced a fine or imprisonment.

Disappointed over poor production by nationalized plantations and other socialist ventures, President Nyerere resigned in 1985. In recent years, privately owned companies have been encouraged and farmers have gained more control over their land. Chiefly lineages no longer have an important political function. People still pay homage to the wealthy and to political and religious leaders, however, and common people cling to their expectations of help during hard times, even though their experiences often suggest otherwise.

Limited Land and Rapid Population Growth

Francis Lema's poverty also has historical roots in the Chagga people's relationship to the ecology of Kilimanjaro, the highest mountain in Africa. A central reality in Chagga myth, Kilimanjaro is an aesthetic inspiration for people in their daily work. Its variable climate, topography, and soils, however, place limits on the growth of population and agricultural production.

According to most Chagga, the middle belt of Mt. Kilimanjaro is the most suitable place to live and farm. This densely settled region has the best conditions for growing coffee and major food crops. Because it is under *kihamba* tenure, it has added value as an asset of the family for generations. Chagga farms are concentrated on the southern slopes, where rainfall is most abundant and the irrigation system allows year-round cropping. Irrigation cannot counter major droughts and has caused soil erosion in certain areas, but generally farming has been successful, contributing to the growth of a large population, which has brought its own dilemmas.

At the beginning of the twentieth century, ample land for new settlement was available in the traditional *kihamba* belt. Most European settlers opposed coffee production by Chagga farmers, who managed to obtain seeds anyway, from Catholic missionaries in the 1890s and an Italian settler in 1900 (Iliffe 1979:154). By 1968, sixty-five thousand Chagga farmers had coffee farms. Coffee gradually replaced most food crops on *kihamba* land, except for banana trees, which produced plantains, a dietary staple. Banana trees were interspersed among coffee trees to provide them with shade. As the shortage of land became acute, the chief often converted *shamba* land to *kihamba* tenure, and the previous occupant had to find *shamba* land elsewhere.

Changes during the twentieth century have increased rates of population growth in many farming societies, including that of the Chagga. In earlier times in most farming societies, it was customary for women to breastfeed their children for two years or more. Frequent breastfeeding can be as effective in preventing pregnancy as oral contraceptives for one to four years after a birth (Jelliffe and Jelliffe 1978; Leridon 1977; Millard 1982).[10] Many societies in East and West Africa have a long postpartum sex taboo; according to various reports, among the Chagga this prohibition lasted at least until the child could walk or for three years after a birth. Like prolonged breastfeeding, the taboo would tend to lengthen birth intervals (Page and Lesthaeghe 1981). In recent years, the practice of these and other customs has declined, and the rate of population growth has increased.

Around 1950, population pressure became cause for alarm on Mt. Kilimanjaro.[11] Permanent crops were being planted in the less favorable upper and lower belts, and average productivity per acre was declining. Since then, the population has almost tripled (see Table 3). *Shamba* tenure is growing increasingly secure, and men often buy *shamba* land to leave to their sons as an inheritance, putting a competitive premium on all arable land. By 1967, population density was a serious problem, approaching two people per acre in the *kihamba* belt proper, and many faced the prospect of being landless. The families whose stories are told in this volume live in an area of extraordinarily high population density for farming. (In the neighboring Kibosho parish of Kitandu, population density was thirty-nine people per square mile in the 1960s [Van Clemm 1964:100].) At the 1988 rate, the population will double within a generation.[12]

Table 3   *Population on Mount Kilimanjaro, 1921–1988*

Year	Total
1921	136,000
1928	147,447
1931	164,141
1948	267,700
1957	365,000
1967	440,239
1978	694,246
1988	840,386

Sources: before 1948, for the former Kilimanjaro District, Maro (1974); 1948 and 1957, for the former Kilimanjaro District, Gamassa 1991:4; later, for the current districts of Moshi Rural, Moshi Urban, Hai, and Rombo, which replaced the former Kilimanjaro District, Gamassa 1991:4; see also Moore 1986.

Chiefs no longer regulate the land tenure system, and councils of elders and the local courts now deal with land disputes, which outnumber all other types of court cases. Despite the strong code of respect for parents, it is not unusual for impoverished men, such as Francis, to refer to their fathers as "mean" because they refused to partition their land.

During the last decades of the twentieth century, land shortages in the middle belt increased, partly because of pressure from coffee, wheat, and sugar plantations, a national park, and a government forest reserve. Government holdings limit expansion up the mountain, and ecological and social constraints limit the downward spread of the population. There is open land on the dry plains at the foot of the mountain, but the Chagga reject living there because they would have to take up a different way of farming with crops requiring very little water, negotiate with the Maasai over their grazing rights, and deal with major health threats, including malaria. Nonetheless, land pressure has led some Chagga to move away.

Much of the production of annual crops has shifted to the drier low-lands, and coffee has gradually replaced food crops and grass on *kihamba* land. The adoption of maize contributed to the shift because it is a relatively drought-resistant crop suitable for the lowlands. Maize yields both food and cash and sometimes substitutes for the milk, beans, millet, taro, and meat production lost to the coffee enterprise.

Early in the colonial period, inequality in land holdings grew when European settlers, missions, and the colonial government acquired large tracts, and it continued when the postcolonial government set up state-controlled farms on Kilimanjaro. Large tracts of farmland remain consolidated into plantations today, compressing family farms and encouraging overuse of land. Land pressure, commercial farming, and the switch to maize from the traditional mixed cropping of bananas, taro, and beans have caused considerable environmental deterioration. Scores of men are moving to Moshi town or leaving the region in search of work, and many are landless and have no means of livelihood on the mountain.

Chagga History and the Generation of Poverty

Poverty and inequality have clearly existed throughout the recorded history of Mt. Kilimanjaro. The phenomena of intractable poverty and boundless accumulation of wealth, however, are more recent. These changes help to explain Francis and Bibiana Lema's predicament and those of many other families during food crises.

The Mt. Kilimanjaro region bore the weight of many early changes under colonialism, and the Chagga people emerged with greater ties to international markets than many other Tanganyikan peoples. The early Christian missions on Kilimanjaro provided education, giving Chagga students formal qualifications and easy access to professional, managerial, and governmental positions. As coffee production expanded prior to independence, the educated invested their cash in land and cattle, giving them further advantages over illiterate farmers. Success in farming and in professional and bureaucratic positions created the Chagga reputation for affluence and the ability to change with the times.

With these changes, new constraints undermined the redistributive basis of the economy. Without cash, land-poor fathers cannot send their sons to secondary school, and without an education, many people fall behind. The need for money stems in part from land fragmentation and the limited access of middle sons to land.

The successful struggle of the Kilimanjaro people to improve their way of life through entry into the cash economy came with a cost. The disconnection of farming from food production and the undercutting of the social order that formerly provided for the poor are two major forces that created a new, severe form of poverty on the mountain. These forces led to the malnutrition of children.

Chapter Four

On the Road to the Margins

1970

〜 "Heshima ni muhimu kushinda chochote [*respect is greater than anything*]," *said a farmer as he gave me a lesson in Swahili. He chose a phrase that reflected the community's concern for human dignity.* 〜

Respect was a concern in daily life on Kilimanjaro, and in times of hardship, loss of it threatened many people. By the peak of the food crisis in 1974, anxiety triggered by economic and environmental crises had come to permeate social relationships on Mt. Kilimanjaro. People had to guard their reputations to maintain the social support of their lineages and neighborhoods. Loss of their reputations could mean being cut off from potential assistance by lineage members. Without social support, a person could be shamed and pushed to the margins of society.[1] Many families with malnourished children suffered shame and were consigned to the social periphery of their neighborhoods.

〜 My earliest lessons about how to fit into the community on Kilimanjaro came from migrants to the mountain who had struggled to assimilate. They knew the necessity of learning the local standards of behavior to establish their good names.

Lucere, the community neighboring our farm, included fifty families living along the lower portion of the Lucere River; 20 percent of the men were migrants. They had married Chagga women and purchased farmland available on that part of Mt. Kilimanjaro. Most migrants had learned the local customs and had become nearly indistinguishable from the other farmers in the area.[2]

Our farm was tied to Lucere in many ways. Villagers brought their grain to our mill for grinding, bought our chickens, eggs, and pork, and asked us to attend to their illnesses.[3] On Sundays, we joined the community for *pombe* (banana-millet beer) drinking at various households.

Like most neighborhoods on the mountain, Lucere included people from a range of economic levels. According to local protocol, the arrival of my husband and me to live on the mountain called for sponsorship by someone of high status. We had to learn to address prominent people with honorific greetings. People went to great lengths to make sure that we learned proper forms of address and deference. For example, during the weekend *pombe* gatherings, an important part of community life, there was a customary way of passing the *pombe* calabash. The host would sip from it first to assure the others there was no poison and then take it to the most revered member of the group, who would pass it to others. The circulation of the *pombe* calabash gave ritual recognition to the social hierarchy of the community.

Some members of our farming cooperative came from Lucere and still worked on their own *shambas* while living and working with us. Among them was Petro Kasulu, who was brought to the Kilimanjaro area from Bukoba during the era of forced labor. He married Ruth, a Chagga woman, and earned the respect of the community for his honesty and generosity. He took in two young Muslim boys from Lucere, Salum and Pazi Komu, after their parents split up. Normally, someone in the boys' father's lineage would have cared for them, but their father was an *mlevi* (an alcoholic) and estranged from his kin. The number of homeless boys living on the streets in Moshi town was increasing, and Petro had saved Salum and Pazi from this fate. His assistance to those in need was seen as altruistic, embodying the best of local values.

My husband and I invited Petro and Ruth to be godparents to Matthew, our firstborn son. It was an unusual honor to have paid a rather poor couple and should probably have been extended to people of higher status. But we had grown very close because of our daily contact, and we were grateful for their guidance as we started the cooperative farm. They patiently helped us adjust to our new home, and as an experienced mother, Ruth gave me indispensable support during my pregnancy and Matthew's infancy. She deferred to her husband, however, regarding business negotiations or politics.

Petro acted with a great deal of deference toward me at first, perhaps partly because of the history of relations between the Kilimanjaro people and *wazungu*. More importantly, like other local people, he prized education and paid me respect as a teacher at the International School. Petro was also careful to respect me because my husband had negotiated the use of the farmland for our cooperative, and the owners held us responsible for the management of their property.

Soon after we arrived on Mt. Kilimanjaro, Petro began to express concern about many of my unconventional ways. As a member of the cooperative, he took me under his tutelage, possibly risking his own reputation over my infractions. I regarded our farm as my home, however, and the people in the cooperative as my family. I assumed I had privacy there and could relax and behave the way I would have at home in the United States.

But Petro knew the power of gossip and did all he could to prevent me from shaming myself. At a time when the government was jailing women for wearing skirts above the knee, he expressed his distress when I wore shorts while playing soccer with the children.[4] "Chagga women wear skirts all the way down to here," he said, and bent over to point to his ankles.

Petro corrected me when I cooked discarded goat placentas to feed our dogs. "No, no, *Mama* Matthew," he said, addressing me as "mother of Matthew." "Here. Let me throw that filth out for you," he insisted as he lifted the polluting matter from the pot with a long stick and discreetly buried it somewhere among the coffee trees. Matters regarding birth are not discussed in polite Chagga society, and the placenta has special powers of contamination.

I later heard Petro scold the boys for laughing at me. They also laughed whenever I publicly fussed about their failure to flush their *mavi* (feces) down the toilet. "*Mama* Matthew," Petro told me in a hushed voice when we were alone together, "people don't talk this way in public—especially about men's feces." My many improprieties drove Petro to distraction in trying to mediate with anyone who might have taken offense.

Petro's worries reached a fever pitch when I spent three days walking about with a small animal nestled in a sock tied to my bra. "*Nipe panya huyo* [give the rat to me]," he said pleadingly after asking about the movement under my shirt. "*Nitakuulia* [I'll kill it for you]."

I wasn't persuaded. The cute little animal seemed to have dropped from nowhere onto my kitchen floor. On inspection, I thought it was an infant bush baby, a small monkeylike mammal that I had heard lived in the area. It drank up the milk I fed it from an eyedropper and became quite content in its new, warm nest. A Swedish friend excitedly brought me a guidebook on East African mammals so that we could be certain of its identity and proper care. We discovered that it was not an abandoned infant bush baby but an adult dormouse! Petro tactfully suggested I not mention my act of kindness to anyone.

These incidents were not his major source of anxiety about me, however. He was losing patience with my lack of fluency in Swahili.

"Please, let me repeat myself," he said precisely as I was loading my motor scooter to go shopping in town. "You must look for a notebook to use for learning Swahili." Petro was a student in an adult literacy program, although he could not yet read and write. When I returned from shopping and handed him my purchase, he led me to a quiet spot with a table and chairs.

"Sit here," he gently commanded. "Open your book. Now write this down." As I picked up my pen, he slowly and deliberately said, *"Heshima ni muhimu kushinda chochote."* He told me to look the meaning up in my dictionary. With some effort, I found that it meant "respect is greater than anything." ⌒

At the time, I took the message personally, as Petro sometimes seemed to consider me bizarre and unruly. He tried to coax me to learn the importance of respecting local custom or at least to behave in a more predictable *mzungu* (white person's) fashion. Later, however, I heard Petro repeat this phrase to other people.

I later came to appreciate how the notions of *heshima* (respect or honor) and its opposite, *aibu* (shame), play into almost all human relations on the mountain. Respect follows lines of authority based on age and social position, and deference is greatest toward elders and those in high positions in the lineage, Church, or government. A respectful person is to be respected in return. Familiarity between unequals in the style I was used to would have appeared presumptuous on Kilimanjaro on the part of lower-status persons and *mjinga* (foolish) on the part of those with higher status. As an outsider on the mountain, Petro had learned the importance of these notions and attempted to teach them to me.

In the 1970s, problems of land shortage increased, making it impossible for the system of inheritance to continue as it had in the past. The problems threatened the fiber of the lineage and reduced the life chances of many people, who were anxious lest they lose their standing and fall behind in the scheme of things. Neighbors and kin stood to benefit when someone lost his economic footing and had to relinquish his land, which then became available for purchase by other kinsmen seeking land to allocate to their sons. In some ways, certain people were selected for failure.

> Sloughing-off of a community "brother" must be rationalized and made congruent with the ideology of community solidarity. If a community must reject one of its own and yet extol the values of community and brotherhood and mutual obligation, it must somehow identify the rejected person as a justifiable exception to these common commitments. Rejection of a member must be turned into an affirmation of community. (Moore 1975:112–113)

~ Figure 11   *Latter-twentieth-century standards on Mt. Kilimanjaro.*

Source of Influence	Standards	Failings	Sanctions
The lineage	Proper reproductive behavior and offerings of *tambiko* to assure lineage continuity; redistribution of resources in a stratified society	Sexual immorality, reproductive failure, and lineage annihilation; stinginess, lack of reciprocity	Shaming immoral and stingy individuals
European capitalism	Progress through competition among individuals in a stratified society, educational achievement, wealth for achievers.	Poverty	Shaming impoverished individuals
Socialism	Equality through self-reliance, cooperation, and social progress; redistribution of resources by a centralized state	Dependency, lack of cooperation, corruption, lowered productivity, and poverty	Shaming dependent, uncooperative, corrupt, unproductive individuals
Christianity	Brotherly love, individual achievement, sex for procreation (Roman Catholic), individual salvation, recognition of the church hierarchy	Hatred, poverty, sexual immorality, "pagan" beliefs	Shaming sinners

People could affirm community by upholding the standards that gave it cohesion and blaming unfortunate people for their own problems. When the unfortunate felt shame and guilt, they lost some of their dignity and became less powerful in defending their reputations and property. Those who failed to meet community standards were blamed for their own misfortune. (See for comparision Ryan 1971 on more privileged individuals in the U.S. who consider the poor to have caused their own suffering.)

During the 1970s, the standards for behavior were a mixture of ideals and moral codes from four main influences: the lineage system, Christianity, capitalism, and socialism. Figure 11 presents a brief representation of ideological and moral pluralism in the area of Kilimanjaro where this study occurred. To the people in that area, Christianity is represented by Roman Catholicism, which is depicted in the figure. At times various influences converged; for example, both Christianity and the lineage system supported social stratification and patriarchal authority. The sanction of shame was a component of all four of these major influences.

The standards also sometimes conflicted. For example, the Catholic Church forbade local customs that tended to lengthen intervals between births. The lineage system did not define poverty as a failing, although the other three influences did. The resulting pluralism left people with a sense of ambivalence about what was proper. They had wide latitude in interpreting events and deciding who was blameworthy and therefore deserving of marginal status.

The Christian emphasis on individual spiritual salvation over fulfillment of the obligations of community life probably contributed to a breakdown of customary forms of reciprocity. With Christianity,

> absolute standards for moral behavior transcend community norms. They allow an individual to defy his community and feel confident within himself that his virtue will reap its final reward. If he does not honor community standards, he will still feel that he is obeying higher laws that are more relevant to his task of finding salvation. (Schneiderman 1995:28)

Although communal values are still strong on Kilimanjaro, individualism is slowly creeping in. Under such circumstances, the shame of failing to meet kin obligations can be replaced by guilt, a more hidden emotion. I have no way of knowing the extent to which better-off people felt guilty when they did not assist their poorer kin. Generally, more-powerful people cast blame on the less fortunate, who were then subjected to scrutiny for any breech of conventional standards (see Kaufman 1980:82). Intense scrutiny of distressed persons could lessen their ability to cope. Better-off people could rationalize discriminatory practices toward "these people," who were set apart by their illiteracy and were visibly distinct because of their tattered clothing and poor housing.

Widows, women without sons, middle sons and their wives, orphaned boys, and unsalaried illiterate men held weak positions in the lineage. They tended to be poor and were subject to considerably more censorship than others (Moore 1986:306). Outsiders were also among those who, through no fault of their own, had little latitude when it came to transgressing social standards. On the other hand, those in good standing through birthright or wealth had greater room to maneuver, participating in a double standard that gave them more latitude.

Petro's immigrant status increased the potential for his being held responsible for a mishap or failure.[5] People who differed from the community in dress, custom, or religion were more likely to be blamed for not upholding local standards. The families in the NURU study were marginalized, most were poor, and some had the disadvantage of being ethnic and religious outsiders. Interpretations people might give of their actions depended on the situation, however, and could be renegotiated with any change in circumstances.

For example, Chagga shifted in their characterizations of Maasai, who herd cattle on the plains below Mt. Kilimanjaro. On a number of occasions, the residents from our farming cooperative insisted that Maasai had not progressed because of their "backward ways." "*Watu wa porini wanaishi kama wanyama* [people of the plains live as animals]," they would say derisively. If a bus driver stopped for a Maasai, other passengers would ridicule the person and send him or her to the back of the bus.[6]

On the other hand, Chagga have historically accepted people from other societies, including Maasai, into their communities. A Maasai man married a woman from Lucere, dressed according to local fashion, and successfully assimilated; he became a respected member of the community and was not ridiculed. Ethnic or religious outsiders gained acceptance in Lucere more easily than they would have on the middle slopes of the mountain, where there was bitter conflict over farmland. Migrants could rise to positions of power in Lucere, as exemplified by two *balozis*, one relatively wealthy and highly respected, the other feared because he was believed to practice *uchawi* (witchcraft) learned in his homeland, the Congo.

One of the most common ways to lose respect and become shamed was to fail to uphold *maendeleo* (progress), which entered the scene with colonialism and became a banner cry of the socialist government. Neighbors and kin sometimes scorned very poor people for going barefoot and wearing tattered clothing. On Sundays, everyone wore clothes that were as *safi* (clean, neat) as possible. Men in brilliant white shirts lined the pews on St. Joseph's side of the church; women in their brightly colored *kitenge* shawls and skirts sat on the Virgin Mary's side. I was always amazed to see the Sunday procession of people emerging from their earthen houses so beautifully attired when their clothes had been washed in a river and pressed with an iron heated with charcoal.

Signs of *maendeleo* included personal hygiene; clean and fashionable clothing; houses of manufactured materials, including tin roofs and glass windows; store-bought foods; and literacy. The list continued to grow as new opportunities developed and new merchandise became available. Upholding *maendeleo* cost money. Being *maskini* (poor) was to have failed, and being *hohehahe* (worthless riffraff) was to be at the bottom of the social ladder.

1972

〜 An elderly stranger appeared when my husband was making preparations for a baptismal feast weeks before our son Matthew's birth. The man took charge of many of the arrangements even though we had never met him before. He was quite tall, darker than most Chagga, and had features uncommon to the region. His distinctively large face was carved with deep lines and accented with a Roman nose and well-defined chin.

Mzee Lamumba had come to the Kilimanjaro area during the period of British control to work on the sisal plantations at the foot of the mountain. He sometimes wore a long, tattered gray cape and an old cap that recalled British authority. He had married a local woman, but his appearance and demeanor made him conspicuous. He was not a mild-mannered man, as one would expect of a poor person on Kilimanjaro, but was instead extraordinarily flamboyant and boisterous. He carried himself with the dignity usually associated with powerful people such as a *masumba* (wealthy man) or *bwana mkubwa* (big man), even though he, his wife, and their six children were the poorest household in the village.

He became involved in the selection of goats for our baptismal feast, two for roasting and one for me to start my own herd. When the day of baptism arrived, *Mzee* Lamumba, acting with his authority as a *balozi*, made sure all of Lucere came. Great tubs of rice, *ndizi na nyama* (a dish of bananas and beef), and beer accompanied the roasted goat. After the priest baptized Matthew, the celebration began and *Mzee* Lamumba took over.

"Where are the drums? And the drummers? We need music here. African music! What's the matter with you people—afraid of the *wazungu*?" he mocked a crowd who were sitting on the lawn enjoying their meal. We had invited some European friends from the International School and the Kilimanjaro Christian Medical Center, where I had been consulting. *Mzee*

Lamumba was probably accurate in his observation that all the white faces inhibited the usual proceedings, for the celebration did not come alive until nearly all the *wazungu* had left.

When most of them had gone, *Mzee* Lamumba gathered everyone around an old water fountain and climbed atop its stone base to be seen and heard. He made a long, formal speech thanking my husband and me for our hospitality, our interest in the community, and bringing Africans and *wazungu* together. Then he opened a bag he'd brought from home.

"All right now, you women, show them you can dance!" And with that command, he took out a bullwhip and herded groups of women into dancing formations. I was astonished! He was quite drunk by then, but people obeyed him and enjoyed themselves.

"Dance, women, dance!" he shouted as he snapped the whip in a drunken frenzy. The women were laughing uncomfortably at first but built momentum as they formed circles and kept time to the rhythm of the drums.

From that day on, I was curious about *Mzee* Lamumba and sought his views on various matters. He assisted me in instructing my International School students in the Chagga crafts of house building, *pombe* brewing, and storytelling. On occasion, when I felt very frustrated with people in the farming cooperative, I'd go to *Mzee* Lamumba with pen and paper and ask him to explain the history of Lucere or answer questions about people's behavior.

Petro was uncomfortable with the relationship I was developing with *Mzee* Lamumba and made it clear that he did not trust the old man. He said it was undignified for him to put himself on display with all his boasting and need for control. Finally he told me that *Mzee* Lamumba practiced *uchawi* (witchcraft). Fear, Petro said, had motivated people to elect *Mzee* Lamumba *balozi*, and he played into it by making occasional threats. I did not pay Petro any heed.

Later, *Mzee* Lamumba approached us with a scheme to rebuild a bridge across the Lucere River that had collapsed some time ago. Only one huge beam remained, and a local woman had fallen to her death while crossing. We were impressed with his apparent concern and civic-mindedness and contributed a large sum as seed money. Others from Lucere contributed, and the amount was sufficient to get matching funds from the government. When the time came to approach the proper authorities, however, *Mzee* Lamumba claimed that the funds had been stolen. No one believed him. ⁓

Like many other poor people, he availed himself of deceit and fraud as one way of coping with scarcity. *Mzee* Lamumba vehemently denied any guilt, but the villagers took him to court anyway. The judges could not find incriminating evidence, but community censorship remained, and gossip about his involvement in witchcraft intensified. He may have gained some power by playing on the fears of others, but the community did not like or trust him.

It was clear that his actions had pushed him to the social margins of the village, and no one came to his rescue in a time of need. *Mzee* Lamumba and his wife were the only members of the village whose children were severely malnourished. Some of them died during the food crisis.

Shame and Stigma

These events occurred in the time of food crisis in the mid-1970s. Trust among the populace was undermined by economic, ecological, and political crisis: failed rains, coffee berry disease, unreliable markets for farm products, a world economy with punishing inflation, and threats by General Idi Amin of Uganda of air raids on Mt. Kilimanjaro's government stations.[7] Rising banditry, swindles in the markets, illegal commerce, alcoholism, corrupt business practices, sorcery, and witchcraft were all responses to these crises. They raised the level of anxiety to such a pitch that even relatively comfortable people had difficulties. Out of this general sense of anxiety, unpredictability, and mistrust came feelings of guilt and shame. These feelings dominated the responses of the poor and hungry, who became socially isolated in the context of widespread intense anxiety.[8]

"To feel shame is to feel *seen* in a painfully diminished sense" (Kaufman 1980:9). A person can feel shame when perceiving the scorn of others, even if it is only imagined.

> Shame can be likened to a border guard who punishes those who overstep a particular moral code's sense of dignity and respectability. Transgressions of such borders offend good morals and can result in social sanctions or at the very least, a certain loss of face. (Jacoby 1994:46)

The possibility that they will be shamed pressures people to maintain social standards, be conscious of the judgment of others, and preserve their human dignity. Fear of shame moves people to preserve their integrity and privacy and to protect themselves from collective condemnation. Being shamed can bring loss of self-respect because it involves other people's learning of a disgraceful matter; a person who feels guilty can try to avoid being shamed by making amends or projecting the blame onto others (Jacoby 1994:2; see also Donahue and McGuire 1994; Finerman 1994; Finerman and Bennett 1994).

The experience of shame varies in its effect on a person's dignity. It can mean a slight embarrassment, a temporary loss of regard, or the more fixed state of stigma. Being stigmatized sets an individual apart from others, whether for merit or failure.[9] Polluting aspects of stigma can be "deeply discrediting" to a person's social identity, according to Goffman (1963:4). Negative stigma can occur on the basis of physical difference, abnormality, or a moral failing such as sexual impropriety or theft (Goffman 1963). Any deviation from the group, including a religious or ethnic difference, can become a stigma (Goffman 1963:12–19). Stigma can "carry with it a series of moral imputations about character and personality" and can lead "normals" to regard the stigmatized as "their psychological, moral and emotional inferiors" (Goffman 1963:4).

Many factors were involved in the tentative fixing of negative stigma on Kilimanjaro. The person's status, the norm that was violated, and the number of transgressions could have a bearing on someone's reputation. Negative stigma may have been one factor contributing to the reported domestic abuse in some of the families in the NURU study. Adults humiliated on a daily basis by their condition may vent their anger on their dependents—men sometimes on their wives, some older women on daughters-in-law, and any of them at times on children in their own households.

The flexibility of people in weighing elements of blame became evident in a case of theft at our farm. Stealing was considered one of the most despicable and shameful offenses. Once I observed a homeless boy stripped naked and nearly beaten to death for stealing food in the Moshi town marketplace. Later, one of the adopted boys at our farm became involved in an accusation of theft.

1974

 ∿ We had a herd of eight milk goats on our cooperative farm. Four youths took them out to graze during the early morning hours. Among the herders were Ndesario, a retarded nineteen-year-old boy; Petro's adopted sons, Salum and Pazi Komu; and my two-year-old son, Matthew. The boys took Matthew along for fun, another diversion besides their flutes in dealing with their monotonous work. Salum, five years older than Pazi, took primary responsibility for the goats and the welfare of the other three boys. He also took a fatherly attitude, protecting and admonishing his younger brother, Pazi.

Pazi was a handsome, bright, lively eleven-year-old when he and Salum came to live at our farm. He spent a lot of time perfecting his game of soccer, for he hoped one day to join Tanzania's national team. He dominated conversations about the various players when the boys all gathered around our radio to listen to soccer matches. Charming and self-confident, he had great dreams for the future.

When the two brothers first moved to our farm with Petro and took up residence, Pazi was moody and had occasional bouts of depression. I had heard of his father's drunken violence and assumed Pazi had been beaten or otherwise abused. He became extremely sensitive and easily took offense, yet he also expressed a great deal of warmth and sympathy to anyone else who was suffering. Pazi grew especially close to me, and he was the first person to sit by my side and throw an arm over my shoulder after I had quarreled with someone or was sad for some other reason. He was tender and loving toward Matthew and delighted in teaching him to walk, appreciate Chagga food, and speak Swahili.

I grew attached to the boys; I made sure they had nice clothing and good food and gave them reading lessons. As Pazi began to feel more self-confident, his depression lifted. He developed a wonderful sense of humor and began telling lengthy jokes with a dramatic flair in our evening fireside conversations. Pazi started learning the new songs that came over the radio and seemed interested in almost everything, including animal life, different cultures, and girls. As his outlook improved and he began adolescence, he took a sudden interest in his appearance.

One Sunday after everyone had returned from church, I found Pazi wailing in his room.

"What happened, Pazi?"

"Nothing. Go away!" he sniffled, and covered his head with his sheet.

Salum entered the room, and I repeated my question.

"He was caught stealing a shirt from a neighbor's clothesline, and they beat him up."

"No, I didn't, you bunch of snake shit!" he protested in a rage, throwing off the sheet and leaping up to struggle with his brother. We saw that he was covered with cuts and bruises, and his face was bloody. Salum laughed in embarrassment while Pazi did what he could to fend off his shame. I could not console him.

From that day on, Pazi was suspected of having stolen anything that was missing. He constantly had to defend his reputation. Some people explained that without an intact family to give Pazi guidance, once he began to steal, he would continue. An act of theft by a child would usually be overlooked if he lived in an intact, respectable household. Broken families were said to produce thieves, and their children were watched closely, often creating a self-fulfilling prophecy.

Pazi became defensive at the smallest hint of rejection. He also became domineering and cruel, especially toward Ndesario, the retarded youth who herded the goats with him. He taunted one of the high-school boys for his habit of wetting his bed at night and encouraged my son to swear and say unspeakable things in Swahili. For Pazi, the shame of theft and the beating resulted in a profound loss of self-confidence. ⌒

When I returned to Lucere in 1989, I asked Petro about Salum and Pazi. In a short time, Salum came in from cultivating the fields and appeared to be doing fine at thirty-three years of age, although he had not yet married. Pazi jogged from his workplace in the hot sun and arrived covered with sweat and cement dust. He explained he had become a *fundi* (expert) in bricklaying, although Petro informed me later that Pazi was merely a day laborer. He was still defensive, and at twenty-eight years of age, his appearance alone was cause for shame. His hair had grown out in dreadlocks, which at that time on Mt. Kilimanjaro were a sign of being crazy or a lost soul. Pazi no longer held his head high as he spoke with me, and he avoided meeting my gaze.

A bad start in a life marred by misfortune was one pathway to becoming shamed, as was evident for Pazi and some of the fathers of malnourished children. Some neighbors had compassion for those who were struggling with misfortune, but for the most part, they ascribed bad fortune to individual weakness. Shaming a person on the basis of misfortune was not an automatic process, however. All people had occasional small lapses, mishaps, and misfortunes, but some could manage negative public opinion about themselves in such a way as to avoid being shamed.

If enough discrediting incidents occurred, however, it was harder for some people to manage the impressions others had of them. As Goffman explains, all people have their "half-hidden failings, and for every little failing there is a social occasion when it will loom large, creating a shameful gap between virtual and actual social identity." Those with minor failings "form a single continuum" with those who have been stigmatized, "their situation in life analyzable by the same framework" (Goffman 1963:123).

On Mt. Kilimanjaro, small injuries to personal dignity were the stuff of daily life and could happen to anyone, yet they caused embarrassment, and people made an effort to cover the mishaps. For example, the struggle to prevent damage to one's identity was obvious in the response to stumbling, which was an important concern on the dangerous mountain terrain. A small stumble often was an occasion for laughter, but when people suffered injury or death from stumbling, suspicions of sorcery arose. Blame for loss of life or limb also could be fixed on injured persons themselves, if they had previously fallen into disrepute.

People who were wealthy and powerful were somewhat less vulnerable than others and often managed to deflect blame. Any scapegoats were usually people with less social standing who found themselves in a bitter contest with better-off kin or neighbors.

A Double Standard and Stigma

Better-off people's misfortunes seldom bring them disrepute since they generally maintain strong social ties by fulfilling obligations to kin and neighbors. Should an impoverished person enter a dispute over harm that has occurred, he or she may be accused of sorcery or witchcraft.

1973

〜 During my stay in Lucere, two women died. The first was Salum and Pazi's grandmother, Gertrudi Komu, who was very old and married to a poor farmer. Her son, Salum and Pazi's father, was an alcoholic, and she did not respect him, nor did his sons, because he failed to provide for them. His neglect was especially harmful during the food crisis, when many elderly made public complaints of *njaa*.

Gertrudi had not fit the Chagga ideal of the stoic woman in her old age; she had been irritable and bitter. She had reason to curse her son from her deathbed—a mother's curse being the most feared of all. At the time, people whispered that she practiced witchcraft. As Gertrudi lay dying, Salum and Pazi became distraught and borrowed large sums of money to buy whatever she might request. They also made visits to a local *mganga* (healer) for fetishes to ward off any harm that might come if their grandmother should curse their father or them.

Early one morning, I heard a knock on my door. I was expecting Salum and Pazi to fetch Matthew for herding the goats. When I opened the door, I found only Pazi, who looked very agitated.

"She died," he said, wringing his hands.

"*Pole sana* [I am very sorry]. Come on in. When did it happen?"

"Before the sun rose."

"Is there anything we can do?" I asked.

"Yes, *Mama* Matthew. Salum wants me to bring a white sheet for her burial. And because of the funeral preparations, we won't be able to herd goats today. Ndesario can manage."

Upon Gertrudi's death, a momentary hush fell over the neighborhood, and then a flurry of activity arose. When we arrived at Gertrudi's house that night for the funeral, a group of women sat outside in their farming clothes, snorting snuff. Ruth took me inside to present the sheet to Gertrudi's daughter.

"*Ayee!*" exclaimed Ruth when she came upon Gertrudi's body. She handed me the sheet and quickly left. Others had similar reactions after peeking in to check on our progress. As we bound her, Gertrudi's daughter wept quietly.

Another older woman, perhaps Gertrudi's sister, begged, "Please, please, Gertrudi. Forgive me for being so clumsy." She made the request to temper any malevolence of the dead woman in her last rite of passage.

A group of men came to carry Gertrudi's body to the grave freshly dug behind her house. Once she lay in the grave, the mourners checked with one another about the proper procedures. No priest was present, and she may not have converted to Christianity, but her kin and neighbors decided to say Catholic prayers anyway. Then each of us threw a shovelful of dirt on her corpse. I never heard Gertrudi's name mentioned after that day.

Gertrudi's complaints roused community fears that she would use her power to seek vengeance in the afterlife. Her impoverishment was a sign that she had been neglected, and her loud complaints drew attention to the disrespect of her kin. Anyone who wept uncontrollably or displayed great sorrow at her funeral might have been blamed for neglecting her. Gertrudi's funeral rites were too rushed and the attendants too tense for the death of a normal old woman. During drought and crop failure, the elderly had increasingly complained as they received less and less from their adult children, who were also undergoing hardship. The common response in the community was to blame the elderly for any misfortune instead of those entrusted with their care.

The other person who died in Lucere during my stay in the 1970s was Mary Kalanga, who at the age of forty succumbed after a long and painful illness. Even though they knew it was coming, Mary's death shocked the whole community. Mention of her name brought tears to women's eyes and woeful expressions from men. People greeted each other with, "*pole* [my sympathy]" instead of exchanging their usual salutations. Mary was the first wife of Filippo Kalanga, the *bwana mkubwa*, the wealthiest resident of Lucere. His two wives lived in large brick homes at opposite ends of the village. The community admired both Mary and her cowife and felt that their presence brought respect to the impoverished village. When Mary died, the community was greatly saddened.

Voluntary collections were taken up to pay for four Catholic masses on her behalf, each costing twenty shillings (U.S. $2.86), more than two days' wages. Her funeral was celebrated by the parish priest four days after her death, and all of Lucere came dressed in their finest Sunday apparel. They extended their condolences to all those sitting nearby, and for a month afterward, people spoke of their loss. For an even longer time, people discussed Mary's thirteen-year-old daughter, her only child, with great concern, as the loss of a mother is regarded as a severe blow to a young woman.

Compared with Gertrudi's death, Mary's posed no moral threat to the community in terms of the guilt of kin and fears of harm by the spirit of the dead. Mary was considered to have lived a virtuous life as gauged by her wealth and her husband's position as benefactor to the community. In a poorer woman, the failure to have more than one child might have brought ridicule and accusations of sorcery. Instead, her death brought the people of Lucere together in their regret.

The difference between Gertrudi's and Mary's funerals exemplifies the double standard applied to poor and wealthy persons. Gertrudi fulfilled traditional ideals by having sons, and Mary did not. Producing male heirs had led to Gertrudi's successful incorporation into her husband's lineage. Her status as an elder would normally have brought her respect and authority. Mary died before attaining elderhood. Although she was personally distressed about having only one daughter, her wealth and involvement in *maendeleo* (progress) brought her favor and respect and overrode any suspicions people may have had. A poor old woman like Gertrudi had little to contribute to community life in times of crisis except to act as a scapegoat for many people's ill feelings. Hiding any shame for failing to care for her, they instead whispered accusations of witchcraft and fears of her curses.

Wealth and Shame

Themes of *maendeleo* echoed through the valleys and ridges of Mt. Kilimanjaro during the 1970s, along with respect for the personal quality of *akili* (intelligence, cleverness). Upwardly mobile people were said to have *akili*, which was partly a local assessment of intelligence and partly a matter of good fortune, often having little to do with intellectual ability. In contrast, poverty and misfortune were frequently associated with *ujinga* (foolishness), as was illiteracy. Advanced education was useful to better-off people in differentiating themselves from impoverished others and ensuring "that new generations of local leaders have values and orientations similar to those of their predecessors" (Samhoff 1979:68).

Meeting customary obligations costs money; those who are better off generally are more able than the poor to live according to Chagga custom (Moore 1986).[10] Wealthier people can also pay for Catholic masses and provide expensive food, drink, and gifts for celebrations of baptism, first communion, and confirmation. They can pay fines in the customary court and offer bribes; cash buys education and social position. Wealth thus brings many advantages, allowing better-off people to defend themselves from insult and their reputations from harm.

Although they have more leeway than others, wealthy people are not free of the constraints posed by local norms. In the 1970s, well-educated people who saw themselves as living in accord with *maendeleo* sometimes underwent economic crisis because of drought, falling coffee prices, and other problems, and they had to guard against being shamed. Those who maintain their wealth must manage it successfully to keep their social standing. Conspicuous displays of wealth can provoke intense envy, resentment, and potential bewitchment or sorcery. People will make fools of themselves if they enumerate their belongings publicly. If a poor person asks for a gift from a better-off person and can promise no return, conceding would be considered foolish. Being *mjinga* (foolish) is to invite enormous disregard. Any increase in wealth tends to bring both higher taxes and more demands from kin. These pressures may play a role in agistment, the custom of placing some cattle with another household, sometimes miles away. Through agistment, men are able to relocate some of their wealth, partly to hide it and partly to gain power and control over kin. Government officials still complain about the difficulty of getting accurate reports of land and cattle holdings on Kilimanjaro.

In the mid-1970s, some conspicuous consumption, in the form of luxurious housing, the latest clothing styles, and automobiles, was acceptable and brought honor to the whole lineage. In the company of outsiders, a person could take pride in the property of wealthier relatives. Any envy that might have been provoked among kin was counterbalanced by expectations of future assistance.

Formal education, brought to Kilimanjaro by Christian missions, eventually superseded coffee farming as a primary means of becoming wealthy (Samhoff 1979; see also Kerner 1988). In 1966, to distribute primary and secondary education more evenly throughout Tanzania, the government stopped constructing new schools in Kilimanjaro and built them in regions with relatively few schools. Kilimanjaro parents and local leadership worked with Catholic and Lutheran church officials to meet the educational needs of a growing population. All members of the community cooperated to build dozens of church schools and eleven private secondary schools which had to charge fees for building and operating expenses. The fees, associated costs such as school uniforms, and loss of children's labor on the farm had the effect of limiting more advanced education for the children of better-off parents. Limited access to public schools intensified competitiveness, which sometimes came to involve deceit, bribery and corruption. Public officials often used their influence to gain access to education for their children in Kilimanjaro. As one study showed,

> access to wealth leads to access to schools, which in turn provides access to power. Church initiative and finance enable more schools to be opened, which enable Kilimanjaro children to be more educated, which enables them to provide a major portion of the national leadership. And it is the ties to the metropole, in this case via the churches, which both in the past and in the present provide access to the wealth used to expand schools. (Samhoff and Samhoff 1976:82–83)

This pattern was perpetuated in part by the value placed on *akili*. *Akili* and *ujinga* were not a simple dualism, and their tie to notions of *maendeleo* sometimes involved manipulation of government bureaucracy. Government rules restricted commerce, but a person with *akili* could learn to bypass them by mouthing the party rhetoric, gaining a government position, and directing government resources to kin. He might arrange admission of his sons to selective schools, manipulate the courts in land disputes, and have ways of obtaining scarce goods.

Better-off people do not make gifts and loans to poor kin simply out of altruism. Gifts and loans can display wealth, enhance prestige, promise future returns, and increase power over others. Wealthy people recognize their obligations to less fortunate kin but are discouraged when they see them making bad use of loans and gifts.

For example, in 1972, Katrina Jones tried to assist her cousin, Alicia, whose husband had recently died, leaving her with ten children to support. Katrina bought Alicia thirty hens at eighteen shillings each. When the birds had just come into lay, instead of keeping them to sell the eggs, Alicia either sold them or cooked them for her family. When Katrina returned with a second month's supply of feed, she found the enterprise gone.

Since poor people normally have no surplus goods or cash, they usually spend loans and gifts to meet immediate needs. Although they understand this bind, wealthier kin are also hesitant to make loans because of it. Inflationary prices for commodities, lowered income from coffee, and increased school fees would place their own families at risk if they were to exhaust their savings to help their poorer kin.

To avoid draining their resources, most wealthy members of the lineage make it known that they are more likely to help needy relatives on a short-term basis. People always turn to the *bwana mkubwa* of their area for use of a car in emergencies. He can be a source of loans for investments if he decides a project is worthy and will bring him a return. The *bwana mkubwa* is sought out for counsel in matters of importance to the community, especially when his power is necessary for a transaction with Moshi town politicians. All these activities tend to enhance his status and secure his power. People look to him not only because he might provide help for short-term problems but also because of customs of respect for those with wealth and power. Keeping continuity with the past by upholding the privilege of wealthy people gives the community a sense of security. It persists even though better-off kin frequently fail to provide help to poor relatives with problems of a long-term nature.

Wealth insulates people somewhat from censorship, and when they are accused of an infraction, they sometimes react defensively, stubbornly maintaining that they are correct. Their lack of flexibility can have dire consequences for those who have become dependent on them. Neighbors may dislodge a *bwana mkubwa* if his cleverness, cunning, and competitiveness become too predominant in his dealings. Being *kali* (mean, stingy) is not admirable. In fact, failure to give assistance, especially regarding emergencies, directly violates lineage solidarity. Being consistently stingy lowers the wealthy person's social standing and can result in his being shamed.

Defending against Shame

To navigate the complex interpersonal realm on Kilimanjaro, people sought ways of protecting themselves from insult, guilt, and shame.[11] The strategies they used varied with temperament and family background. Pazi, for example, was an extroverted child who initially reacted to being accused of theft with rage and aggression. Francis Lema withdrew from the larger community and acquiesced to a collective judgment that he was a hapless individual, but he struggled to maintain a quiet life of dignity with those who knew him well (see Chapters 1 and 3).

Some defended themselves by seeking positions of power. *Mzee* Lamumba may have sought power as a means to defend himself from the potential judgments of others. Once he achieved a position of power, he could more easily deflect blame onto others, and he did so with relish. On reflection, it seems that Fatima Ruaha's anger and revenge toward me may very well have been a means of coping with her public humiliation when I accused her of theft (see Chapter 2). If she tried to bewitch me, she may have been reacting to the death of her nephew, Roberto.

Accusing someone of sorcery is a way to exercise power and to shame an errant lineage member. Use of curse and sorcery was specified or implied in the situations of Gertrudi Komu and many of the families with malnourished children. Someone found trying to harm a person by supernatural means is usually forced to take defensive action. In general, the direction of blame follows the line down the social hierarchy. Passing the blame down the social ladder makes the problem of shame intractable for the poor, who today are the least respected members of their lineages.

Without sufficient cash, a person's moral standing weakens in all spheres—lineage, church, and state. Those who are well off have proof of high status in contemporary terms, and they can afford to uphold customary obligations to kin, enhancing their status in customary terms as well (Moore 1986:130). Those who are poor need assistance from better-off kin and tend to be tied to the system of customary values for that reason.

Poorer people sometimes said, "You can't get help from anyone," but I observed cooperation among them, despite competition and hostility. Poor people lament the loss of old forms of reciprocity. According to them, what one person can count on from another has changed for the worse, and money is to blame. Better-off people explain, "Everyone has his own problems now and must see to them first." The anxiety of most people that their "half-hidden failings" would be discovered could be relieved somewhat by projecting blame onto someone else. The argument "You can ask once for help but not a second time" suggests that wealthier people see the chronic problems of poor kin as a potential drain on their holdings. The statement may also further shame needy lineage members unable to resolve their problems after a single act of generosity.

When they broke the local standards for sexual propriety, became inebriated, or were accused of sorcery, poor people were cut off from normal forms of social support. Worse yet, when their children became ill with kwashiorkor, they were blamed. In a very real way, social interaction on Mt. Kilimanjaro ensured that impoverished people would remain poor and be blamed for it.

Chapter Five

"These People"

Institutional Discrimination and Resistance by the Poor

1974

~ *In the company of Francis Lema, I was interviewing parents of a child who had been in NURU. At one point, the father broke in and said vehemently, "What good are all these questions to us? Find me a job if you want to do good!"*

Watching him chastise me, as another man had done a few days before, Francis seemed embarrassed, though he understood the man's outburst. Walking down a path with me afterward, he said, "You know, Mama Matthew, perhaps we could organize an ushirika *[cooperative]. With your help, we could apply to the government for loans and materials. Nathaniel, Paulo, and I hardly make enough money at the mission plantation to buy a pint of milk for our children. Everywhere we are hearing about* ushirikas. *Even this morning at the mission clinic the radio explained that the path to development is through cooperation."* ~

Francis had already discussed his concept of a woodworking cooperative with his cousins, and he had then waited for an opportunity to present it to me. His approach to me came at a good time because I was beginning to despair of the hardships people were facing. Francis's request was an opportunity to try to help him create work and earn more income. The men had heard radio announcements about government programs to assist commercial initiatives and asked me to mediate for them with the bureaucracy.

Our team leader, Marja-Liisa Swantz, had designed our study as "research in action," with university students from the area collecting information and, with community members, initiating solutions to community problems. We had anticipated involving local women, but the poorest women simply had no time, and they may have feared that they would arouse opposition from men if they took collective action. I took the men's case to local church and government officials, who at the outset seemed eager to help. Eventually, I was cautioned about "these people," and I came to understand how inequity was reinforced by the institutions offering assistance.

〜 I met with Francis and his cousins and we began to lay the groundwork for the cooperative with government officials. Next I searched for a place to formally present Francis's idea to all of the fathers of malnourished children in my study.

Father Patricio, who had sometimes accompanied me on daily visits to the families, suggested we use one of the church buildings. We decided on a date and time for our meeting, sent word to the men, and planned to get the pastor's approval to use the church grounds.

The pastor was continuously unavailable to see me, and his refusals began to worry me. Finally, as a last resort, I sent him a letter with Father Patricio requesting permission to use a room for our first meeting the next day.

Late that evening the priest's servant brought me a note. It read:

> Dear Mrs. Thomas,
>
> I heard that you wanted to see me but unfortunately whenever you came to my office you always found me occupied. I would like sometime to see you but I don't think I will because as I am a Dean I am always out.
>
> *What I would like to bring to your attention is that you come here for research and for heaven's sake adhere to that goal otherwise I will have to change my mind. I hope this is clear.* [Emphasis his.] I know your intention is to help us and I praise you for that. If you want to help us you can but you must first let us know.
>
> Thanks,
> Father Cambrian 〜

With the note, Father Cambrian canceled our meeting, refusing to allow the men a place to organize. He also admonished me for attempting to help families in need without waiting for his approval. My mind was spinning all night trying to understand his motives. Hadn't I waved to him daily as he sped down the road to Moshi? Hadn't I done what was proper by receiving communion from him on a regular basis? And hadn't I acknowledged his authority by attempting to introduce myself to him? This part of Kilimanjaro was largely Catholic, and I saw the Church as having considerable responsibility for neighborhood families in crisis. By dawn, I was no longer worried about being offensive, and I stubbornly planted myself outside his office waiting to speak with him when he returned from the 6 A.M. mass. It would be our first encounter outside mass.

⁓ "Father Cambrian," I said so assertively that I surprised myself, "we have some important matters to discuss."

Startled, he invited me into his chambers while he regained his composure. "I've been looking forward to talking with you, Mrs. Thomas. The sisters and Father Patricio tell me of the fine work you are doing with our very poor families."

"Then why did I get this note last night?" I rudely interrupted, omitting the usual exchange of pleasantries.

"Please hear me out," he insisted. Getting up from behind a large wooden desk, he motioned for me to join him next to the window. "Do you see those buildings? Down at the bottom is our primary school, and these large buildings are for our secondary students. You should know by now the workings of our clinic, as I have permitted you to use one of the rooms for sleeping quarters. The sisters supervise twenty nursing students, who must eat, like the primary and secondary students. We have developed programs to give technical training to young adults; it is the youth who will help us make progress, and I cannot even meet all their needs."

Father Cambrian was explaining why he had refused the organization of another program on church grounds. "But we simply asked for a room for our first meeting in case it rained," I persisted, ignoring his attempt to explain that his refusal was not capricious.

"Don't misunderstand me, Mrs. Thomas, but do you really think these people would feel comfortable in schoolrooms? What real future do they have? We already have to turn away many promising girls and boys because we don't have enough classrooms for them."

"We're not cold-hearted and careless. As I said in my note, I praise you for your concern. We help these people already through the St. Vincent de Paul Society, where they can get clothing or food when they need it." ⁓

I heard Father Cambrian's phrase, *hawa watu* (these people), time and again in conversations with clerics, government officials, and community leaders about very poor families. Francis and his cousins may not have known how they were talked about, but they did know that they lacked the power to convince officials to take them seriously.

Francis had tried to consolidate power by getting me involved, probably because he thought my status, connections, and bureaucratic skills would open doors. On the men's behalf, I went to officials to try to get support, but the wide range of responses made it difficult for me to proceed. Their reluctance to support the men can be understood only in light of the history of the institutions and the orientation of their officials.

Christian Missions and the Distribution of Wealth

The first serious missionary activity in the Kilimanjaro region began in 1885, when British missionaries of the Church Missionary Society established an Anglican mission in Moshi. When the German government took over administration of the area following a Chagga uprising in 1892, Anglican missionaries, suspected of conspiring with the Chagga against the Germans, were ousted, and the Leipzig Lutheran Mission moved in (Bennett 1964:229). Meanwhile, a Roman Catholic mission had been established in Kilema by French missionaries in 1890 (Shann 1956:27). Soon other missions arrived, and eventually the mountain was carved into separate, often competing, spheres of religious influence, divisions still important in local politics today.

The missionaries of the late nineteenth century brought more than Christianity to Kilimanjaro; they also introduced the people to a formal European educational system, the cash economy, coffee farming, and European goods. The Chagga welcomed formal European education early, and mission schools still inspire the enthusiasm of clerics and the Chagga people alike. The hierarchical organization of European churches paralleled that of chiefdoms, enhancing the appeal of Christianity and promoting rapid adoption of European institutions on Kilimanjaro.

> Their [missionaries'] very presence in Chagga communities created a market for raw materials such as food and building materials and a demand for labor which they preferred to pay for in cash. Thus they introduced to the Chagga the concept of money as payment for goods and labor. Life in Kilimanjaro began to experience the gradual but revolutionary change from barter to a money economy. The ramifications were considerable. Time became a commodity to be bought and sold; traditional labor patterns of shared work in the fields changed dramatically. New patterns of agriculture emerged; new crops were planted, not for consumption but for sale. Men learned trades such as bricklaying, masonry, carpentry, and printing.
>
> Over the first 15 years, from 1897 to 1912, the missionaries noted with both pleasure and concern the increasing wealth of the Chagga people—much of it in an expendable form. The growing opportunities for paid workers in mission and government stations to earn a regular wage and for agricultural produce to be sold as cash crops created a new consumer demand. In place of traditional weapons, tools, utensils and clothes—all made in Chagga households—people began to purchase European-manufactured steel axes, knives, and cooking pots; china plates, cups and dishes; cotton shirts, trousers and dresses. A whole range of imported luxury goods such as umbrellas, boxes, chairs and leather goods, etc., also appeared in shops and was bought by the more affluent Chagga. (Lema 1973:51–52)

Some people say that the Catholic Church donated the first coffee seeds to the Chagga, although others claim that an official in one chiefdom purchased seeds from an immigrant farmer and began the first successful Chagga coffee farm (Iliffe 1979:154). In the 1920s, many Chagga people readily took up coffee farming as a means of acquiring cash. Once the cash economy took hold, the Church did not relinquish its role in continuing the transformation. The majority of parishes acquired huge coffee plantations and large tracts of farmland.

In establishing schools, the missions used education to propagate the faith, and the government gave them a free hand in controlling the curriculum (Samoff 1974:37). The mission schools received financial support from the colonial administration, and by 1914 they had enrolled twenty thousand children on Kilimanjaro (Shann 1956:25). After World War II, the British government hesitated to continue giving the schools more than token resources, but by then, Kilimanjaro had already established its lead over the rest of the country in education.

Christian-educated people came to exemplify modernity in local society. Through formal education, some gained access to salaried positions; many found they could claim social and political authority. Educated people could use their newfound power and influence for personal advantage in accumulating wealth. As they pursued their economic ambitions, however, they paid less attention to customary lineage obligations. The activities of the missions intensified social and economic differentiation at the expense of the customary routes to prestige, including providing work and food for needy kin, land and bridewealth for sons, and support for the elderly.

The missions introduced an economic system to Kilimanjaro that built on some features of Chagga society while eroding others. Social and economic differentiation increased, based in part on differences in education obtained from mission schools. The missions stressed individual achievement and undercut kin obligations and many other traditions. Mission-initiated economic transformations changed patterns of redistribution and reciprocity, especially food sharing. The activities of the missionaries were partly responsible for changing the face of poverty on the mountain and making it more intractable than it had been in earlier times.

The Role of the Pastor

The Kilimanjaro people feel that the presence of a pastor in their community enhances their spirituality, much as the presence of the chief did in the past. Lay people view the accumulation of property by the Church as appropriate, in part because of similarities between pastors and chiefs in both the religious and economic realms. The pastors' fine manors, surrounded by expanses of well-kept lawns, have antecedents in the huge banana-thatched round houses built for chiefs.

Under the direction of pastors, the Chagga have built churches and church schools, which have become symbols of progress. Beautiful cathedrals abruptly appear in the midst of the mountain foliage, and their imposing Gothic architecture is a source of pride for the people. The churches give the Christian God an imposing home, evoking the majesty of Ruwa's resting place in Chagga cosmology, the snow-capped peak of Mt. Kilimanjaro.

The pastor maintains the comportment of a chief, and the people treat him with the greatest *heshima* (respect) given to any mortal, surpassing even that accorded to the *bwana mkubwa* (big man). Like the court of lineage elders that formerly advised the chief about judgments in civil disputes, the Church Council makes judgments and advises the pastor. The Church Council deals with many disputes, frequently leaving civil courts as the last resort in disputes among family members. For the majority of people, the pastor in Chagga society has replaced the chief as mediator between God and the people. Christian rites of baptism, first communion, confirmation, and marriage have replaced former rites of passage.

During the 1970s, Christian rites included offerings solicited with a collection plate passed through the congregation or placed in the center of the church. Contributions were thus public and a matter of respect or shame. When the priest officiated at other events, such as a memorial mass, he was given a donation, usually twenty shillings. Church income was not redistributed directly to community members, as religious offerings of meat and other food had been in earlier times. Instead, the money supported Church personnel and paid for programs in health and education. Although family feasts accompanied Christian ceremonies, food redistribution was not a Church concern.

To preserve vital ancestral ties, household and lineage heads continue to make ancestral offerings. The notion of honoring ancestors resembles the reverence for saints and is not opposed by the Church. Pastors regard sacrificial offerings of slaughtered animals, however, as pagan superstitions or consorting with the devil and an affront to Christian morality. By prohibiting animal sacrifice, the Church has challenged customs of food sharing and other mechanisms of redistribution that upheld lineage solidarity. Pastors did not give recognition to the patrilineage as a key institution that kept life going on Mt. Kilimanjaro; instead, they undermined it and partly usurped its power.

Church teachings also undermined customary sanctions, including curse, witchcraft, and sorcery, against those not fulfilling their customary obligations. The Church attacked these realms of supernatural power as the work of the devil. Pastors frequently preached against seeking the services of an *mganga* (traditional healer), who was believed to have the power to counter a hex. Church pressure against the *mganga* had to be tempered, however, because he was too important to most parishioners. Pastors would temporarily suspend parishioners for visiting an *mganga*, but if they had expelled everyone who did so, the churches would have been empty (Moore 1986:263).

When I first arrived on Kilimanjaro, I could appreciate the position of the churches on curse and sorcery because of the suffering caused by accusations. I now also see the importance of these customs, as they give people means to force others to pay debts or redress other wrongs.[1] These means are particularly important to those without resources to pursue other remedies.

Living far differently from ordinary people, many priests drive cars, eat fine food, have servants, and supervise Church plantations. All the decorum surrounding Catholic clerics serves to perpetuate their authority and their comfortable way of life. Some clerics on Kilimanjaro, however, including Father Patricio, disregarded the allure of power and took a more egalitarian approach. I asked Father Patricio to take the lead in working with the cooperative until it was viable, and he accepted. He was soon transferred to another parish, however.

The variety of perspectives of clerics and nuns could have strengthened the Church's response to social change and economic crisis, but the institution was so hierarchical that it could not make use of diverse observations and proposals. While the rigidity of the hierarchy made decision making simple, the results often were at odds with some of the institution's main principles.

Ambivalence Toward the Church

Although the Church supported many local customs, including respect for elders and honor for the dead, and brought popular innovations to Kilimanjaro, some people were ambivalent about its activities.

During two years of drought in 1972 to 1974, household and crop theft increased. While most robberies were small-scale, the ire and fear of the population were aroused. I was swept up in this chaos, as our farm was raided by seven men who arrived in a truck, seized the children of one of the residents, and beat them to force the parents to surrender their belongings.

Other terrible assaults occurred elsewhere on Kilimanjaro, and I even heard of the beheading of a child. By the evening fire, people told stories of banditry and embellished them with tales of their own bravado. Villages organized to protect themselves.

Lucere, the village closest to our farm, set up a night watch and finally decided to raise money to pay the parish priest to give a ceremony asking for God's protection against this scourge. After our priest arrived in his car and began the proceedings, Yesiah, a blind old man who was drunk, walked up to the gathering. He shouted blasphemies, accused the priest of being a thief, and then urinated in full view of everyone, as if to underscore his words. His wife, although horrified and ashamed, found it hard to hold back her giggles, and it was obvious that the rest of the congregation also sympathized with his protest. ⁓

On other occasions, people complained about their obligatory work in Church fields or about requests for money during worship. People seldom made these complaints publicly because of their reluctance to criticize the Church and chance offending God. They usually relied on the *vichaa* (deranged people) or drunks to publicly air common sentiments discussed privately by more prudent members of the community.

Church Assistance to the Poor

During the course of the NURU study, I lived in an empty maternity room at the mission clinic. In addition to the schools and clinic, the parish managed a huge sacristy, a convent, a priest's residence, and numerous agricultural and community programs. I became friends with the Chagga nuns at the clinic and with Father Patricio, who had been born on Mt. Kilimanjaro. Sometimes, unfortunately, our conversations had bad repercussions for the clerics and nuns.

⁓ I met with Father Patricio to discuss the woodworking cooperative. He listened patiently while I reported on my survey of woodworking enterprises in Moshi town. I also explained that I had arranged with the Medical Center to send the chief carpenter to teach the fathers woodworking skills for two hours a week. Father Patricio and I sat discussing our plans outside the room at the mission clinic where I was staying while working on the NURU study.

"This is all good. Very good. Now tell me, just what kind of a woodworking business did the fathers have in mind?" he asked.

"They suggested furniture making, but there are already a number of carpenters in this area, and the market in Moshi seems flooded with stalls selling furniture." I jumped up from the bench where I was sitting to retrieve something I had brought back from Moshi. "I can assure you, there's a big market for these," I declared as I pulled an assortment of large wooden toys out of my shopping bag. "I've looked everywhere for toys for my son. We've even had to make our own because no one has them in stock. There's a grocer in Moshi who sells these. He says they're a hot item and he has to go all the way to a carpenter in Arusha to get them."

Father Patricio had greater wisdom than I regarding the willingness of a group of poor men to start making toys. He must have thought that the men would refuse; Chagga men do not make toys, and children generally make their own. Rather than disappoint me, however, he kindly suggested I keep the trucks and trains under wraps until the meeting. That way, the men "would be surprised." Then, perhaps trying to distract me, he gently spoke of the men we were preparing to meet. "So many families here need help these days," he said forlornly.

"What exactly does the Church do for very poor people?" I asked, thinking he would expound on his own efforts—visits to their homes, intercession with wealthier relatives on their behalf, and other daily routines. But he repeated the list Father Cambrian had given me the day before, though without the same conviction. I got the impression that he felt ambivalent about the Church's efforts to prevent poverty. He seemed to have internalized the values of meekness and humility viewed as proper for men of a lesser station in the Church, and it would have been inappropriate for him to challenge his superior.

"We do our best to provide work on the coffee plantation of the Church—charitable hiring, if you will." ∽

This program of employment on the mission's coffee plantation was designed to give employment to fathers of needy families. Most of the mission workers were women and girls, whose earnings the Church did not consider essential for family survival. Father Patricio did not specify the exact number of people hired by the Church, but it appeared to me to be between thirty-five and fifty. Three of the fathers in my study, Francis, Nathaniel, and Paulo, were steady employees of the mission at five shillings a day. With most plantations paying seven shillings a day and government minimum wage set at nine shillings a day (U.S. $1.35), the wage at the mission was low. It was legal, however; as charitable institutions, churches were permitted exceptions.

Churches usually command some free labor from men's and women's service organizations, and many people in my neighborhood saw such service as a privilege. Some aspired to use their service as a stepping-stone to positions of community leadership. On the other hand, I often heard people complain of the priest's solicitation for funds during church services.

⌒ "Another way we help is through the St. Vincent de Paul Society. Church members donate used clothing or money for a fund to purchase food during times of hunger."

"Which parishioners have been asking for assistance?" I inquired. I was curious to know if any of the families in my study made use of this resource.

"See Stephen over there?" He pointed down the hill to a series of steps leading up to the front door of the church. There sat a disheveled middle-aged man holding a loud conversation with himself.

"He's a bit strange. That's how he came back from World War II—shell shock, I believe. The society's funds provide for all of his needs except housing. He has a small home next to his brother's on their father's land."

I wondered, but was hesitant to ask, if this program didn't inadvertently excuse better-off parishioners from their obligations to poor friends and relatives who could now be referred to the Church for help. Even Francis, who walked about in burlap sacking, told me he would be ashamed to ask for clothing from the St. Vincent de Paul Society. Father Patricio said that the only people who went there were *wakichaa* (crazy); they tended to be unaware of the stigma associated with the Christian notion of charity and the personal failure it implies.

I thanked Father Patricio and hurried to meet one of the younger nuns, who had agreed to take me on a tour of the mission's plantation. She showed me the coffee plantation, which she estimated to be over 2,500 acres. The vegetable gardens were large enough to feed the whole convent and all of the priests, nursing students, clinic patients, servants, and hundreds of schoolchildren whose noon meal was included in their school fees. The mission was also self-sufficient in milk and poultry. Sister proudly guided me through the animal shelters, where a herd of sixty milk cows, dozens of pigs, sheep, and goats, and six hundred hens were housed. ⌒

The next day I found out that the nun had been chastised by Father Cambrian for freely enumerating the mission's possessions. In addition, Francis informed me that the wage for him and the other fathers had been suddenly raised from five to seven shillings a day.

The reluctance of some members of the clergy to assist the poor appears inconsistent with some tenets of Christianity, such as egalitarianism, charity, and brotherly love. Most of the priests on Kilimanjaro, however, had been born on the mountain, where more-privileged people, including clergy, often espoused views supporting their high status and protecting their power over others.

Officials' Efforts to Maintain Privilege and Power

Although some farmers still loan cattle to relatives and friends, local lending organizations have encouraged people to keep their wealth in assets other than cattle. In the 1970s, poor farmers requested loans from the Kilimanjaro Native Cooperative Union (the coffee cooperative). The cooperative would loan local entrepreneurs money, but the poor lacked credibility as business-people.

For example, in 1974, I asked Francis Lema why he didn't have a cow or goats. He responded that no one would loan him animals because he could not guarantee that they would be secure; the door to his house, where he would keep them, was falling apart. He went to the coffee cooperative to ask for a loan to buy a cow and was rejected. He applied later for a loan to purchase the wood necessary to make a door and was also turned down.

Like all Chagga coffee growers, Francis paid dues to the cooperative; however, he did not get many benefits. In the 1970s, and probably still, only well-to-do farmers were considered good risks by the cooperative's loan program to support cattle raising; even so, their default rate was high (Zalla 1982). In effect, the poor were subsidizing the rich. Thus, the stereotype, "these people," formed part of the systematic discrimination against the poor and the preservation of more privileged peoples' control of resources.

Leaders of Tanzania's socialist government were also supposed to help to create a more egalitarian society. Impoverished farmers, however, faced difficulties in making claims for government entitlements.

1974

〜 One of the fathers of malnourished children, Richard Moshi, confronted me in a rage one day in response to my questions about why his child was malnourished. He didn't want me to ask questions, but instead demanded that I help him find a job. Another father had made the same demand two days earlier. Some of the parents seemed very defensive about their situation. I called Ulla-Stina (Tita) Henricson, a member of my research team and director of the Medical Center's Community Health Program. We arranged a meeting with the District Development Commissioner's office in Moshi to ask for food relief for the families.

At the commissioner's office, Tita and I were taken from one official to another by skipping ahead of long lines of Chagga men, many of whom were *balozis* (ten-house leaders). Normally, the men would have had precedence over women, but Tita's position and our status as professionals and perhaps as *wazungu* overrode our female disadvantage in this case.[2]

We went first to the clerk in charge of the Office of Hunger, which had been instituted to distribute food to families affected by the drought. The clerk was friendly and responsive but seemed overwhelmed by the task.

We specifically asked him what had been done for the division where the families in my study resided, and he said that ten bags of maize flour had been sent for distribution by the Kilimanjaro Native Cooperative Union. We asked if the office provided beans as well as maize flour and were told none were available. With further probing, however, he indicated that beans were not considered a famine food. We tried to argue that a weanling child needed more than maize flour to keep from being malnourished. He suggested we discuss the matter with the district development commissioner and immediately escorted us to his office.

The commissioner, an educated man from Tabora, was a delightful person. He gave us an hour of his time, listening to descriptions of the families' conditions. He seemed appreciative of our detailed stories of the impoverished families' plight, much of which, he informed us, was news to him. I had been prepared to encounter a tired, apathetic official who would be all too willing to let a few people's cases go untended. I thought that the fifty thousand households in food crisis in the Kilimanjaro region would make him feel that special attention to a few would be a futile waste of energy.

The commissioner made a number of phone calls in our presence, authorizing our requests for other food and ordering beans and bean meal. He mentioned that the Chagga wouldn't eat *dagaa* (dried fish), but we assured him tastes were changing, and he ordered it as well.[3] He then made a phone call to the district welfare officer, who soon joined us.

In an authoritative manner, the commissioner demanded to know what the Welfare Office was doing for poor peasant farmers with hungry children. The officer responded defensively that hunger was not under his jurisdiction. The commissioner said he would *make* it under his jurisdiction and added that food was basic to the survival of the people. The welfare officer then turned to us and requested that we document observed cases of malnutrition so he could petition Dar es Salaam for the release of emergency funds.

Buoyed up by our apparent influence, I told him about the fathers' interest in a woodworking cooperative. Would he be able to help us get access to government funds set aside to encourage such enterprises? The commissioner responded by telling us about the possibilities for joining the *ujamaa* villages initiated by the government on the plains below Mt. Kilimanjaro. Each family would be given five acres of land, some construction materials, and assistance with water and irrigation. I nodded politely. I did not want to suggest the likelihood that the families would refuse such an offer. They would see leaving the mountain as forfeiting their membership in their own neighborhood and, to an extent, in their lineage.

We persisted in asking just how the men could get loans for beginning an enterprise. The Commissioner then told us that all *ushirikas* of this sort are funded by the government. He informed us that the fathers needed to develop a written proposal for the project, describing an initial activity. I took this as approval to help organize the men. He encouraged us to bring him more information and requested our presence in a planning session to be held on Friday. The commissioner added that his office had a list of projects that the government had already designated for each area. ∿

On reflection, I thought about how quickly we two Europeans had reached the seats of power while *balozis* had to wait in line. I wondered how far a group of mostly illiterate, ailing men could proceed in writing a proposal and demonstrating the requisite initiative. This question arose again when I pursued funding for the fathers' venture at the head office for *ushirikas* in Dar es Salaam. The minister for government cooperatives lauded our efforts but requested the same extensive paperwork and evidence of ongoing activity as the other office had.

∿ Six men had agreed to participate in the development of a woodworking cooperative, but only Francis demonstrated any real enthusiasm. A local district head who knew the men was immensely supportive of the idea, at least in my presence, and offered to lead the first meeting with the fathers. There was heavy rain the day of the meeting, and when no one, including Francis, showed up, the official hastened to explain, "These people are just not reliable. They drink too much and don't know the value of planning ahead."

Middle-class and wealthy Chagga also complained about their frustration with the poor. In a discussion with neighbors regarding the fifty thousand heads of household and their emergency food requests to *balozis*, one man said, "These people will say anything if they know a handout is available." Those surrounding him concurred about "these people" and their failure to plan ahead. ∿

Despite the reluctance of some government officials to recognize a severe food crisis, the pressure from the *balozis* and others prevailed. The quick responses of the government and International Catholic Relief Services in delivering food prevented a full-scale famine. Without the extra wheat and maize provided by food relief, many more children and elderly people would have died.

Socialist Efforts to Reduce Inequality

Beginning with independence in 1961, the government developed policies to meet the needs of rural people, stem the tide of migration to the cities, build national unity, and legitimate itself in the eyes of the people. A revolutionary movement had to transform itself into a political party with a coherent set of plans that could consolidate popular support by immediately improving economic conditions for most farmers. The failure of overly optimistic plans and other problems brought on sporadic resistance and revolt by the general population and an attempted mutiny by the army (Kerner 1988).

President Nyerere and other politicians developed socialist policies to transform the economy through rural and agricultural development. The growing gap between wealthy and poor greatly disturbed politicians, who passed legislation aimed at encouraging cooperative enterprise and reducing economic inequality. Most of the Kilimanjaro people, however, reacted negatively to these measures.

Education continued to provide the principal entry to employment in the private sector and the civil service. On Mt. Kilimanjaro, people value education highly, partly because of the development of an elite who are relatively well educated, well-off, and powerful (Kerner 1988). Middle sons and other land-poor young men look to education as their only possibility for gaining a position with a good salary. At the time of the 1967 population census, Kilimanjaro District had twice the proportion of children enrolled in primary school as the average found in all other districts and a slightly larger proportion enrolled in secondary school. Children from better-off families, especially middle sons of prosperous farmers, were likely to get the most support from their families and go furthest in school.

One of the earliest egalitarian efforts of the socialist government focused on education. To promote more even educational opportunities across the country, the government restricted secondary-school admissions and prohibited any new secondary schools in the Kilimanjaro region, intensifying competition for educational opportunities as the population in the region grew rapidly (Moore 1986:219). Restricting education, which has been economically and symbolically important on Kilimanjaro for decades, alienated the Chagga people. While egalitarian policies may have been warranted on a national scale, they tended to affect poor people disproportionately on Kilimanjaro. Without influence to gain admission and funding to further their education, boys from poorer households were destined to become poorly paid wage laborers, further exacerbating the growth of poverty. In spite of government efforts to provide educational opportunities in a balanced manner, Chagga still maintained a considerable educational edge over other ethnic groups in Tanzania, and the wealthy elite continued to dominate educational opportunities.

In reaction to the growth of an educated elite, President Nyerere, in his 1967 Arusha Declaration, made a radical change in national development policies. He called for nationalization of the major means of production and democratic control of public institutions by workers and peasants. Stating that because Tanzania was predominantly agricultural, agriculture must be the basis of national development, the Arusha Declaration attempted to reverse the trend toward industrialization and urbanization.

It was not until 1972, with the beginning of the second five-year plan, that Tanzania began implementing the Arusha Declaration policies in rural areas. These policies were based on the principles of *usawa* (social equality), *kujitegemea* (self-reliance), *maendeleo* (economic and social transformation), economic integration of African states, and *ujamaa* (brotherhood). *Ujamaa vijijini* (brotherhood in the village) was a principle designed to bring dispersed rural people into villages to facilitate integrated rural development.

On Kilimanjaro, however, population density was already high, and in the *kihamba* belt nearly all the available land was being farmed. There were no open spaces for creating villages. As a result, government efforts were focused on developing *ujamaa* villages on the plains and encouraging farmers on the mountain to join agricultural and small-scale industrial cooperatives. Later, the districts of the former chiefdoms were renamed "villages" and district heads were appointed to carry out the central government's policies (Moore 1986:316).

Kilimanjaro reacted to the Arusha Declaration and its ensuing policies with outright hostility. In 1972, I witnessed the nationalization of a British-owned coffee plantation that had become Kilimanjaro's largest producer of poultry and purebred swine. After being informed by radio that the plantations now belonged to the people, neighboring farmers rushed to the area with sisal twine to put their claims on the land. They were chased off by armed soldiers, who informed them that the government had control of the plantation, and after all, the government was "the people."

The farmers became especially discouraged when they witnessed the corruption of those in charge, who pilfered poultry and swine and threw large parties at which enormous numbers of animals were consumed. The locally hired staff began to complain and were all fired, only to be rehired later at a lower wage. One year after the nationalization and a series of such disappointments, the plantation's workers contributed seven hundred shillings (U.S. $100) toward the medical expenses of the plantation's ailing British founder. Although done partly out of compassion, this act also seemed to express their outrage toward the government's false promises regarding land distribution. It also conveyed the offstage, silent protest of ordinary farmers who feared official reprisal should they hold public demonstrations (see Scott 1991 on weapons of the weak).

People who had welcomed the nationalization of large plantations realized that they personally would not benefit, and they became mistrustful. On the contradictions between the socialist ideals and the realities of everyday life, Moore observed in the mid-1980s:

> In practice, remarkably asymmetrical relations exist even locally between the party higher-ups and their unlettered brethren. The hierarchy between educated and uneducated is central to party structure in practice, though it is otherwise in theory. According to party doctrine and national ideology, all local development plans are supposed to originate with the peasantry. The peasant's proposals are supposed to be polished and put into bureaucratic language, complete with budgets and formal plans . . . and proposals then compete for funding before regional committees. In 1974, at local party political meetings in different wards on Kilimanjaro, the major items on the agenda of the subvillages were identical. This happy coincidence of "spontaneous" peasant interest had been produced by suggestions emanating from the central regional party organization. (Moore 1986:314)

Apparently not understanding local affairs, the government appointed officials to take on responsibilities normally held by lineage elders. The Kilimanjaro people criticized socialist measures aimed at closing the gap between wealthy and poor partly because they undercut the power of the patrilineage.

"Why Don't These People Just Move Away?"

Some government officials asked, "Why don't poor families move down to the plains where they can have more farmland? Why do they continue to struggle on the mountain?" The socialist government had encouraged emigration to the plains through the *ujamaa* village program, which offered assistance with constructing irrigation systems and other infrastructure to offset agricultural disadvantages such as an arid climate. Many of the Kilimanjaro people, however, spurned these offers; today, land in the plains is more affordable, but few people move from the mountain to farm.

Outsiders find it difficult to understand what a poor person would lose by moving. Despite the economic constraints of living on Mt. Kilimanjaro, mountain neighborhoods remain a source of security, support, respect for Chagga ways, and aesthetic pleasure in the natural beauty of the surroundings. Obligations of reciprocity among kin in patrilineages are eroding, but by staying in the neighborhood, poor households still have greater promise of receiving resources from relatives than if they moved away. The sense of social support gained by living among patrilineal relatives in the case of men, or near their natal patrilineage in the case of women, grows out of emotional attachment to kin and awareness of ancestral bonds as well as material exchanges. In familiar surroundings with neighbors close by, the poorest person may feel safe from thieves. Even if the impoverished have no belongings, they at least hope to hold on to their personal *heshima* (respect). Wealthy neighbors and relatives bring added *heshima* to their community with their fine houses and possessions. Consequently, poor people often identify with the rich, and in their fashion, the rich return the respect to some extent. *Watu wa porini* (people of the plains) are considered to be backward, totally alien to the value of *maendeleo*. Mountain folk believe themselves to be more virtuous than those who live below, and they say their children should be reared in an environment where virtue prevails.

A general respect for financial shrewdness justifies better-off people in denying loans or favors to poor men who cannot repay them. Those who are better-off thus avoid appearing *mjinga* (foolish). A poor man does not wish to appear *mjinga,* either. It would be foolish of him to move his family to a dangerous, immoral environment away from familiar support when he still has a chance to inherit a *kihamba*. He may anticipate earning enough money to purchase a plot of land on Kilimanjaro, or his father may eventually grant him a plot. Regardless of the course of his life, after death his remains would be placed near those of his ancestors. His sons would remember him with ancestral offerings, ensuring him a rightful place on the mountain and continued existence for his spirit.

Socialist Policies and Daily Life

Wealthy Chagga sometimes do fulfill their customary obligations to poorer relatives, especially in offering nonmonetary help, although they are rapidly adopting the nuclear-family independence found in larger urban, industrial societies. In everyday life, however, poorer people largely fend for themselves in small groups of similarly disadvantaged. They help sick neighbors get medical treatment, exchange food in barter, and listen to one another's woes.

In the 1970s, I was perplexed at first with the anger of most people at the government's plan to nationalize privately owned cars. In spite of frequent government messages about the long-term benefits of this measure, poor peasants resented it, even though none had any hopes of purchasing a car. Ordinary people, however, definitely valued their own right to purchase affordable European-style products including ready-made clothing, watches, radios, wheat flour, cooking oil, and sugar.

The automobile had other important meanings to peasant farmers. On the one hand, it symbolized Chagga modernity and the progress of wealthy individuals, with whom poorer kin identified. On the other hand, poorer Chagga expected a wealthier neighbor to provide transportation by car for medical emergencies, especially injuries and births. Not to do so would be a grievous offense and cause for a lineage council hearing.

Smaller crises did not always prompt assistance, however, and resentment brewed until it exploded in ways confusing to outsiders. Automobile drivers venturing into the network of mountain roads might be greeted by hand-waving, welcoming children or by people making mocking requests for rides. If the driver complied with the request, the petitioner might feign surprise and gratitude; occasionally, if the driver refused, the car was bombarded with stones. As dust-spewing vehicles sped by, irritated pedestrians frequently shouted insults while brushing off their clothes. Outsiders were often warned that if they ever hit a pedestrian, they should not stop lest they encounter "instant justice," immediate brutal retaliation. It was not only injury or death that elicited such a reaction from pedestrians but also their ambivalence toward the automobile; the car separated nonowners symbolically from the main stream of progress.

People also expressed disappointment and anger at government officials and members of the educated elite who manipulated situations to take advantage of others. My neighboring community collected money to buy materials for building a footbridge over their river. They entrusted the funds to the *balozi Mzee* Lamumba, who congratulated them for consulting him. When the time came to begin the project, *Mzee* Lamumba claimed the money had been stolen. The community members felt impotent in confronting him; they never recovered the funds.

Events of this kind were common, and on rare occasions, desperation propelled people toward public protest. In the neighborhood of our farm, people took action in various ways to try to secure access to farmland.

1973

~ We assisted members of our cooperative in applying to a government-sponsored program to gain ownership of the land we had cultivated for almost two years. Although we compiled reports demonstrating that our cooperative farm had been successful, the administrator for cooperatives was not impressed. He knew that the farm would end up in the hands of the other members of the cooperative, who were poor, illiterate farmers.

The land was eventually sold to a Kilimanjaro member of Tanzania's parliament, who built a home for his second wife and family there as well as a large shelter for herds of cattle, sheep, and goats.

Near our farm, the Medical Center owned farmland that it allowed neighboring farmers to plant with maize and beans. As a requirement for continuing use of the land, each farmer had to keep it under annual cultivation. When a minor hospital official heard of the Medical Center's plans, he planted bananas in an effort to claim a large plot that included land already being farmed by others. When he found all his banana plants uprooted the next day, he called the police.

To my surprise, the farmers gathered with hoes and machetes in hand and went to the hospital to demand their rights. A formal court hearing was held to deal with the dispute between the farmers and the hospital. The farmers were granted continued use of the fields nearest their homes but were not given any additional land to expand their crop production. Additional land was awarded, however, to the hospital official because he could claim that his land would be productive. ∼

"Proof of productivity" seemed to come from an individual's social status and personal connections rather than from any past performance. Poorer individuals, whose farms appeared to be risky investments, could not secure loans to pay for cattle or insemination services for cows.

In the mid-1970s, the high rate of inflation, compounded by the enormous expense of a war with Uganda, threw the country into an economic crisis from which it has yet to recover. These pressures undermined the Tanzanian government's financial support for many initiatives to improve conditions in the countryside (on the large decline in export earnings as a percentage of gross domestic product, see Kerner 1988:37–38; World Bank 1981:23). Infrastructure began to collapse, and hardship increased for many people. The rising price of petroleum-based products raised the cost of farm supplies, from fertilizers to pesticides, putting them out of reach for many farmers. All of these pressures brought the people of Kilimanjaro to further resent socialist policies, conceived in idealistic ways but implemented problematically.

> The demands of socialism have added new strains to life in the countryside and have put new pressures on close relationships. Many property arrangements that were legal and legitimate before independence are now against the law. Many illegal or extralegal transactions nevertheless continue. Not all party pronouncements are heeded. The knowledge that kinsmen have of the affairs of their agnates and neighbors now implies a possibility of betrayal to unfriendly authorities. The friendly ones look the other way, and their number is legion. Every man was

> always his brother's keeper in some sense. Now a new dimension has
> been added. A multiple-plot landholder has anxieties about confisca-
> tion, a new-house-builder about inquiries into the source of his means.
> The arena of local politics involves many tacit understandings about the
> new modes in which old business must be done. The general shortage
> of goods, the limited stocks of the price-controlled government stores,
> and the exorbitant prices in the private sector make for a peculiarly dis-
> torted economic life. Influence is needed to obtain many necessities.
> Personal networks loom larger than formal organizations, and goods
> and information move outside the official system. (Moore 1986:308)

Cooperatives were being promoted by Tanzania's socialist government, but the policies were ineffective in changing the behavior of elites and promoting greater economic equity on Kilimanjaro. The entitlements people expected were mostly out of the reach of extremely poor individuals. My effort to initiate the woodworking cooperative met with failure in part because the community seemed to regard "these people" as hopeless and a bad investment. The Kilimanjaro people on the whole did not support socialism, and government efforts to redistribute the profits from private property did not reach the impoverished families in this study.

On my visit in 1989, I found that strains between the community and the government had continued. Old friends spoke of painful experiences when the government attempted to offset the growth of the informal market (evading government taxation and regulation) with increased vigilance and arrests. Many Chagga went to prison, and fear and mistrust had spread through the countryside.

Friends also told me about another severe drought that had occurred on Mt. Kilimanjaro in 1984. Child malnutrition had surged again, necessitating food relief, but not to the same extent as ten years earlier. By then, many households had expanded their vegetable gardens to protect against food crises. Even professionals and officials had taken precautions against food shortage. In 1989, for example, a physician at the Medical Center, who had arranged to meet me one morning to discuss health issues, apologized when he arrived late. "Do you know any other doctors who must shower after two hours of work on the farm each morning?" he asked. "We are all concerned about having enough food." Some farmers had even made space for vegetable gardens by uprooting coffee trees. In 1974, it had been illegal to convert coffee acreage to vegetable gardens; government policy had aimed to ensure large coffee harvests for desperately needed exports. The country needed foreign exchange to pay for the rising cost of imports and to repay interest on loans from abroad.

The welfare office in Moshi town was inadequately staffed and financed to address the needs of townsfolk, let alone the farmers on the mountain.

With the exception of emergency food relief widely distributed in the time of *njaa* in 1974 and again in 1984, government relief programs carried a heavy burden of shame for recipients. Church-organized welfare for the poor also conveyed stigma. Other Church social programs were oriented toward educating the youth and investing in the health and welfare of better-off Chagga who could pay small fees or membership dues and who would not prove an embarrassment to the ideals of progress.

National Budget Crises

Severe budget crises hit Tanzania in the 1980s for many reasons, including unusually severe drought, increased expenditures for imported oil and petroleum products (Kerner 1988:38), and its poorly run nationalized farms. Rising oil prices and declining self-sufficiency in food struck many less developed countries in that period, including Tanzania (Kerner 1988:37; see also Kavishe and Mrisho 1990: Tables 9 and 10). When the government imposed taxes on farmers to pay for assistance in marketing their products, the informal market extending across the nearby border with Kenya exploded. Government sales tax revenues fell, squeezing budgets for maintaining roads and other infrastructure. Deciding that his economic policies had failed, Nyerere resigned his presidency in 1985 and was replaced by his vice president, Ali Hassan Mwinyi.

One of Mwinyi's first moves was to apply for loans from international lending agencies. The International Monetary Fund (IMF) extended a loan, but only after the government agreed to structural adjustment. The austerity program floated the shilling, and the cost of living rose; social, educational, and medical services were severely cut. The government agreed to privatize its companies, cut back on import duties, and allow investment in Tanzania by international corporations. Under the banner of "free trade," Tanzania no longer restricted imports and exports, and the government gave up its one-party structure.

Tanzania's embrace of socialism was over. It was clear to me during my visit to Kilimanjaro in 1989 that most of the infrastructure built during colonialism and the first fifteen years of independence had collapsed. With it went many of the people's hopes for *maendeleo* (progress). Roads had deteriorated considerably, buildings were in need of repair and covered in dirt from crumbled roads, transportation and communication systems had become unreliable, and no new government buildings were being constructed. The only active development was in private housing north of Moshi town at the foot of the mountain. Some had profited in the informal market or at the expense of poorer relatives, who had sold out and migrated in search of work.

When we authors visited Tanzania in 1993, structural adjustment measures required by the IMF had been in place for some time. Loans from the IMF and the World Bank were given as short-term support for national economic difficulties, not to solve long-term national social and economic problems.

Inflation had made life difficult for most. A head nurse at the hospital reported that a whole month's salary would buy her only "a good pair of shoes with nothing left over." In discussing the austerity measures, people expressed the most concern over the privatization of the health care system. Hospital and clinic costs rose and included charges for medicine that had once been free. Many people feared that health care would soon be too expensive for ordinary Tanzanians.

The socialist government had attempted to transform the rural sector to make it more productive and egalitarian. Although well-meaning, socialist policies failed to take account of the capitalist orientation of the Kilimanjaro people. Even if the poor on Kilimanjaro had wanted to support socialist policies, they could not, because it would mean opposing the interests of important members of the patrilineage who, on the one hand, supported capitalism and resented government constraints but, on the other, were eager to take advantage of any new opportunities. If poorer competitors had expressed enthusiasm for socialism in hopes of monopolizing its benefits, they might have risked losing respect in the patrilineage and the possibility of assistance from their better-off kin.

Socialist policies inadvertently hurt the poor on Mt. Kilimanjaro in some ways, but the end of socialism did not improve their situation. Religious and economic inroads into the unity, wealth, and authority of the patrilineage did not cease. The undoing of socialist institutions put more pressure on better-off people, local communities, and churches to take up the burden of the poor. In the meanwhile, however, views solidified that "these people," the rural poor, were unable to plan ahead, irresponsible, and beyond hope.

Chapter Six

Sex and the Shame
of Kwashiorkor

⌒ *Some explanations for child illness involve the parents' sexuality. A couple's having children at the wrong time or under the wrong circumstances is evidence of their sexual transgression and can lead to ostracism and shame, especially of very poor parents. The puffy skin of a child with malnutrition is said to be an ancestral warning, and the child's death may be a sign that an ancestral spirit has not been appeased.* ⌒

1974

⌒ The first day I arrived at the mission, I noticed a shy young man in tattered clothes who seemed interested in my research. He joined the group of men who escorted me to Francis's house, but he didn't contribute to the derogatory remarks they made about Francis along the way. In fact, he seemed rather protective of Francis and eventually gathered the courage to stand next to him as the local *balozi* loudly blamed the hapless man for his misfortunes. I thought at the time that his sympathy for Francis came from their common poverty, implied by the dirty, torn shirt on his back, but I understood later that there were other reasons.

I also later discovered that the young man was Nathaniel Lema, Francis's cousin and neighbor. Nathaniel, who was 26 years old, appeared at most of my visits with Francis and generally said very little. Finally one day Francis was moved to tears while describing the loss of his mother at five years of age—a tragedy he saw as casting a pall of misfortune over his entire life.

"I also lost my mother while still a young child," Nathaniel interjected into a moment of silence that followed Francis's story. Nathaniel's father had migrated from Kilimanjaro to the Arusha area, where his wife had died; then he had converted from Catholicism to Protestantism and remarried. He had not yet given any land to Nathaniel, who lived with his young wife, Cecilia, on one corner of the farm. Their home was a squalid two-room mud structure with no furnishings. Cecilia was not Chagga; she was from Arusha, where Nathaniel's father had met her and arranged her marriage to his son. Like Francis, Nathaniel worked as a wage laborer at the mission for less than a dollar a day.

"I would appreciate it very much if you could help my wife," he continued. "She's had four children and is pregnant again. None of our children has survived."

I was immediately taken with Nathaniel's plea, especially when he mentioned the deaths of his children; Chagga do not usually enumerate their children or speak of their deaths. I thought that my background in nursing might be useful and that I might find a way to alleviate some of the poverty surrounding me.

Nathaniel, Francis, and I went to meet Cecilia. We found her cultivating a small vegetable plot by her house. She seemed concerned about my comfort and borrowed a chair from one of her neighbors for me to sit on during my visit. She was lively, attractive, and in good health, and she spoke to me in a more open and assertive manner than many of the poorer women I had encountered. As she lived close to the Catholic clinic, distance from medical care was not a factor in the lack of medical attention to her sick children. Only once did I dare to probe for reasons for her babies' deaths. "It was the will of God," she said with conviction, and I left it at that.

The passivity implied by this statement did not dominate other aspects of her existence, however. A bright woman, Cecilia was interested in finding ways to improve her situation. She planted the seeds I gave her and constructed a chicken coop with the help of her husband. Cecilia and Nathaniel shared a tenderness and love for each other that was seldom apparent in poorer households during the food crisis. Neither complained about the other, and he seemed in awe of her beauty, while she valued his kindness and friendship. I just couldn't comprehend why all four of their children had died.

One morning I went to visit Philippe Lema, the wife of Edwardi Lema, Francis and Nathaniel's wealthy cousin who was also their neighbor. I was accompanied by Martha Mboya, a twenty-year-old nursing student from the area who had been my companion and assistant throughout the research. When I asked Philippe why Cecilia had lost all of her babies, she replied, "Cecilia took no rest between births. As soon as she gave birth to one she got pregnant again, just like Bibiana [Francis's wife]."

"I assume she continued to breastfeed the children while pregnant?" I asked.

Philippe and Martha looked horrified and exchanged glances, then Philippe politely explained in a patronizing manner, "It is not proper for

Chagga." Later, I took up the issue with Martha again, feeling obliged to educate her with the biomedical perspective. "You know, it does a woman no harm to continue breastfeeding while pregnant. And if she eats adequately, she'll have plenty of milk for her baby."

"No, *Mama* Matthew!" she insisted. "The milk becomes poisoned and will make the child swell." According to Martha, mothers often unknowingly breastfeed their children into the succeeding pregnancy. When they discover their condition, they abruptly wean the child, but often it is too late—swelling has started, kwashiorkor has begun.

I tried to point out the fault in her logic—that rather than developing kwashiorkor from continuing to be breastfed during the mother's next pregnancy, a child could get it from being weaned abruptly—but Martha retorted, "It does not matter, because the ancestors would be enraged!" ∽

I was reluctant to accept Martha's explanation at the time. The Chagga university students who belonged to my research team dismissed this perspective as superstition. On the other hand, some parents in the NURU study insisted that we listen to their explanations, which turned out to be essential for understanding child malnutrition on Kilimanjaro.

Child Malnutrition and Breastfeeding

Contemporary ideas about breastfeeding and child illness belong to a larger realm of Chagga knowledge about sexuality, the continuity of life, and the spirit world. Notions of proper sexual behavior derive from a central cultural theme about the connection of human reproduction to the fertility of plants and animals. These concepts are evident in writings about Chagga knowledge and ritual earlier in this century.

Customary rituals and other practices celebrated sexuality, the reproductive powers of men and women, and birth, and they also clearly delimited timing and circumstances for conception. Birth at the wrong time or under the wrong circumstances was to be avoided, and there were customary means for doing so. Parents were not to start childbearing if the husband was not making bridewealth payments or if the wife had not been circumcised. They were to stop childbearing when their oldest child was circumcised.

Threads of these earlier ideas persist today and may be used in a discretionary manner to discredit and reject certain wrongdoers. In the 1970s, some people explained children's malnutrition as the result of their parents' sexual misconduct. The term most people used for the puffy skin and swollen belly associated with malnutrition was *kuvimba*, meaning "swelling." The swelling was taken as a sign of displeasure on the part of ancestral spirits. The silent withdrawal and irritability of a child with this form of malnutrition probably strengthened any suspicions of ancestral displeasure. The word *kuvimba* thus evokes notions of parental sexual transgression, ancestral displeasure, and threat to the continuity of the lineage.

Although most local people in the 1970s spoke of *kuvimba*, health professionals and well-educated Chagga used the biomedical term "kwashiorkor." Local health professionals used either term, depending on the context. By the 1990s, everyone commonly used the term "kwashiorkor," in part to avoid the criticism implied by *kuvimba*.[1]

Kuvimba was highly stigmatic because it implied that the parents had not restrained themselves in having sex and that their irresponsibility was endangering the lineage. Many women were reluctant to take a child to the clinic once swelling was evident because of the shame they felt about the child's condition. Some of these notions are also connected to kwashiorkor, but not so directly as with *kuvimba*.

The children's illnesses in two of forty-two families in the NURU study, including Cecilia's family, were said by neighbors to have resulted from the mother's continuing to breastfeed while pregnant. Neighbors explained that illness of two other children had resulted from the father's failure to pay bridewealth to the wife's family. In another case, *kuvimba* was said to have resulted from the mother's failure to be circumcised. The NURU study's interview questions tended to discourage people from expressing these views; therefore, we believe that the ideas were probably more widespread than the numbers indicate.

According to some people, Cecilia suffered the loss of all four of her children because they were born in rapid succession. Ideas about proper reproductive behavior had forced Cecilia, upon becoming pregnant again, to abruptly wean her children. Kwashiorkor was and still is commonly associated with the weanling child. The symptom of swelling was believed to have resulted from an improper combination of bodily fluids linked to reproduction. Semen was believed to cause the breast milk to spoil. The power of semen as a life-giving substance, combined with the powers in mother's milk, apparently created an excessive life force lethal to the breastfeeding child.

This belief was associated with a broad metaphor equating eating and sex (Moore 1976). In this metaphor, the body is considered to be a container: feeding the mouth maintains life, while feeding the vagina during intercourse produces new life. The mouth of the baby is fed by the mother's breast, and the mother's vagina is fed by her husband's penis to sustain the chain of life. The proper sequence of feeding must not be altered; that is, one must not have been feeding the vagina of a mother at the same time that she is feeding the mouth of her child.

This requirement for order contributed to a postpartum sex taboo and an expected interval of three years between births (Raum 1940). It protected the mother's nutritional status and her ability to care for the nursling while making other contributions to the family economy. In the past, if parents broke the taboo and had sexual intercourse before their child was weaned, they were supposed to abort any resulting fetus or kill any resulting child at birth.

In some cases, the child was not killed, but the child's paternal grandmother, caretaker for the whole clan, could punish the parents for immoral behavior by withholding meat from the child. In another form of social sanction documented by ethnographers, the whole lineage could reject the parents by withholding meat until they made the necessary rituals of reparation.

1930s

> It still happens that a woman commits suicide when she becomes pregnant inside the three years prescribed by custom. This shows the pitch of sensitiveness to which she has been trained on this point, and the relentlessness of her companions in castigating her for her lapse. (Raum 1940:88)

The illnesses of Cecilia and Nathaniel Lema's children were said to have been brought about by the ancestors to restore the balance upset by the inappropriate behavior of the parents. In the 1990s, pressure on women to prolong nursing and child spacing are still strong. A birth soon after the previous one reflects poorly on a mother-in-law, who feels shame for not having properly instructed her daughter-in-law. The daughter-in-law's lapse creates tension with the person she is most dependent on for help with child care.

During the 1970s, women were still expected to breastfeed for a long period but to wean immediately upon becoming pregnant. In the clinic survey, 65 percent of 399 women said breast milk was bad for a child once the mother became pregnant (see Appendix B, nos. 23–25; see also Lindner 1972). Seventy percent of women stated that it was ideal to breastfeed at least 18 months, and 61 percent did so. Women generally did not breastfeed as long as they preferred, but only 1 percent said they preferred to breastfeed for six months or less. Generally, women felt that a long period of breastfeeding was crucial.

Lucere, 1972

∼ I was enjoying the companionship of three of my women friends on a particularly bright, sunny day. We were sitting in a compound in the community neighboring my farm. I had my baby on my lap, and my friends were instructing me in child care. They frequently expressed how sad they felt for me because my own mother was so far away.

"Put the cloth over his face," Anna insisted, and then adjusted the colorful cotton *kitenge* so it covered Matthew's view. (The rearing of children was not a private venture on Kilimanjaro, and it took me a while to accept intrusive suggestions. I had attempted to follow this instruction before but found that Matthew would get agitated and eventually develop a heat rash.) "Now the mosquitoes won't give him malaria," Anna said.

"And he won't look at the sun," added Anna's sixteen-year-old daughter, who was caring for her eight-month-old baby.

Ruth, Matthew's godmother, added, "Evil eye. Some people can bring harm to Matthew. You must keep him covered in public."

Just as I was thinking of a response to Ruth's warning, a woman walked by on the public pathway next to the courtyard. "*Shimbony shafoo maye,*" she greeted us in Chagga. "*Aya koo maye,*" my companions responded in unison. The woman stopped in her tracks and stood with one hand on her hip and the other balancing a large, heavy bundle of bananas. She inquired about everyone's health, family, and workload in the usual courteous salutation.

I was very surprised by my companions' response. "*Sawa sawa* [fine]," they muttered in Swahili, without any of the usual enthusiasm of local greetings. The woman seemed to sense she wasn't welcome, politely excused herself, and moved on.

As soon as she was out of sight, all three women spat on the ground.

"Why did you do that?" I inquired.

"*Uchawi* [witchcraft]!" Ruth said with a look of disgust on her face.

"How can you tell?" I persisted, noting that the woman was very thin. (I had been told thin women could be suspected of witchcraft.)[2]

"She refused to breastfeed her children!" Anna asserted, as proof of their neighbor's status as an undesirable person. ⌒

The message I received that day illustrated the ambivalence of many people in the 1970s about changes in their society. While there were probably many reasons that contributed to my friends' rejection of the woman, failure to breastfeed was, and still is, a significant failing. Many people saw lack of breastfeeding, whether a conscious choice or not, as an act against the lineage, against the values for cooperation and commensality, and against ideas about mother's milk as an essential link in the life cycle.

Nonetheless, breastfeeding seems to be generally on the decline today, most often among women who cannot afford other nutritious infant food. Prolonged breastfeeding is associated with lack of *maendeleo* (progress). By the 1970s, powdered milk formula, usually mixed with porridge, was common as a supplementary weaning food and was often fed from a baby bottle without a nipple. Today, stores are forbidden to sell baby bottles.

A woman today seldom enjoys the customary three months of postpartum confinement. Traditionally during this phase, her chores were done by others, and she was given extra food, which supported her recovery and the earliest phases of breastfeeding. By the 1970s, confinement periods of women in Lucere had dropped to only one month. Even in the most affluent households, women have commitments soon after birth for social events or employment outside the home. Perhaps their obvious good fortune, attractive appearance, and physical health during an active postpartum influences others, tending to erode the confinement period throughout Chagga society.

Birth still brings considerable attention and assistance to women on Kilimanjaro. A woman is justified in complaining if her work burden is too great in the second and third months of her child's life. In poorer families with limited resources, however, a woman's complaints are often futile—her family's survival depends on her work in the fields. Increased demand for their labor in the fields makes it difficult to continue prolonged breastfeeding. In the household, they also have to work at various tasks and care for many other children. Most families cannot afford to lose a woman's labor for three months.

Interference with breastfeeding is a problem not only for a child but also for a mother. Birth intervals of two to three years are normal in populations where women practice prolonged breastfeeding in the absence of pharmaceutical contraceptives. Curtailing breastfeeding stops its contraceptive effect and brings a rapid return of ovulation, increasing the chances of an ensuing pregnancy. Most women do not use other effective contraception; thus, they are caught in a vicious cycle of increased childbearing and increased workloads.

In one of our discussions, Cecilia explained that she thought it improper to breastfeed while pregnant. She was probably concerned about propriety rather than thinking consciously of cosmological issues or the wrong combination of sexual fluids. Sex with her husband was a private matter, but breastfeeding while pregnant would eventually become public knowledge and could result in condemnation and shame. Any failure to act according to local custom could raise questions about her, especially because she had been an outsider, and she could lose community support.

Order in Chagga Cosmology

Remnants of precolonial beliefs are embedded in people's explanations of *kuvimba* although most of the associated rituals are no longer practiced.

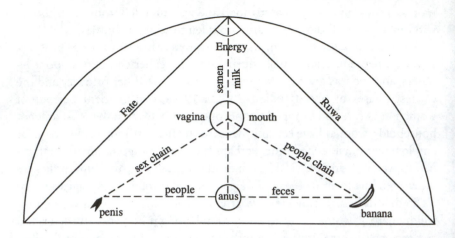

~ Figure 12 *The cycle and chain of nature and culture in Chagga cosmology.*

They stem from notions of order used to address the mysteries of life and death and the place of humans in nature (see Figure 12).[3] In descriptions of Chagga cosmology by German missionaries and researchers during the first half of this century, apparent opposites are understood to be extremes of the same reality (Gutmann 1926 and Raum 1942 interpreted by Moore 1976). For instance, light and dark, life and death, were part of each other in a mutually necessary continuum. In the figure, the outer sphere represents the snow-capped volcanic mountain environment, mother's breast, and father's penis—all sources of moist energy. It is within two opposing energy sources, dryness and moisture, that the dramatic life chain is enacted, and death as well. In the center of the diagram is the small sphere representing the negative poles of life—the mouth and vagina, both dark, moist orifices. The death of substances (people) produced from the vagina fed the male line with ancestors. The "death" of substances passed from the mouth through to the anus produced fecal material that fed the earth. The smaller sphere at the bottom represents the anus. The two opposing positive poles represented by the penis on the left and the banana on the right fed into the negative poles to produce life. Proper feeding assumed the penis to have been eaten by the vagina and the banana to have been consumed by the mouth. Crossing the projectiles over into inappropriate orifices (the penis into the mouth or anus, or the banana into the vagina or anus) was a logical as well as actual possibility and may in part be responsible for much of the humor associated with the banana.

People had to maintain order in their lives in specific ways to contribute to the cyclic renewal of generations of people, animals, and plants and the continuity of day and night and the seasons (Moore and Purritt 1977). Maintenance of order would ensure continuation of the chain of ancestors and descendants, giving the dead a continuing existence in the spirit world. The watchful eyes of the ancestors were thought to oversee all of these processes. The complexity of Chagga cosmology, which extends far beyond the scope of our book, is apparent in the many ways in which themes of sexuality and reproduction were woven through ritual, myth, and practices in daily life.

Sexual reproduction has become a metaphor for the Chagga in understanding powerful forces in the universe. It is also a key to balancing the related forces of life and death.

> The proper combination of male and female in marriage was in keeping with social order and produced healthy new life. The wrong combination, out of wedlock, incestuous or anomalous in some other way, made disorder, sickness, and death. . . . The powers of destruction could be used against an enemy for protection of self. Hence the powers of destruction were not unambiguously evil, merely dangerous, and the direction in which they were sent determined whether they were operating positively or negatively for a particular person. Similarly ambiguous were some of the most fundamental of the life-maintaining processes such as the taking in of food and drink. What entered the body could nourish and sustain it, or it could poison and kill. Thus the persons with whom one shared food, drink, and physical contact were the most trusted and intimate, and yet were the very persons to whose bad intentions one was most vulnerable. (Moore 1986:334)

The powers inherent in food and drink affected the dead as well as the living. A recently deceased person was admitted to the life of the spirit through a ritual involving slaughtering an animal. The animal's death symbolized the release of the dead person; its spirit "fed" the dead person; its carcass provided food for the living. The dead were thought to need continuing nourishment from the spirits of ritually slaughtered animals. People regularly gave small offerings of milk, blood, meat, and beer in special sacrificial spots in their banana groves. Many of these practices continue in fragmentary and somewhat hidden form.

People appreciated the fact that an offering, when consumed by the living, added to soil fertility and the life of plants through defecation. The cyclic nature of human and plant reproduction was expressed in concepts that connected digestion and sexuality to fertility (see Figure 12). Cattle manure spread among the banana plants and human feces deposited there were seen as having magical qualities that brought fertility to the plants. The practice of using manure may have been related to psychosexual images involving digestive processes and feces recurrent in Chagga ritual and myth (Moore and Purritt 1977:49). Men own the banana groves and pass them on to their sons. In the past, their circumcision astride a banana stem magically gave boys the capacity to produce male offspring for the lineage.

Concepts of male and female imbued many other parts of life with meaning.

> This double association of femaleness and maleness, each and both with life and death and each and both with blood and milk and feces, helps reveal what seems to be a general circumstance about many Chagga symbolic categories, that they are dual and then doubled again. It may also explain in part why, though female is associated with the left, with misfortune and impurity and life negative categories, she is also associated with the luckiest number of the Chagga, the number four, which is used to announce the birth of a girl (Raum 1940:96, 97). Three is for males. . . . Female has two aspects: inauspicious, dangerous, menstruating, polluting, death-bringing, castrated, penis-less female . . . and the other aspect, pregnant, non-menstruating, childbearing, maternal, feeding, life-bringing, peaceful, femaleness associated with the lucky number four. Equally, male has two aspects: auspicious maleness associated with purity, cleanliness, strength, virility, completeness (i.e., having a penis). . . . But maleness is also imbued with violence, the death-pollution of killing in war, animal slaughter, and characterized by male incompleteness in not bearing children and not producing milk food. (Moore 1976:366–367)

Chagga concepts of sexuality and reproduction are thus tied in many ways to the balance of female and male, of humans with the natural world, and of good and evil. Neither males nor females could proceed in isolation from the other sex; they had to recognize that they were part of one another (Moore 1976). Ways of balancing the apparent differences were symbolized by the distribution of food. Throughout the rites of passage, food was used to mark changes in a person's identity and role. Choice of food corresponded to a person's needs, which were perceived to change over the life cycle.

Kwashiorkor, Initiation, and Circumcision

The initiation rites were the main way of communicating ideas of order. The rites themselves showed that life and death, male and female, and purity and pollution were not polar opposites but were shared aspects of human experience that needed to be balanced (Moore 1976). Instructions and myths told during the initiation rites conveyed these notions.

Circumcision was one of the rites of initiation, and it was required before childbearing. A mother-in-law, under whose jurisdiction a bride was to reside, had an interest in maintaining the requirement for female circumcision. Her daughter-in-law's circumcision was supposed to prevent the death of her own son's heir and to perpetuate the lineage of which she was an honored member. The first child of an uncircumcised woman was likely to contract *kuvimba* and, ultimately, to die (Gutmann 1926).

Descriptions of the initiation rites by Gutmann show the Chagga attention to balancing the powers and activities of male and female (Gutmann 1926). In the rites, each sex claimed to formerly have had the power to reproduce without the other sex. Women were said to have originally had penises; men had wombs and the capacity to become pregnant. Even though each sex came to need the other to have children, young men still had to be reminded that they were not solely responsible—women had a role in producing offspring as well. The reminder was necessary because male initiation emphasized the men's role in conception and traits inherited from fathers. Boys were taught that nine months in the initiation camp were necessary for them to father children later. Painful and unpleasant ordeals and tests of stamina during the nine-month male initiation supposedly counterbalanced the difficulty and pain of pregnancy and birth for women.

Initiation emphasized other parallels between the sexes. Men went through a mock hunting ritual using spears to symbolize their sexual prowess. Girls also performed a mock hunt in which they caught grasshoppers and tadpoles and wrapped them in a grass bundle, symbolizing a fetus, an image of women's sexual power. Men mimicked warfare during initiation, while women were taught ideals of stoicism during birth, which in the Chagga view was as heroic as the brave deeds of warriors in battle.

A theme in the myths was the idea that the anuses of adult men were permanently closed.[4] Because their anuses were said to be plugged and stitched during initiation, they were able to fully digest their food without defecating, without polluting the earth as do women. Their anuses had to be altered because men were believed once to have had the capacity to be impregnated by other men. Giving birth would have resulted in the death of both father and fetus (Moore and Purritt 1977:60). The myth portrayed ideals of men's purity, superiority, and authority. Only children were duped by the myth, however, because the truth about adult men was exposed as part of female and male initiation. Adults knew and swore to keep secret the fact that in reality male anuses were open, as were women's.

The male anal plug myth symbolized the male as closed in contrast to the woman as open. Men were retainers of feces and blood, remaining pure, while women polluted the earth with their feces and menstrual blood. In pregnancy, on the other hand, at the height of their reproductive power, women were considered closed because they no longer menstruated. Pregnant women had special powers that could bring misfortune to men;

and men, as all adults knew, did defecate, and thus were open. The symbolic categories of open and closed were connected not only with sexuality but also with life and death. A man's feces or a woman's menstrual blood could, for example, be used in sorcery to make that person sterile. The threat of sterility was serious because lack of sons meant that no one could make the ancestral offerings required to sustain a person's spirit in the afterlife. Death would be complete; the spirit would not survive (Moore 1976; Raum 1940).

The connection between *kuvimba* and rites of circumcision, especially of girls, involved the integration of many important cultural themes. Circumcision prepared young men and women for marriage and stopped their parents from having more children. The rites divided one generation from the next, maintaining an orderly succession.

During customary rites of circumcision, adolescent boys and girls went through painful surgical procedures. The circumciser would cut off parts of each sex's genitalia. The ordeal, which involved no anesthesia, was to ready boys for their future pain from warfare and girls for the pain of birth. Each person offered this bodily sacrifice as a testimonial of willingness to accept the rights and responsibilities of adulthood. Their community received them with great fanfare once they had successfully endured the ordeal.

The operation itself supposedly lasted only moments but must have entailed enormous pain. Some East African groups use trance and other techniques to reduce pain (today, often anesthesia). In the case of boys, the surgeon removed the foreskin with a sharp instrument, frequently a blade of obsidian (volcanic glass).[5] Removal of the foreskin symbolized removing the "open" or femalelike aspect of the male sex organ. For girls, the operation (known technically as excision) varied from region to region on Kilimanjaro and usually entailed removal of part of the clitoris and the labia minora. The removal eliminated the "closed" or malelike aspect of the genitalia. Today, many girls, or even young married women, elect to undergo a small cut instead of the surgical procedure.

Circumcision involved some health risks, as did the months of duress for males during their period of initiation into the warrior age grade. For both sexes, heavy bleeding, tetanus, and other infections could occur. Although there are no gynecologic reports from early studies on the Chagga, physicians in other parts of East Africa reported complications later in a woman's life, especially in the Horn of Africa, where a much more severe form of surgery is performed on girls.[6]

The customary Chagga rites make it clear that the focus was on the girl's transformation into an adult. The effect on her sexuality probably depended mainly on the interpretation given the operation by her family. European missionaries and physicians felt comfortable with the male surgery because it was customary in their own society. They reacted strongly against female circumcision, however. In their crusades against it, they focused on the danger of infection from the operation.[7]

A cornerstone of the lineage was the sexual division of labor. It rested on two basic facts: only men were warriors, and only women gave birth. These facts were emphasized by the separation of male and female workplaces and food. Chagga classified most foods into predominantly male or female categories and required that they be stored separately. For example, a man could not take milk from his wife's calabashes without her permission, nor could a woman enter the millet granary without her husband's permission. These and similar distinctions permeated daily life.

The differences between the sexes were also expressed in distinct diets. Ordinarily, a man who slaughtered a cow distributed the meat to certain household heads; each man who received a share was expected to keep most of it for himself and distribute the rest to household members in proportion to their status. Men's control of the prized portions of meat corresponded to their ascendancy in the lineage. In contrast, a Chagga boy's initiation involved nine months of extreme duress and hardship isolated in the wilderness, often on the brink of starvation.

On the other hand, women received abundant milk and *mlaso* (a blood and butter mixture), seen as female food, during critical rites of passage. They were supposed to become fat on this favored food, in recognition of their crucial part in producing new lineage members—a triumph ritually celebrated in the same manner as a successful hunter returning home with a kill. In the past, a girl was isolated from the rest of society for three months before circumcision and up to six months after her operation, symbolizing the duration of pregnancy.

Care that women ate well during their reproductive years was customary. An almost immediate sequel to circumcision for a girl was the commencement of her wedding ceremonies; thus, a young woman had an ample diet prior to her first conception. The celebration of circumcision was one of the greatest days in a woman's life, commemorated with the largest number of gifts she would ever receive (Moore and Purritt 1977:61).

Circumcision was required for both men and women before they became parents. Circumcision was more important than marriage in legitimating offspring. This is underscored by the contrast between the penalties for premarital conception and those for conception by the uncircumcised. Bridewealth payments could be adjusted if a circumcised girl became pregnant before her betrothal ceremonies, and a sacrifice could be offered, perhaps a goat, to appease those offended, including the ancestors. If uncircumcised youths had sex that resulted in pregnancy, however, they were to be impaled with a spear, one on top of the other, in a public place (Raum 1940:69).

Circumcision also had repercussions for others in the family. Daughters were circumcised individually or in twos and threes (as opposed to group rituals for boys), and the rite had to precede the beginning of their menstrual periods. A father whose firstborn child was a daughter would have to withdraw from his age grade when many of his age mates were still "administering the law of justice." Because sons' circumcisions occurred in large groups, all their fathers resigned at the same time.

1920s

Why did a man have to resign from his own age grade as soon as he had to have one of his children circumcised? The name for the act of resignation will give the answer: *ikuwuta mohoju* which means literally, "to take oneself off the banana stem." The banana stem is the one on which the man has been circumcised. The banana shaft signified the alliance of procreation [marriage and childbearing], and this alliance lasts until the firstborn himself seeks consecration for the preservation and renewal of the alliance. The father makes way for his son and the mother is not allowed to give birth any more after her daughter gets married. "If the child jumps over you, you must die. Take yourself quickly off the banana stem." To be jumped over by the child means to still belong to the alliance of procreation while the child is being received into this alliance. (Gutmann 1926:324)

People saw a daughter's circumcision as advantageous for her mother because it would stop the mother from further reproduction and ensure bridewealth payments before the daughter conceived. These reproductive restrictions on the order in which women gave birth reduced the toll of childbearing on older women. "If the child jumps over you, you must die" was not only a ritual incantation, warning of the wrath of the ancestors, but seemed also to warn of potential conflict if interdependent generations were to compete over the same resources. The restrictions also tended to make older women available for child care because they would have no infants of their own.

Circumcision brought a daughter adult status and gifts. By customary law, a circumcised girl had control over the farm products resulting from her labor, and her father could no longer demand them (Moore 1986:48). At circumcision the elders declared, "We have handed over our child to the ancestors" (Raum 1940:68). People feared that the ancestors would kill those who refused to be circumcised or to circumcise their children (Raum 1940).

These features of Chagga culture provided for an orderly succession of new entrants into the lineage. A father's act of resignation from his age grade publicly dramatized the maintenance of this balance. If his wife were to become pregnant and breastfeed a newborn, he would face the conflict of trying to simultaneously provide cattle for his son's bridewealth and special pregnancy foods made of cattle products for his wife.

Male circumcision ceremonies, which were once mass rites for large groups of boys, are no longer held. Boys go to a clinic for circumcision. Neither boys nor girls undergo the long seclusion of earlier days, and much of the information formerly taught during that period is being lost. Female circumcision is still practiced and celebrated on an individual basis.

During the 1970s, many youth openly debated the value of female circumcision. Boys almost always voiced opposition, and girls usually expressed ambivalence about circumcision. Some girls supported the institution, and one sixteen-year-old I interviewed did not seem hesitant in preparing for circumcision. Like other girls I knew, she may have focused on the gifts she would receive and the security and praise she would gain. The current incidence of female circumcision on the mountain is unknown, but in the 1970s, an obstetrician-gynecologist at the Medical Center told me that about 40 percent of his maternity patients had not been circumcised, suggesting that this custom was changing.

Circumcision of one's pubescent child is still supposed to end childbearing by parents, but two women in the NURU study continued bearing children in middle age, when they were already grandmothers. Grandmothers are increasingly bearing children, even though in the eyes of some this practice is still implicated in kwashiorkor.

Kwashiorkor and Failure to Make Bridewealth Payments

The payment of bridewealth legitimates marriage and spiritually joins the husband's and wife's kin for all eternity. Bridewealth payments cement the bonds between the bride's and groom's families, ensure the legitimacy of the couple's children, and lead to continuing social support for the couple. The families tended to live close together, making their ties potentially important in practical ways. According to one study, people usually married within two miles of their parents' compounds (Moore 1986:238), and the clinic survey found that nearly 70 percent of couples grew up in compounds less than six miles apart (see Appendix B, no.8).

Bridewealth payments were customarily in the form of cattle paid in ten payments over a long period. Final payments were made by the couple's own sons when they got married. Failure to complete the sequence of payments was a shameful infraction, upsetting the proper order of things, possibly bringing revenge from the ancestors. Children born to a marriage not sanctioned by bridewealth payments might die or bring misfortune to their lineage (Swantz 1969:155, 167). Two children in the NURU study were said to have become ill with *kuvimba* because of their fathers' failure to complete the payments.

If a young man squandered his bridewealth and failed to make payments on time, his own father could curse him to avoid shame for the rest of the family. Frequently such cursing was directed at the son's children. This drastic measure was usually a last resort to force the son to make the payments when all other forms of persuasion had been exhausted.

Today, better-off Chagga have the means to pay bridewealth, often in cash and new forms of wealth, such as automobiles. The financial crisis in Tanzania over the past twenty-five years, however, has inflated bridewealth payments, prohibiting many parents from accumulating enough cattle or cash for their sons. As a result, many men are delaying marriage until their mid-thirties and forties, and abortions and illegitimate births are increasing (Kerner and Cook 1991). Some young men strongly advocate ending the system.

Changes in Birth Intervals

Women customarily had means of avoiding sex with their husbands. One method involved the custom of a woman having her own house, constructed after the birth of her first child, where she resided separately from her husband. She would bolt the door of the house to keep from having sex. This custom was not working well in the 1970s, however, as one woman testified.

1972

∼ My UNICEF research team consisted of two women from Kilimanjaro, a European sociologist, and me. We were on our way to Masama to hold one of nine focus group discussions with women.

"I hope we won't have any men around this time," said Helena Klein, a sociologist and a committed socialist who was quite critical of the government's failure to improve conditions for the poor. "Not that I have anything against men, but the last discussion in Lyamungu really bombed with those two government officials."

"Perhaps it was the size of the group," said Margaret Matingo, who tended to take offense at Helena's more critical view of her people, especially those who, like herself, were well-off. "I counted forty women, and that simply is too large a group for any good discussion to take place." Margaret was a highly educated Chagga woman who had two master's degrees from universities in the United States. She had returned to Tanzania shortly after independence and opposed socialist policies.

Realizing that she had inadvertently affronted Margaret once again, Helena reluctantly agreed with her. "You're right. Our last discussion on Kibongoto with the nine women church leaders was quite frank. I think, on the whole, the Chagga people tend to confront their problems openly. If anything, information almost seems exaggerated for dramatic purposes. Perhaps that's part of the oral tradition, or maybe it's because *wazungu* need things spelled out more clearly."

The last comment was meant as a joke, but no one laughed.

"What will our topic be today?" asked Catherine Meela, a university student from Kilimanjaro. She sought to curtail the ideological jousting between the two researchers that had become a strain on all members of the team.[8]

"Well, we're headed for a prenatal clinic. I thought we'd consider issues around family planning and birth intervals."

Helena was in charge of the research. She had done extensive demographic and economic surveys in her position as a researcher at the University of Dar es Salaam, and she was a supportive and encouraging teacher for me and Catherine.

When we pulled up to the clinic, there was a crowd of women waiting to be seen by the doctor. Some were gathered under the shade of a nearby tree. Others were sitting beneath the porch roof of the clinic's veranda. "Make sure you spread out," Helena reminded us in a whisper as we approached the group. Because Catherine and I generally said little, we were able to observe women's reactions and hear their muttered exchanges, helping us to understand their points of view. Helena made our observations an official part of the research methods.

Margaret greeted the women standing outside the veranda and began to explain the purposes of our research.

"We're part of a larger group who are studying conditions for children. Five areas were chosen in Tanzania, including Kilimanjaro. We have gone to many health and education programs and have interviewed their staff to understand their perspectives. We've spoken with schoolchildren and have asked them to write about a day in their life. We're especially trying to understand the difficulties mothers face in bringing up a healthy and happy child. So we've arranged to meet with several groups of women. How fortunate we are today to be with all of you mothers. Tell me, who better knows what hopes and concerns people have for young children than a group of expectant mothers?"

This direct public reference to pregnancy made everyone laugh because normally people don't speak about such matters openly. Margaret had a way with words and conducted herself in the authoritative, somewhat patronizing manner expected of an educated, wealthy person. By saying things considered rude and improper, she could catch people off guard and joke with them.

After a while, everyone in the clinic, including the two nurses, joined the group. Seventeen women gathered around and seemed to enjoy the unexpected interruption of their morning.

Helena asked the first question. Women expressed their concerns about small children, as usual. Safe drinking water was at the top of the list, as most people knew that irrigation water was contaminated, and children often had parasitic infections. The women spoke of the need for more clinics because of the difficulty of walking miles, often over rough terrain, carrying a sick child. Others complained about the cost of food, especially milk, and everyone said she knew of a malnourished child in the area. It was a typical meeting until Helena started asking questions about family planning.

"Are you concerned about spacing births?"

A few women nodded. One said, "About two to four years is best. That way each child can be cared for properly. It's very bad to have children every year, as more and more of us are doing."

"Do you know any women who go to family planning clinics to help them space their births?" Helena asked.

At first there was an uncomfortable silence. A few women snickered, and others muttered something about it not being anyone's business to know about such things.

Then one woman spoke up. "My sister was divorced because she went to a family planning clinic."

The women burst out laughing—a sympathetic gesture that must have given another woman the courage to share her story.

"I'll tell you what happened to me when I went to the family planning clinic." She glanced at the other women for support. "I had been unsuccessful in keeping my door closed, and my husband gave me nine children. So I went to the clinic for some assistance to stop having more babies without informing my husband. They gave me a prescription for pills and I locked it in my personal box, but he found it and exploded. Right then he took me to bed, and that's why I stand here before you, pregnant for the tenth time!"

Again, everyone burst into laughter in sympathy with her unfortunate experience. I noticed that the exchange that day had brought Margaret and Helena closer, at least momentarily, as they identified with the women's struggle to control childbearing. ⌒

It was clear that the women who desired to increase birth intervals or stop childbearing were not having much success. Chagga expectations for long intervals between births developed before colonialism and continue today, but such expectations are clearly undermined in practice. In earlier times, polygyny may have contributed to long spacing between births by providing men with an alternative sex partner when a wife was still breastfeeding (Moore and Purritt 1977). In 1903, observers reported that women in monogamous households had more children than polygynously married women, and polygyny was reported to be more common in precolonial times than today (Moore and Purritt 1977).[9] Men who could not afford more than one wife were allowed to have sex with a barren woman or a woman past childbearing age.[10]

Christian churches condemned extramarital sex and polygyny, however, and women's protection from a rapid succession of pregnancies diminished. In the 1970s, only about 5 percent of households were polygynous (Moore and Purritt 1977:2). Among people I knew in the 1970s, the university-educated Chagga were monogamous, but a number of wealthier Christian and Muslim entrepreneurs had two wives living in different areas on the mountain. An older man who was newly impoverished was finding that the custom of keeping two wives on the same *kihamba* created conflict because he had too little farmland to provide enough for his sons. The community came to associate the conflict with polygyny.

On the other hand, a newer form of extramarital liaison was becoming established in the 1970s. Some secondary-school girls enter sexual relationships with wealthier married men, who reciprocate with gifts of money. Their pregnancies have led to increased rates of abortion and illegitimacy. An out-of-wedlock child usually lives with the grandparents, supported partly by money sent home by the young mother from her work in a city (Stambach 1995).

Abortion and infanticide have been punishable by imprisonment in Tanzania since earlier in the century. Some doctors on Kilimanjaro would risk performing abortions, but usually only for people of their own class. The poor had to rely on midwives, some of whom would perform abortions for high fees. Women were said to assist their daughters in bringing about abortions with uterine massages and herbal remedies. Some girls would attempt abortion themselves by using the midsection of a long dracaena leaf to provoke miscarriage. There were rumors that dead fetuses or infants were found and attributed to girls who had feared telling their parents.

Other customary methods of reproductive control included coitus interruptus, ejaculation between a woman's thighs, and the use of a smooth river pebble said to act as a barrier when placed against the woman's cervix. These methods, as well as the pill, diaphragm, injection, condom, and sterilization, are condemned by the Catholic Church. Instead, the Church teaches people to use the rhythm method, but, as one woman remarked, this strategy did not work when her husband was drunk. Many women are ambivalent about modern contraceptives. They fear the potential physical side effects and their husbands' disapproval.

One ethnographer suggests that changes in birth control methods may have played a role in the explosive population growth over this last half century:

> How much . . . population increase has been the result of public health measures which decreased infant mortality and how much to the interference of Christian monogamy with indigenous customs regarding the spacing of children is not clear. It had been Chagga practice to breastfeed children for several years and not to have a new baby until the nursling was weaned. Christian priests and pastors are said to have told Chagga that it was all right to have a child a year, that polygyny was wrong, and child spacing unnecessary. (Moore 1986:110)

Men publicly decried modern contraception during the 1970s. A wealthy man behind me in a line at a grocery store in Moshi loudly exclaimed, while pointing to the condoms near the cash register, "The government just expects Chagga men to be like Europeans and have only two children!" Male sexual prowess is sometimes measured by number of children, although many men buy condoms. Husbands who work outside the Kilimanjaro region are said to keep their wives pregnant for fear they would engage in extramarital affairs. Men also control the government, churches, and medical system, and it wasn't until 1995 that women were allowed to go to clinics for contraceptive pills and tubal ligations without their husbands' signature. Many women persist in trying to get access to modern contraceptives despite their fears and legal restrictions. A Chagga nun told me that she even sent women who were exhausted from childbearing to a nearby family planning clinic.

Despite the religious pressure against many of the customary practices that increased birth spacing, the pride of men in producing children, and women's fears of modern contraception, the Kilimanjaro region has the highest rate of contraceptive use in Tanzania (Tanzania Demographic and Health Survey 1992:9). Over one quarter of the people surveyed reported using a modern method of contraception, compared with the next highest reported regional contraceptive usage of about 10 percent (see Table 4). Although not remarkable for urban populations, the contraceptive rate on Kilimanjaro is significant for rural people, and it may relate to the region's relatively high educational levels.

Table 4   *Contraceptive Prevalence in the Kilimanjaro Region*[a]

Type of contraception	Prevalence
Married women using	
Oral contraceptives	9%
Intrauterine device (IUD)	5%
Sterilization	8%
Other methods	3%
Total	25%
Men using modern contraception	29%

[a] Source: Tanzania Demographic and Health Survey 1992:9.

Change, Child Spacing, and the Shame of Kwashiorkor

Customary sexual practices indirectly promoted long birth intervals and a relatively short reproductive span. Having many children in quick succession was understood to result in scarcity of food and assistance for the new mother and an increased workload as well. In the 1970s, *kuvimba* was commonly associated with poverty, and both *kuvimba* and poverty were viewed as shameful failings on the part of the parents.

Breastfeeding while pregnant, failure of a woman to be circumcised before childbearing, and failure of a man to make bridewealth payments were some of the explanations given for *kuvimba* during the NURU study. Even though some of the customary reasoning behind these explanations has been lost, notions of proper timing and spacing of births persist. In the realm of human sexuality, Christianity often contradicts some central tenets of Chagga morality, especially regarding the spacing and timing of births.

Despite the teachings of Christian priests, pressure has been maintained on women to sustain long intervals between births. The people of Kilimanjaro, including some Catholics, are increasingly adopting birth control. In the midst of these sweeping changes, people have difficulty knowing what to expect from one another or when and if it is appropriate to impose sanctions for undesirable behavior.

A discretionary pattern of condemnation nevertheless was present in the 1970s and continues. Affluent individuals have more freedom to transgress customs than others. Few criticized wealthy parents such as Philippe and Edwardi Lema, who successfully fed, clothed, and educated all nine children born in quick succession. They could cite church teachings about the value of many children and the evils of birth control. The obvious failures of the impoverished to secure resources and prevent malnutrition, however, could be compounded by community censorship for lack of propriety. To many who observed the struggles of their neighbors during the food crisis, kwashiorkor came to symbolize the shame of very poor people.

Chapter Seven

The Meaning of a Child

1930s

~ *When the child is born, there is a hush to hear its first cry. . . . As soon as it utters the first sound, the women, led by the husband's mother, raise a long and high-pitched trill; kyulilili, the call of victory, shouted by the women on the successful completion of a hunt or raid. The word is quickly passed round the whole neighborhood that another woman has succeeded in her test of courage and mortality. (Raum 1940:85)* ~

The spirit of triumph and joy recorded by Raum fifty years ago still describes birth on Kilimanjaro.[1] In the past, the celebration of a birth began a series of rites of passage taking the child through times of transition and providing protection for the lineage. Although many of the rites are no longer widely practiced, the beliefs that underlie them influence contemporary ways of dealing with children and childhood illness.

Childhood Rites of Passage

Accounts from the first half of this century show that the Chagga viewed children not as wholly dependent on their caretakers but as beings with powers of their own (Raum 1940). People ritually obligated to a child saw the transitions marked by the life cycle rituals as especially dangerous periods during which the child's power was activated, threatening both the child and its kinsmen.

Both the fetus and the neonate were seen as links between the living and the dead (Raum 1940:67). A fetus had the power to bring misfortune to a sibling who was still being breastfed and thus competing for maternal nurturing. It was also believed that spirits could use an abnormal fetus or child as a vehicle to signify their displeasure with parental misbehavior (Raum 1940). Rituals were required to ward off danger, evil, impurity, or pollution. Many of the rites were believed to reveal the child's potential as a member of the lineage, thus giving relatives a basis for favoring some children over others.

The literature on childhood rites of passage among the Chagga contains some variation, which may reflect lineage, regional, and historical differences on Kilimanjaro as well as differences between ideals and practice. Here we focus on the concepts of a child's need for protection and its potential to do harm. The rites of passage were occasions for assessing these needs and potentials in children, revealing the centers of power and authority and potential sources of conflict in the patrilineage.

The rites defined stages of development in the infant from birth through weaning. Breastfeeding had particular significance in Chagga culture as an expression of kin relationships that helped define the lineage.

The First Feeding Rite

1930s

> The paternal grandmother received the infant at birth. She licked it, rubbed it with butter, massaged and shaped the head, and then wrapped the child. The baby was then handed over to the other women in order of prestige and rank, in the same sequence as beer or food distribution. Soon after washing, the baby was to be shown "the food of this world"— two roasted bananas steeped in milk and butter, then chewed by the husband's mother and spat, piece by piece, into the baby's mouth. Several medicines were added: *kyana* dracaena to "open the mouth"; *kilau* tubers to prevent threadworm; bark from a *msesewe* tree masticated with finger millet to combat roundworm; and others to clear the alimentary canal of meconium. (Paraphrased from Raum 1940:95, 96)

This rite was the first test of a newborn. The child, and the ancestor linked to it, would choose to grow or die. Eating was a child's first responsibility, and if a child refused to eat, it could be left to die.

Three further rituals were performed before the infant was weaned: the rite of the first tooth, the naming ceremony, and the covering rite. The covering rite signified the end of infancy and marked the introduction of meat into children's diets.

The Rite of the First Tooth

The newborn was referred to as *mgeni* (visitor) (Swantz 1969:94). In later infancy, prior to the expected eruption of the first tooth, at about six months, the baby was called *mnangu* (the incomplete). Any delay in tooth eruption was attributed to the paternal grandfather's displeasure at not having been supplied with beer and meat. If the parents brought him his provisions, he spat into the child's mouth, retracting his spell (Swantz 1969).

With the appearance of the first tooth, the paternal grandmother performed a rite called "to take up the child," in which she rubbed a special herb on the gums while uttering a blessing to ensure the completion of the set of teeth (Raum 1940:296). The eruption of the lower incisors was evidence of a child's normality, and kin celebrated the passage of the child through one of the first crises of life.

A boy was regarded as potentially dangerous to his mother's lineage, since he could not be incorporated into it. In addition, any abnormality in a son was believed to be lethal to his own father. Had the upper incisors appeared first, the whole community would have known there were evil forces at work. A boy would have been killed, while a girl and her mother would have been returned to the mother's lineage (Raum 1940). The proper eruption of the first teeth signified that the baby was maturing normally and, hence, was not suspected to be a possible agent of malevolent spirits.

The Naming Rite

Ordinarily, a child received a name only after starting to utter some words. The firstborn could not be named without the offering of a sacrifice (Marealle 1963:10). The first daughter was the namesake of her paternal grandmother and the first son that of his paternal grandfather. The secondborn children of both sexes were named after the maternal grandparents and the thirdborn of both sexes after the paternal great grandparents. Later children were given names of uncles and aunts or other names somehow connected with special lineage events or circumstances at birth (Marealle 1963:10). A child's becoming ill before receiving a name meant that its dead grandfather wanted the naming to take place (Raum 1940:297).[2]

The Covering Rite

In the covering rite, a ring made of animal skin was placed on the child's finger to prevent the spirits from putting a spell on the child. The rite, performed independently or in conjunction with the naming ceremony, was a petition to the ancestor after whom a child was named.[3] It was the last of the infancy rites, removing the child from the special protection of the ancestors and marking social incorporation as a person (Raum 1940:298).

These rites began at birth and marked the maturation of an infant in the first and second years of life. The rites required a child's mother, father, and paternal grandmother to assess its suitability for membership in the lineage. Concepts of a child's potency and responsibility were balanced by opposing notions of vulnerability, dependence, and need of protection.

Food and Social Life

Giving food to children was an element in the rites of passage as well as part of daily life. Patterns of distribution of food expressed social ties, especially obligations and reciprocity in households and lineages. Customary rules governing infant feeding emphasized the importance of maternal milk, which was regarded as crucial but not sufficient to nourish the infant. The mother was responsible for food distribution and used food to teach children their first lessons in reciprocity. Access to food took on social significance early in a child's life.

Breast Milk and Breastfeeding

Reports about a baby's first introduction to breastfeeding are not uniform. One early report said a baby was not fed colostrum, the antibody-rich clear liquid produced by a woman's breasts immediately after birth. The mother was to wait to feed her baby until milk appeared (Raum 1940:97). In the area in which I worked in the early 1970s, colostrum was also believed harmful to infants.[4]

Lema, however, cites another practice immediately following birth (1973:371). The infant's paternal grandmother gave it ground seeds of a certain herb to prevent future roundworm infection (ascariasis). The baby then began nursing slowly, obtaining the colostrum. According to Lema, colostrum was thought to be good for a baby. Even animal colostrum was regarded as food for young children, and when a cow delivered, the milk obtained in the first two weeks was drunk only by children.

In addition to having special life-enhancing qualities, mother's milk was considered able to transmit evil and sickness. Women were supposed to cover their breasts during pregnancy for protection from the entrance of spirits. In some cases, a magician was called to scarify the areolas and close up the nipples with a charm to prevent what Chagga considered unfit or "burning" breast milk, said to cause colic in infants (Raum 1940:103).

A number of sayings and practices conveyed the image of mother's milk as powerful. The relationship among brothers and sisters was characterized by the phrase *waleonga ve limu* (they sucked the same breast) (Gutmann 1926:4). The lineage was said to draw its strength not only from descent from common ancestors, but also from mother's milk. An unrelated child was accepted into a family when the mother offered her breast. An alliance was completed and secured with a few drops of mother's milk, and the life-giving qualities of milk from women were seen as equal to those of cattle (Gutmann 1926:9). Like many other aspects of infancy, breastfeeding could bring good or harm to a child.

Other Food and Weaning

Infants were believed to require food in addition to mother's milk in early life. After the first-feeding rite, a mother regularly placed masticated food into her newborn's mouth (Gutmann 1926; Raum 1940:105). Milk and butter added to cooked porridge made with *mchare* bananas and *magadi* (bicarbonate of soda) usually made up these early meals.[5] Infants also ate other special foods, some of which required considerable maternal labor.

> The mother peeled one or two green bananas and a small ripe banana, cut them open to remove the central fibers, then boiled them in milk in the baby-pot until they were cooked soft. She then poured off the liquor and mashed the bananas to a soft mass using a special instrument *(uwiri)*. The so-called baby milk was added to form a thick porridge, which was then diluted with water. The mixture was allowed to stand and later the supernatant fluid was poured into a bowl and given to the baby using a wooden spoon or by mouth-to-mouth feeding by the mother or nurse. If the mother was in a hurry she filtered the food through a grass mat. As the baby grew more teeth, less filtering was done and the food was less diluted, so that by the age of one year the food was taken unfiltered and undiluted. At this time, or even earlier, the mother chewed adult food and offered it to the baby from her mouth. (Lema 1963:373)[6]

The mother was the one to receive credit if her baby flourished. At three months, infants were permitted to eat a greater range of adult food, but not meat (Raum 1940:105). An infant was allowed to mouth but not swallow certain foods until the first tooth appeared (Lema 1973:372). An infant's food was prepared in a special small pot with cow's milk that was kept in a separate gourd to prevent souring.

Prolonged breastfeeding was widespread and generally continued for at least two years; customs of the father's lineage determined the time for weaning (Raum 1940:206). Both Lema (1973:373) and Gutmann (1926) reported that breastfeeding longer than three years was believed to spoil the child's character. Extended breastfeeding would have helped to postpone a succeeding pregnancy until the child no longer needed to be carried, a situation most women desire.

Women were permitted to use strong discipline in weaning children who were reluctant or had to be weaned prematurely for some reason. They could smear red pepper or a bitter substance on their nipples (Raum 1940:106; Lema 1973:373). Relatives could mock children to make them feel ashamed of being dependent (Lema 1973:373). Grandparents might help by taking a weanling to their household; the household of maternal grandparents was likely to be at some distance. Some of these weaning regimens, especially abrupt removal from the home, could upset some children enough to threaten their health (see also Cassidy 1980).[7] Most authors, however, viewed the change in diet when breastfeeding ended as less traumatic than might otherwise have been expected because the child had been accustomed to other food throughout its life.

Food and Reciprocity

A mother's authority and right to respect was derived partly from her control over the household food store. There was a general prohibition against entry of children into the food store, and for boys it was a disgrace to touch a milk calabash. Women apportioned food among their children with larger amounts for their smaller children and for sons who worked as herders.

The good health of her child enhanced a woman's social status. As she provided nourishment for the child, the mother used food to teach the child responsibility. A mother gave a first lesson in sharing food when she tasted what was in her weanling child's bowl.[8]

> She may refuse a meal to a child that has annoyed or offended her. . . . The mother expects a return also after dispensing food. When sharing out a meal, she has no plate. She eats directly from the pot or, in times of famine, may go without food. Each child is then expected to leave a handful on its plate for her. To a child who refuses to give this return, its starving mother retaliates: "Look, you haven't given me any food. Don't be astonished if I do the same to you next time!" (Raum 1940:127)

The practices of leaving food on the plate to share with the mother and of small children eating from a common bowl with their older siblings were being discouraged in the 1970s through clinic and radio campaigns that admonished mothers to give weanling children separate bowls. Schools have also taught children that the customary practices are unhygienic. Poorer households, however, persist in giving children a common bowl.

In times of plenty, I have seen mothers and other adults persuade a child to eat by pretending to enjoy a succulent morsel. Upon reaching for some, the child was given a piece and upon reaching for more, the whole portion. At this point, the adult became the petitioner and mimicked the face of the pouting, sad-eyed child. Then the child responded by giving the adult food, and the adult responded with loving gratitude. If the child reciprocated, the adult's reaction made a considerable impression on the young child.

When faced with overwork, economic crisis, or family conflict, people have little time for playful lessons and close attention to how a child eats. Feeding a small child becomes one more burden, especially when there is not enough food. When children share a common bowl without enough food for all of them, it is easy for the youngest and weakest to be left hungry.

Child Care

Ideally, a mother enters a dyadic relationship with her infant, who spends much of its time being carried by her and sleeps with her until weaning. In most compounds, mothers-in-law and others care for an infant occasionally. After three months of confinement, a woman carries her baby secured on her body with a cloth, giving the infant access to her breast whenever it is hungry.

A mother learns to offer her breast to her baby before it starts to cry; shortly afterward, she holds the baby out in an appropriate place to allow it to excrete without soiling any clothing. She knows the rumblings in her infant's stomach and is sensitive to the length of time before it eliminates. The baby becomes accustomed to her handling, and their timing becomes synchronized.

~ Figure 13 *Three generations, including a grandmother who took her daughter to NURU in the 1970s.*

Women deal with their babies calmly, without great displays of affection. Most people reason that a baby's lack of verbal capacity makes attempting to converse inappropriate and ridiculous. They rarely talk to their babies and never do so in public. If a woman isn't carrying her baby, a grandmother or older sibling is, and babies seldom cry. Being carried constantly and handled quietly introduces an infant to the social life of the lineage. A child's initial sense of belonging comes through physical contact with its mother's body; later, the sense of belonging comes from membership in the patrilineage.

By the 1970s, the intense, two- to three-year contact between mothers and infants was weakened. Women left their babies at home when they went to market or worked in the fields. According to a Chagga friend and colleague in research, leaving the baby at home while the mother goes to market is a radical change from the past. She had suggested that we go to the market in her home area to observe how women dealt with their children. When we got to the market, hundreds of women were buying and selling, but there were no children in sight. My friend had not frequented the mountain markets, and she was shocked to see that children were not present. When she inquired why this was so, she was told that older children were in school, and babies should not be in an area where so much *uchawi* (witchcraft and evil eye) abounds.

Women today have less time to spend with their children for other reasons as well. The *shamba* they farm may be as far as two hours from home by foot, removing women from the home compound for most of the day. In addition, women working as wage laborers cannot take children along.

Separation of mother and infant when a woman is breastfeeding can result in nutritional deprivation for the infant. If the baby is not fed often enough, the woman's milk production is reduced, further contributing to nutritional problems for the infant and bringing an early end to the contraceptive effect of lactation. Pharmaceutical contraception is unusual, so the result is often a rapid return to pregnancy and the early weaning of the existing child. Thus, the economic and social changes that reduce the intensity of the mother-infant interaction burden the health of the existing child, the mother, and the child to come.

Nurses and Siblings

In the past, a figure of major importance during the early months of life was the nurse. An adolescent, nearly always a girl, she took substantial responsibility in day-to-day infant care and in rites of childhood (Dundas 1924:201, 279; Raum 1940:137). Special care was taken in her selection, and she was often a niece and a member of the patrilineage or a trustworthy child of a neighbor. The grandmother supervised the nurse's work while preparing the family's food. The nurse was usually on duty at least during the mother's three-month confinement period. She received room and board (if she lived far away), and if her charge was without blemish at the end of her stay, she received a goat (Raum 1940:193; Gutmann 1926:279).

Like other relationships in Chagga culture during the precolonial and colonial periods, the institution of the nurse had ritual expression.

> Thus it is the nurse who ritually announces the eruption of the first tooth, even if the mother has actually discovered it. The baby is made to laugh, whereupon the nurse calls the mother; "Look, the house has got a new prop!" It is only now that the mother may express her joy. Likewise the first calling of the child by its name is performed by the nurse. Having been informed of it beforehand, she hands the baby to its mother to be suckled, saying: "Here mother. Take Such-and-Such!" The mother, simulating astonishment, asks: "When did he get his name?" To which the nurse replies: "He had to wait a long time for it!" Only now does the mother's face brighten up and she receives the child, wishing him luck and his grandfather's blessing. Here quite definitely the nurse assumes before the world of spirits guardianship over the child. (Raum 1940:138)

Raum's account implies that the nurse assisted the mother for well over a year, until the child began talking. In the 1920s, changes were already beginning in the nature of nurses (Gutmann 1926:279). The age of nurses dropped drastically, so that they hardly seemed capable of carrying their charges about. Gutmann attributed the change to the "result of great thrift which modern economic conditions demands from parents."

By the early 1970s, the position of nurse no longer held ritual significance. Better-off women still employ adolescent girls as nurses, but poorer women must often leave boys and girls between the ages of four and eight in charge of younger siblings. Although children are supposed to start school at eight years of age, sometimes parents keep a daughter out of school to care for other children. Often a young child looks after a still younger child when their mother is at home but busy with other work. The mother prepares meals, but when she is absent, her children often eat leftovers and sometimes go without. Care by young siblings presents risks to babies, especially in bottle feeding. Even if the mother is aware of the hygienic precautions necessary to food and bottle preparation, young children rarely follow them.

In better-off families, a child who cares for a small brother or sister is rewarded. In happy circumstances, holding and carrying the baby is a treat for children. Since the parents are often busy, older children spend hours

~ Figure 14   *A ten-year-old girl caring for her younger sibling while playing* bao *in the sand with other children.*

coaxing babies to sit, walk, and talk, and they take credit for any of the babies' achievements. Babies and toddlers often become a focus of older brothers and sisters in their play. Close bonds often grow between an older and a younger child and persist through their lifetimes.

In times of hardship, however, the relationship becomes erratic, with the older sibling sometimes becoming resentful of his or her charge and easily distracted by other activities. Because women have reason to worry about infants being cared for by small children, they often resort to instilling fear in child caretakers to force them to be responsible. I never heard of physical violence toward an infant by a sibling, but neglect is common. Often when the parents return home, children left in charge immediately drop their disinterest to make it appear that they have been intensely involved with their younger siblings the whole time. The increasing reliance on small children for child care and the decreasing availability of mothers add new uncertainty to child care.

Grandmothers

In the past, a paternal grandmother had major responsibilities in caring for her grandchildren. By custom, she was forbidden to bear children after one of her own children had been circumcised, making her available to care for her grandchildren. A daughter-in-law had many heavy demands in farm work and regularly left her small children at home; the grandmother was the most likely member of the extended family to take over the child's care. Under normal conditions, her way of caring for an infant closely resembled that of the mother. She carried the baby on her body, and many older women let their grandchildren suckle at their breasts. In the past, if a woman died, her mother-in-law had the responsibility to try to induce the return of her own breast milk for the baby. Breastfeeding helped to continue the lineage, and the infant received the warmth and closeness recognized by Chagga as important.

Paternal grandmothers were expected to lavish affection, food, and care on grandchildren. The older woman's ambivalent position of dependence and power in the patrilineage came out clearly in her relationship to her grandchildren. She needed the goodwill of grandsons, who were supposed to care for her in her old age and to make sacrifices after her death to ensure the continuation of her spirit in the afterlife. A grandmother could be weak, vulnerable, and dependent because of her frailty and inability to do heavy labor. On the other hand, as an older woman, she was considered powerful. She had the ability to inflict misfortune through the worst form of curse conceivable, a curse by the mother on her deathbed. Because of the older woman's significant cosmological power, a daughter-in-law was wise to defer to her mother-in-law.

It was a grave offense for a daughter-in-law to neglect the customary provision of meat to her mother-in-law, whose body had provided breast milk to sustain members of the patrilineage. Milk and meat had a symbolic equivalence and were important to lineage perpetuity; hence, a woman who had been offended by her son's or his wife's behavior might have felt justified in with-

~ Figure 15   *A grandmother with her granddaughter.*

holding food from her grandchildren when she was responsible for their care.

The grandmother was both a lineage's most powerful living member and one of its most vulnerable ones. Like the tiny infant in her care, a grandmother could be a barometer of the problems in a lineage. Her judgment took into account the emotional and economic environment of an infant and shaped her verdict at the first rite of passage on the infant's capacity to survive in a family possibly weakened by conflict or poverty. If a grandmother was having bitter conflict with the child's parents, she might negatively assess a child.

During times of economic crisis, meat is scarce, especially for poorer families. Older people spoke of the time of *njaa* (hunger) during the height of the drought and food crisis in 1974, when they were going hungry. In these circumstances, a grandmother might not have enough to feed her grandchildren well and, being hungry herself, might lack the energy for many child care tasks. Grandmothers continue to care for grandchildren, including increasing numbers born out of wedlock and left on the mountain while their mothers work in faraway cities. Most older women's obligations are not as strong as they were in the past, however, partly reflecting the decreasing strength of lineage ties. This situation contributes to lack of attention to small children and the food they eat.

Fathers and Grandfathers

Fathers and grandfathers normally have no day-to-day responsibilities in child care. Customarily, it was the paternal grandfather who interceded with remoter ancestors or Ruwa when his grandchild's life was at stake. In this role, he dramatized the authority of men and elders. Although a grandfather is not expected to care for children, he occasionally holds and plays with them. For the most part, however, a grandfather remains a distant, yet concerned, adult in a child's life.

Fathers, like grandfathers, are expected to remain remote. Men are regarded as superfluous in the day-to-day care of newborns. Customarily, their responsibility in the postpartum period was to see that their wives' confinements ran smoothly, with ample food and assistance with their tasks. When their babies become more responsive (at three to four months of age), fathers hold and interact with them, but only in the privacy of their compounds. Public displays of affection are considered unmanly.

In the past, a man was to act as diviner and healer when his children were ill. These responsibilities emphasized a father's authority and ritual leadership in the patrilineage. People said that children must be taught to fear their father, since without fear there is no *heshima* (respect for authority). Children reacted by showing the proper deference while in their fathers' presence, and as soon as they or any other authority figure left, they often let down their guard in mocking laughter. "*Ng'ombe akiondoka, mijusi hutawala* [when the bull is gone, the lizards slip out to sun themselves]" was a common reference to such behavior. A child knew from the twinkle in a father's eye that there was some merit in certain forms of defiance, despite harsh reprimands.

It was more acceptable for men to express affection to another's child than to their own. When they dealt with small children, men tended to be more playful than women. Playing with a child provided relief for men from their other responsibilities, and they tended to have more fun at it than women. Most men were familiar with handling children, because they had taken care of younger siblings.

On a few occasions in the 1970s, I observed a father playing especially tenderly with his child, who was learning to talk. Pointing to an animal, the child said, "*Kuku* [chicken]."

"No," the father said, "it is *ng'ombe* [cow]." The child argued with a mixture of irritation and laughter, and his father responded with an affectionate hug indicating his pleasure in his child's intelligent defiance and self-assurance.

I have seen men hold babies in public only in cases of emergency, and they never carry them on their bodies in a sling. Highly educated men who have traveled hold infants in public occasionally. Men in hard-pressed households, including Francis and Paulo Lema, cared for infants while their wives were otherwise occupied. Francis could not count on his mother for extra assistance during his wife's postpartum confinement, and he often carried his young child at home. Paulo also cared for small children when he was too

~ Figure 16 *Paulo Lema holding his son Revocarte, who is ill with kwashiorkor.*

ill to work and his wife was working in the fields. Even when they were forced by circumstances to care for babies, men did so rather awkwardly. The usual playfulness of fathers faded when they had to deal with the moment-to-moment needs of a child and felt the shame associated with doing women's work.

As their children mature, men become less physically affectionate, but their children come to rely on them. In the past, men were responsible for guidance, support, and judgment, and they remain the teachers and models for their sons. They struggle to find the resources to send their sons to secondary school, and education takes priority over farm work for most boys. They still assist their sons to accumulate resources for bridewealth. For their daughters, men often pay for schooling if they have the money and can spare the labor from the farm. They discourage undesirable suitors and take charge of arranging marriages.

The instability of the coffee market and increasing land shortage drive more and more men to leave home to work as day laborers. They need to earn cash to pay for their sons' schooling and other expenses. The relationship of fathers to their children thus tends to be even remoter than in the past.

Neighbors and Kin

Children were customarily sent to live with kin to complete weaning or simply to get to know other relatives better. Kin and neighbors may help a woman care for her child although they do so less frequently than in the past. As the power of the lineage declines, there is a trend toward considering children the responsibility of kin in their own housing compounds rather than the larger kin group. Neighbors still look after visiting children playing at their compounds but tend not to invite them to share in meals. Growing fears of being accused of or victimized by sorcery make women hesitant to cook for neighbor children unless there is an emergency. Competition over scarce land has eroded lineage ties and intensified concerns over sorcery and evil eye. The wife of a landless man is likely to be suspected of sorcery against a landowning brother-in-law and his household (Moore 1986). In the 1970s, people gave neighbor children freshly roasted bananas or maize as snacks but avoided offering mixed dishes, regarded as more suspicious.

Newcomers to a community can extend care to needy local children, and others sometimes also do so, enhancing their reputations as good neighbors. Pazi and Salum Komu, the two boys who lived on our cooperative farm, survived a difficult childhood partly because of neighbors. They stayed with their grandparents after their mother left to escape abuse by her alcoholic husband. Their grandparents were too poor to feed them, however, and Petro Kasulu, in the village of Lucere, took them into his household. He had married a local woman and already had children and local respect. Because he had relatively few financial problems, he could easily take the children into his household, further enhancing his own acceptance by the community.

Care of an unrelated child is less likely in the more densely settled middle belt of Mt. Kilimanjaro, where there is little ethnic pluralism and localized lineages are well established. Higher up on the mountain, Pazi and Salum might have been shut out by relatives who were hard pressed to provide for their own children. Many children, especially boys whose parents are unable to care for them, end up hustling in cities, where the number of street children is growing at an alarming rate.

A Child's Significance

Perceptions of children have changed in many ways since the ethnographic observations of the 1920s. In the past, rites of passage asserted and illuminated the potential of infants to bring good or harm. If an ancestral spirit was thought to be trying to punish immoral parents by sickening their child, the parents might withdraw their affection and care from their child. The rites provided a basis for judgment and may have given some families reason to reject a defective or weak child. The scrutiny of a child by parents and kin certainly considered both the child and the condition of the whole family. Economic crisis and interpersonal conflict may have affected the interpretations of the child's behavior during the rites of passage.

I seldom heard of the performance of any of the early childhood rites of passage in the 1970s, yet families who more closely followed local custom may still hold them. Even though the rites themselves are no longer widely practiced, some of the ideas that underlie them persist. Parents, grandmothers, and other kin draw from the shreds of customary notions in partial, unsystematic ways in dealing with day-to-day issues of child rearing. Neighbors who see a child with kwashiorkor sometimes say the child is less well cared for than brothers and sisters in the same household, implying that the child has been judged somehow less worthy than the others.

In recent decades, many birth practices have changed because of a growing tendency of women to go to clinics and hospitals for birth. Mothers-in-law, however, continue their central role in managing births that occur at home. Relatives continue to bury the umbilical cord and the placenta, and new mothers continue to be provided with special assistance during confinement.

Ideas about the power of breast milk are still important. Colic is thought to be brought on by bad or "burning" milk and is the most commonly cited reason for the scarification of infants.[9] Nursing a baby while pregnant is still prohibited because the milk is thought to become poisoned (see Appendix B, no. 25). Prolonged breastfeeding is still an ideal, but time constraints and work requirements of women interfere.

Parenthood continues to be a major anchor of personal identity and a central part of life. The practice of teknonymy (addressing a parent as "father of" or "mother of" the first child) underscores the significance of parenthood in the pattern of life. To become fully adult, a person had to become a parent. A son was necessary for making the ritual sacrifice required for entry of a dead parent's spirit into the ancestral realm. Sons were also responsible for *tambiko*, regular sacrificial offerings to ensure that the spirit of the dead continued in the afterlife. Daughters participated in rituals held at home but could not carry out the major rituals required for survival of the spirits of parents and other ancestors. A dead parent was buried in the *kihamba* and required *tambiko*, without which the spirit of the deceased would wander about aimlessly, creating havoc and misfortune among the living until eventually vanishing from existence. Upon their deaths, children and childless adults were thrown into the bush to be eaten by wild animals, metaphorically signaling their wild, chaotic state. Their spirits were not incorporated into the ancestry of the lineage. Parenthood remains required for adulthood, but *tambiko* is no longer universally practiced.

1974

〜 Ruth, Petro, and their children left our farm for the safety of the village of Lucere, where Ruth would give birth to her fifth child. Groups of bandits were roving the countryside, making everyone afraid. A gang of thieves had brutally assaulted the family at our farm and systematically beaten each child while demanding that Ruth and Petro relinquish all of their valuables. Another assault would be less likely in Lucere than at our farm, which stood in isolation on a green hill surrounded by dry, brown fields. Birth in Lucere would give Ruth the support of nearby kinswomen, and she would also more easily be able to follow local customs, including rituals of purification and the special disposal of the afterbirth.

When we received the news of their baby's arrival, we carefully wrapped gifts for Ruth and set out on the path through the maize field to her house. I had selected two matching pieces of *kitenge* cloth for a skirt and a sling for carrying the baby. I thought Ruth would be delighted, since her friends had told me what would please her. I had chosen the colors with care, and I knew the cloth cost about a fourth of her husband's monthly income.

"*Shikamo, mzee* [greetings, revered elder]! *Habari gani* [how are you]?" I asked as I approached Petro, who was busy in the courtyard preparing food for Ruth and the children.[10]

"I'm fine," he said. "How good of you to come."

"I brought these for Ruth," I said. He quietly took my presents and walked into the house without one word of thanks. I did not see Ruth unwrap the presents, either. I was disappointed with his response, but I later learned that the lack of fanfare was the normal manner of receiving gifts.

At Ruth's request, her husband led us inside the house, where I pulled up a chair beside her bed. Matthew clung to my side in anticipation of seeing the baby, who lay asleep next to his mother in the dim light.

"What a beautiful little boy," I said.

"Not really," Ruth responded. I noticed that women were in the habit of responding this way. Eventually, I realized that they were trying to avoid the envy of others because they feared that compliments could be related to evil eye or sorcery.

"Matthew, come here. Do you want to see the baby too?" Ruth asked. She knew my son would soon have to cope with the birth of a baby brother or sister.

We were enjoying Matthew's fascination with the baby when Ruth decided to give me some advice. Typically lighthearted, Ruth seemed especially serious when she said, "You know, *Mama* Matthew, children are the greatest gifts we'll ever receive from God." ∼

On numerous occasions, I heard other people make statements similar to Ruth's about the great value of children. In the 1970s, the first child born to a married couple was a cause for celebration. Relatives often joked about the parents' "silliness," and they too felt giddy about the arrival of a new member of their lineage. Young parents had difficulty suppressing their joy, but they worried that others might envy them and bring harm through sorcery or evil eye. Parents had to take precautions, leading to a routine in which the infant received little overt attention in public.

During the twentieth century, Christianity has either rejected or replaced many of the childhood rites of passage. Christians have been taught by church leaders that God will punish them if they harm a fetus or newborn. According to Catholic doctrine, a child's right to exist is neither ambiguous nor subject to judgment. Church teachings have discouraged the negative evaluation of children along with the rites of early childhood, and the need for the regular assessment of infants may exist nowadays only as a vague notion.

Some people still participate in *tambiko*, the ritual ensuring continued existence for ancestral spirits, although church leaders try to portray it as a pagan practice. Because a son is required to carry out rituals of *tambiko*, boys represent the future of their patrilineages. Indeed, during the period of crisis in the 1970s, many people sought help from the ancestors to ward off misfortune.

Children continue to have economic importance from a very early age. They bear messages, fetch water, gather firewood, collect grass for cattle, sweep the compound clean, herd animals, carry infants, and do many errands. As they grow older, children work alongside parents of the same sex, eventually reducing the parents' workloads considerably. In the past, children could be "loaned" or "pawned" to kin or neighbors to offset debts or extend obligations (Moore 1986:86).[11] Currently, when a family simply cannot afford to lose a child's help (especially true of daughters), the child does not go to school. Students may be kept home at certain times to work in the harvest, care for an infant, or do other tasks. When sons marry, they bring wives to assist their mothers in their work, and when daughters marry, they bring their families bridewealth payments in cattle or cash. Children also provide aging parents with food and care during illness, old age, and infirmity.

Much of the spiritual, economic, and social significance attached to children in the past continues today. The structure and specificity of some of the childhood rites of passage have disappeared, but people still draw from earlier notions in handling and scrutinizing young children. Mothers and fathers still follow many of the unspoken conventions from the past. Shreds of many of the earlier concepts about children's potential for good or evil continue, particularly in relation to ancestral spirits and sorcery.

Reports by some observers early in this century stated that some children were neglected and allowed to die because of customary judgments against them. It is impossible to know whether childhood illness or death actually resulted from such overt judgments. It is clear, however, that in the 1970s, neighbors thought that certain children were being neglected while their brothers and sisters were healthy. In the 1990s, fears of witchcraft, sorcery, and ancestral spirits are still active and, in some cases, are drawn on to explain kwashiorkor.

Chapter Eight

Conflict in Families

The forces of social and economic change that are reshaping Chagga society are heightening conflicts in Chagga families. Tensions are building between spouses and between generations in the same compound. Most women are working longer and harder, while many men face dwindling opportunities to earn wages. Family resources wane as farmland is fragmented into smaller and smaller plots.

The drought from 1972 to 1974 heightened a sense of crisis, making even wealthy families feel besieged. Under these conditions, the relations between spouses and between generations were laced with conflict, sometimes endangering children. A child suffering from kwashiorkor increased the anxiety of parents already humiliated by their poverty.

1974

⁓ *Mzee* Bernardi knocked at the clinic room door and interrupted me as I was cooking lunch over a small Bunsen burner. "I heard you have been helping families with malnourished children," he said after introducing himself as a *balozi* (neighborhood leader). "I would be very pleased if you took the time to visit Magdalena Minde, who lives in my neighborhood. She has four children, and two are severely ill."

The *balozi* was acting out of his responsibility for the families in his unit. I hadn't anticipated being placed in such an official role, but I was happy that the community was beginning to put their trust in me.

It was a half hour's walk from the clinic to the *balozi's* neighborhood, and I had a hard time keeping up. I followed *Mzee* Bernardi until we reached a tall, forbidding stone wall surrounding a compound. When the gate opened, I stood dumbfounded at the sight of one of the wealthiest compounds I had seen in the area. "This is Magdalena's home?" I joked.

"Yes," Bernardi said with a nod. After extending our greetings, we were welcomed into the compound by a young male member of the household who escorted us past well-built cattle barns to a small, one-room mud house on the edge of the property. The walls were smoothly plastered and flowers had been planted below the only window. It was the home of Magdalena and her children. Much of the compound was quite impressive, with a main house constructed of stone, two houses of cement block with glass windows, a separate house for cooking, and barns with milk cows.

The contrast shocked me—exceptional wealth coupled with extreme poverty, all in the same family compound. My effort to joke with Bernardi had come from a misunderstanding; I had assumed that we were stopping at the wealthy compound for refreshments or out of courtesy to the *bwana mkubwa* (lit., "big man") of the neighborhood. ⌇

Magdalena Minde's poverty, I discovered later, arose partly from the ambiguity that surrounds a widow with small children. Her situation put her into conflict with her mother-in-law with no apparent means of resolution.

Women's Place in the Patrilineage

Most Chagga women work as farmers on land belonging to their husbands' families. Farmland is generally owned by men, and women normally gain access to it through marriage. A bride moves to the compound of her husband's family and begins building ties to his patrilineage, usually under strained conditions at the start. A woman earns a place in her husband's family through proper wifely behavior, motherhood, and obedience to her mother-in-law.

⌇ During my first visit to the compound, Magdalena's mother-in-law sat in a plush chair in the shade, surrounded by relatives, including two well-dressed sons, their wives, and their healthy small children. She received their deference in honor of her position as the senior woman.

When I asked about Magdalena's children, her brothers-in-law reported that the children had become ill from hookworm. In subsequent visits, however, the same men told me privately that Magdalena was doing everything she could. The children's health was failing, they said, because of neglect by the children's grandmother, who was responsible for them while Magdalena cultivated her fields.

During my visits, the grandmother expressed no interest in any effort to get medical attention for Magdalena's children and remained aloof whenever I appeared.

It was not difficult for me to understand how conflict could develop between mother-in-law and daughter-in-law. What was difficult to understand was how a grandmother could neglect her own grandchildren. That the grandmother was not an eccentric but was herself a typical older woman, who was in some way defending her own position of authority, became apparent to me over a period of time.

According to neighbors, Magdalena had a complicated relationship with her in-laws. At the beginning of her marriage, life went smoothly. She moved to their *kihamba* at marriage and assumed her position as the most junior woman in the compound. She produced a son and then a daughter in accord with the expectations of the time and in the process gained respect from her husband's family.

Later, however, Magdalena argued with her husband over her efforts to earn money for household expenses by working in a low-prestige, low-paid position as a day laborer. Eventually she left and went to stay at her parents' compound. Soon after, her husband was killed in a fight at a beer club.

Her mother-in-law apparently blamed the tragedy on marital discord, and she seemed to have held Magdalena ultimately responsible for her son's death. Magdalena felt compelled to return to her deceased husband's compound to care for her children, despite the conflict brewing with her mother-in-law.

Magdalena had not taken her children with her when she left because children belong to their father's patrilineage and must stay with his family. To live with her children, Magdalena had to return to her deceased husband's compound and to farm whatever land she was allotted.

She eventually developed a sexual relationship with Wilibald Minde, one of her husband's younger brothers, as encouraged by Chagga custom. Custom also would have required ritual sacrifices to mark the legitimacy of this union, but the Church opposed it. Instead, Magdalena developed a more casual relationship with Wilibald. He was the father of her last two children, both girls under the age of five years. From the Christian perspective, they were illegitimate. These girls were the children who had become malnourished under their grandmother's care. ～

Magdalena's difficult marriage and the ensuing death of her husband strained her ties to his relatives. As a Roman Catholic, she may have experienced additional tension because the Church forbids the levirate, the custom of a woman marrying her deceased husband's brother.[1] The church encouraged brothers to take financial responsibility for widows and their children, but sexual relations were no longer permitted (Moore 1986:284). It seemed that the younger two of Magdalena's children had become the grandmother's scapegoats, viewed as markers of Magdalena's transgressions of both customary and Christian standards. The conflict between Magdalena and her mother-in-law thus had a visible outcome, kwashiorkor in the children. Magdalena's problems were all the more painful when compounded with her unending load of farm work.

Powerful trends are challenging the patrilineage. Kin relations have often become brittle, and problems can intensify among people who spend virtually their whole lives in the confines of their own neighborhood.[2] There is no longer sufficient land to distribute to sons, eroding bonds between generations, among brothers, and between husband and wife. Conflict over land is intensified by changes in morality and meaning. Chagga elders complain about their adult children failing to provide them with food or cash regularly, men complain about lack of land, and women complain about lack of time to complete all their work.

Women's Workload

Each morning, women descend the mountain to work in the fields, cut grass for cattle, or carry huge loads of bananas on their heads to sell at market. In addition to these arduous tasks, they haul firewood, prepare food, clean their houses and compounds, and care for their children. Their pride in their work, the need to prove themselves as daughters-in-law, and economic necessity drive them nearly to the edge of human endurance.

1974

◠ Finally I met Magdalena. An hour before sunset, she returned from a day of work in her fields, carrying a heavy load of firewood on her head. Whenever the weather permitted, Magdalena walked miles to the family's lower *shamba,* where she cultivated maize and beans.

By this point, I had learned not to converse with a woman just after she had unburdened herself from a heavy load. Even Magdalena's two little daughters kept a respectful distance until their mother had taken a moment to rest from her journey and nurse her aching head.

After several minutes of quiet, Magdalena led me into her tiny home, where her few belongings were neatly arranged. As her daughter climbed up on her lap, she slowly began to respond to my questions about her stay at NURU, her daughters' continued illness, and the extent of cooperation between women neighbors.

"The girls are sick from hookworm," she sighed, and added that a latrine was under construction to address the cause of the problem. Throughout our discussion, she never relented in her optimism, nor did she cast blame on her mother-in-law.

Because she seemed intent on portraying a rosy picture of her situation, I was reluctant to probe into the cause of her arguments with her dead husband. She did tell me that women should not inquire about their husbands' incomes—the typical response of a good Chagga wife. ∽

Magdalena was trying to cope with a tremendous workload, conflict with her mother-in-law, and the resulting inadequate attention to her youngest children. The heavy workload took Magdalena away from home all day nearly every day, and her mother-in-law did not feel compelled to follow custom and care for the children. The clash of Chagga custom with Roman Catholicism over the remarriage of a widow contributed to disagreement in the compound. Because she did not have the approval of her mother-in-law, Magdalena became isolated from the rest of the family. The conflicts in Magdalena's family developed from economic changes that heavily burden women, as well as from the clash of value systems on the mountain.

An immediate difficulty faced by most women in daily life is their enormous workload. In one study, rural Tanzanian women worked 11 to 14 hours a day (Lukmanji et al. 1993). On Kilimanjaro in 1973, the average number of births per woman who had completed childbearing was 7.9 (Egeno and Henin 1973), and so child care was a major burden for them. Women also take sole responsibility for cultivating food crops for the family larder, while their husbands manage the coffee farms, work locally as day laborers, or travel in search of employment. Children are left at home, often in the care of a young brother or sister rather than their grandmother.

The work of women farmers includes planting and caring for vegetable gardens near home and cultivating substantial fields of maize and beans on the lower slopes of the mountain. Caring for dairy cattle also involves significant heavy work for women in return for the milk for their children and manure for the fields. A Chagga saying is, "When a man has two wives, he gives his favorite fewer cattle." Cattle are not put out to pasture; the mountain has virtually no fenced land and very little open rangeland. The cattle spend their lives in stalls, eating grass brought to the compound by women. In one study, women spent twenty hours a week, on average, carrying grass bundles weighing as much as 120 pounds each from the lowlands (Zalla 1982). Some women spent as many as forty hours weekly at this work.

In the 1970s, the socialist government of Tanzania encouraged women to begin business cooperatives, in part to break up male monopolies over some forms of enterprise and give women greater access to cash. The effort was related to the government ideology of *ugawa* (egalitarianism) that, at least in principle, applied to gender relations. Women on Kilimanjaro responded with mixed emotions to these efforts. In precolonial times, women had worked together as members of their age grade in fulfilling responsibilities to their chief, and they had been in charge of the marketplaces. These activities, however, never led to the development of any group that held political authority (Moore 1986:54).

Political action by women occurs sporadically in response to a crisis or particular injustice but is seldom sustained. In one instance, some men who were local leaders had planned to sell emergency grain supplies on the informal market instead of distributing them to the hungry, as the government intended. Women organized and made a public outcry over the illegal appropriation of emergency grain supplies by community leaders (Cook and Kerner 1989). The weak structural position of women, however, makes them dependent on other women in their husbands' lineages for support. Land shortage increases the likelihood of conflict among sisters-in-law who have married into the same lineage.

Although women want to improve their lot, they are restrained by strong expectations that proper Chagga women are not to undermine their husbands' self-respect by acting without their guidance, whether in decisions about farming or otherwise. A woman's social standing can suffer if she acts independently, but it will be enhanced by her husband's success in his work.

1974

～ Women did not fully accept the injustice of their huge workloads, my research team found in discussions with nine groups of women on child care issues (Von Freyhold et al. 1973). Earlier interviews had led us to ask a provocative question: "If it were not for the children, would you leave your husband?" The response in all nine groups was overwhelmingly affirmative; and even when we took into account the leading nature of the question, we could not ignore the women's tremendous hostility toward their marital situations. ～

Perhaps Magdalena's dispute with her husband had roots in the expectation that money should be in the hands of men. A woman could threaten her husband's authority by earning more than he or even knowing how much he earned. In the NURU study, my research team noted that a number of men who lacked regular income had brought accusations against their wives, who had earned money from beer brewing. They brought the accusations to a Church-related marriage conciliatory board whose secretary said, "This causes the wife to think of herself as being equal to her husband and to show it by coming home as late as the husband does." If the wife was found to "feel herself equal to her husband," the board warned her and imposed a fine to put her in her place (Swantz et al. 1975:52–53). The Church also fined a woman for assuming the financial burden of providing for her family. Impoverished women are caught between the need to generate income for family survival and customs that limit female independence.

Women's Income: Marketing, Wage Labor, and Making Gin and Beer

The notion that women should control their own property (as distinct from cash) is not new to Kilimanjaro. It was customary that women brought their vegetables to market, ran the market itself, and used surpluses gained in bartering to purchase their own cattle. Women's gardens vary by season and altitude on the mountain, where climates range from tropical at the bottom to permanently snow-capped at the top, resulting in an ongoing market for vegetables and fruit. In early colonial times, markets were reported to draw large numbers of women bringing fruit and vegetables from various chiefdoms. In precolonial times, women policed market transactions without interference from men. Women began to lose power over the markets when German administrators assumed adjudication over disputes; as the women were reluctant to comply, cheating in the markets increased substantially according to some reports (Moore 1986:102). Women also resisted colonial orders to centralize commerce by closing three markets; two were closed and one remained (ibid.). It is clear that women's autonomy and economic power were at stake.

In the past, women had a balance of sorts between their autonomy and subordination to men. That is, although men were the major property owners and political authorities, women had activities and control over property that were largely independent of male dominance. A woman could use any extra barter income to purchase cattle and then freely dispose of them over her lifetime. Women thus had the right to own property and amass savings independently of their husbands. Women were not relegated to a domestic sphere to leave men in control of a public sphere, including commerce; gender relations were more complicated, and women had specific rights.

Decades ago, women faced a new disadvantage when coffee cultivation and the cash economy became widespread (Moore 1986). Men directed women to work in the coffee groves but took control of coffee income and most other cash. Such male control over these newer resources was patterned after the Chagga system of land ownership which nearly always excluded women from land inheritance.

> Although women contributed their labor to the coffee, picking and processing, they had no access to the coffee income. Men felt no obligation to share the cash with them. Though men recognize that they must provide certain things for a wife that in this century could only be had for cash, such as cloth for clothing, they were not obliged to turn over cash itself unless specifically to buy such items. Today, the amount of money that women are able to make from their vegetable sales in the markets is a tiny proportion of what is available to men from coffee. . . . Thus, even at the level of the household, coffee changed the balance of relationships. (Moore 1986:117–118)

Involvement in the coffee trade curtailed women's income and autonomy, and the colonial government reinforced and intensified male authority in other ways. Government farm services excluded women as clients, in spite of their contribution of a great deal of farm labor. In the 1970s, agricultural extension workers, foreign agricultural consultants, and researchers still offered services or information to men almost exclusively. The only exceptions I observed to this pattern occurred when the experts were women and when farming lessons were given to women at NURU. The colonial government restricted women from owning bank accounts. Even during the 1970s, I, like other women, had to get my husband's signature to withdraw money from the bank. Eventually, these restrictions were revoked.

During the colonial period, women were also banned from working as salaried employees. By the time I arrived in 1970, however, better-off households had started to send daughters and wives to work as white-collar employees in Moshi town. Wealthier people, in the effort to use situations to their best advantage, could draw on new values that challenged Chagga customs. A wealthy woman pays for transportation to distant fields instead of walking, or she pays someone to cultivate the fields with a tractor and has a relatively light workload because of other hired help on the farm and at home (Von Freyhold et al. 1973). Poorer women lack paid assistants and efficient technology, and they often must hire themselves out as day laborers. They work pruning, spraying, weeding, and picking coffee on large plantations, and they also cultivate and harvest grain crops, cut grass for the finely bred milk cattle of wealthy farmers, and work as maids in their homes.

Most women still sell food off the farm to earn cash. They have rights to sell bananas, beans, cattle products (milk, blood, and manure), chickens, and eggs. Beans are considered women's food, and women have made them into a commercial crop, along with bananas.[3] It would be demeaning for a man to stand by a stall and attempt to sell a woman's crop.

Money has become a necessity for all households on Mt. Kilimanjaro, and women have become responsible for purchasing food to supplement harvests, for paying children's school expenses, and for buying minor household necessities. Most women farmers gain cash income only through ill-paid work, such as the sale of food crops.

Making and selling alcohol provides many women with income, but it can be controversial, divisive, and sometimes dangerous. Women who become prosperous in this work chance jeopardizing their reputations because of it. To provide for their families, some women even risk imprisonment through illegal activities such as making gin and prostitution.[4] ("Gin" is a general term for a clear alcoholic drink.)

1974

〜 Magdalena Minde and I set out once again to try to visit Mamka Akarro. Mamka lived close to Magdalena, and I had attempted to contact her on two other occasions. I knew she was the mother of ten children and that the youngest, a weanling, had been at NURU. I had high hopes of meeting her because there had been a heavy rain, making it impossible for her to work in the fields.

I had other plans, too. Perhaps, I thought, Magdalena and Mamka might form the core of some kind of cooperative for women. Magdalena seemed buoyed by my presence and I was concerned about the isolation she experienced in her compound.

"What are your views about *ushirikiano* [cooperation]?" I asked along the way.

She answered, "I think cooperation is necessary. Without cooperation, people would be at war all the time. The government is right in trying to teach people to work together."

"And what about women's cooperation?"

"That can be a problem," she answered. "My sister-in-law and I help each other in the field but we have separate plots and split the harvests and the cash from sales. We each have our own children, you see."

We continued our conversation all the way to Mamka's house, and by the time we reached our destination, I was convinced Magdalena would be interested in starting some kind of venture. At least she wasn't immediately put off by the idea, like most of the other women.

We approached Mamka's house and called out the customary greeting, "*Hodi! Habari gani, Mama* Mamka!"

Mamka took one look at me, gasped, and fled inside.

From outside, I yelled my introduction. She answered but remained in hiding, and when she finally appeared, I realized that she had been changing to more presentable clothing. Mamka answered all my questions grudgingly, and I soon realized that she was reluctant to talk to me. I could smell alcohol on her breath.

"Do you think a work cooperative with other women might help with problems these days?" I asked as soon as the conversation allowed.

Mamka appeared worn out and much older than a woman in her mid-thirties. Life wasn't going to defeat her, however, and she seized the opportunity to express defiance.

"Oh, sure. I believe in cooperation," she said sarcastically. "In fact, before I left for your hospital [NURU], I planted a whole field of maize with my best friend. When I returned, my friend had stolen the harvest and sold it in the market. Just what did you expect me to feed my children when I came home?"

Magdalena and I laughed nervously. I had no answer to her pointed inquiry and hurried through a few of the other research questions.

On our way back, we stopped to visit Mamka's neighbors to gain more information about her. According to them, Mamka was in a desperate situation. Neighbors later said that while drunk on gin, her husband often consumed enough meat and eggs to feed his hungry family. His income from carpentry was unsteady, and he had become an alcoholic.

Mamka told me that she farmed a *pori* (a type of field on the lower slopes of the mountain), but Magdalena later said it was a lie. In discussing her situation, Mamka spoke highly of her husband, and she blamed his employer for refusing to pay his salary. We had reports that her husband was violent toward her, and Mamka drank gin as well, Magdalena confided as soon as we were out of hearing range.

Other claims by Mamka about the kind of work she did were also refuted by neighbors, although no one ever discussed her distilling enterprise. I concluded that she was in the gin business after seeing an apparatus for making gin and some visitors drinking inside her house. Drinking indoors suggested gin consumption to me because other socializing, even while drinking beer, is done in the open courtyard. ⌐

Although distilling gin is illegal, gin is nonetheless a desirable commodity on the mountain, despite its locally recognized link to alcoholism and violence. Someone who makes gin, like Mamka, often will not be reported by her neighbors, who are also usually her clients or who respect her entrepreneurship. The woman distiller must always be on her guard, however, as the community is ambivalent toward gin. Were she to arouse the envy or enmity of others, she could be reported to the police.

1974

〜 At the Kilimanjaro prison, I interviewed women who had been caught distilling gin. Most had been divorced or widowed; some were nursing infants.

Their complaint was that they had been driven into the illegal enterprise because their relatives had not taken them in. They had no land and no way to provide for themselves.

"After all," one woman remarked, "isn't it better to make gin than to steal from your neighbors?" 〜

Making beer in private homes was also illegal but was a widespread custom with greater acceptance (Moore 1986:350).[5] Both men and women do the work involved in brewing *pombe*, a local beer made from bananas and millet. Men usually oversee the process, and conflict with her husband tends to erupt when a woman brews *pombe* for home sale, establishes her own business for selling to a *pombe* shop (neighborhood bar), or opens a *pombe* shop of her own.

Marital troubles can result when brewing and selling beer take up a woman's time and bring her money. The beer business also can place her in contact with many men, increasing suspicions about extramarital liaisons. A man may spend his time in beer clubs and come home late, but he will always discourage his wife from taking such liberties. Most of the women in my own community who regularly brewed *pombe* had already suffered some break in ties to their husbands through ongoing conflict over lack of financial and emotional support or, in some cases, through separation.

During the 1984 food crisis, women who worked in commercial *pombe* brewing were able to offset the unsteady income from their husbands, according to a study by Cook and Kerner (1989). Contributions from husbands sometimes fluctuate because of inconsistency in cash crop production and livestock sales or because some men overconsume *pombe* and meat at neighborhood bars, at the expense of their dependents.

Table 5 *Mothers' Drinking Habits*

	Mother of malnourished child		Neighbor mother	
	N	(%)	N	(%)
Drinks excessively	6	(14%)	1	(2%)
Drinks moderately	5	(12%)	21	(36%)
Drinks a little or none	31	(74%)	36	(62%)
Total	42	(100%)	58	(100%)
(No information)	(0)		(8)	

Source: Swantz et al. 1975.

Compared with neighbor mothers, more mothers of malnourished children drink excessively (Chi square = 11.52, d.f = 2, alpha=0.05).[6]

Together with the stress and demands of their lives, heavy drinking and alcoholism among a few women contribute to child malnutrition. In the NURU study, 14 percent of mothers of malnourished children were known as heavy drinkers, compared with only 1 percent of neighboring mothers (the difference is statistically significant; see Table 5; see also Swantz et al. 1975). On the other hand, as in Mamka's situation, alcohol production also contributes to many women's autonomy, power, and economic survival. For those who succeed despite the opposition of courts, churches, and some men, it puts food on the table for children.

Sorcery and Explanations of Malnutrition

The tension in Magdalena Minde's compound, the obvious resentment and bitterness of her mother-in-law, and the discomfort the older woman evoked in Magdalena made me wonder, some time later, whether curse and sorcery were involved. Although women have little authority in this world, they are believed to possess supernatural powers, including sorcery and curse. No one, however, explicitly accused Magdalena's mother-in-law of sorcery.

When people in the same lineage find themselves in conflict, sorcery or other forms of spiritual harm enter the picture. Calling on the supernatural was once perceived as a justified and respectable means of last resort in pressing someone to pay compensation for wrongs or make other restitution.

Misfortune is not believed to occur simply out of coincidence or accident. Serious childhood illnesses often raise suspicions of supernatural interference. Sorcery and curse are not necessarily believed to act immediately; any negative event can come under scrutiny and be explained retrospectively. The death of Magdalena Minde's husband, for example, may have resulted in accusations against Magdalena. Sometimes a supernatural explanation relieves anxiety over uncontrollable conditions; at other times it provokes anxiety. For those saddled with the painful emotions of jealousy, envy, resentment, and bitterness, the practice of sorcery may provide relief.

The powers that can harm can also be used for protection from the ill will of others or to bring about good fortune and fertility. In the past, these powers involving the ancestors were the same powers that governed life and death and were manifest in sexuality. Sexual themes abounded in the bodily substances and implements used for sorcery, notably the clay cursing pots shaped into human forms with obvious sexual markings. In the past, an aggrieved individual could legitimately and publicly enter the marketplace and announce his or her intention to curse the offender by swinging or striking a cursing pot. The curse was supposed to announce a dispute publicly and force the offender to make a sacrifice to appease the ever-watchful ancestors and to negotiate an end to the conflict (Moore 1986:38–51).

Today, Kilimanjaro's Christian churches regularly admonish parishioners not to "consort with the devil" by engaging in supernatural harmdoing. Catholic priests remind their followers that only God can punish and then only the unjust. Nowadays, a curse tends to be given by stating "You will see" or "I leave it to God" (Moore 1986:51). A curse by a mother from her deathbed is considered the most powerful and permanent of spiritual threats. A woman may curse a daughter-in-law who fails to uphold lineage rules by such actions as feeding her children in unapproved ways, refusing circumcision, or neglecting to provide meals for her and her husband. The threat of wreaking supernatural vengeance gives older women some indirect control over family matters.

Curse and sorcery were explanations given for the illnesses of two children in the NURU study (Swantz et al. 1975). Neighbors said the children became ill after their mothers had been cursed by their paternal grandmothers. One of the older women had been heard to say that she would continue to make her daughter-in-law suffer, implying a curse. The notion that curse or sorcery can cause a child's illness or death, or a woman's sterility, is part of everyday life on Kilimanjaro. The notion is related in part to the system of land inheritance and the role of ancestors in guarding lineage perpetuity.

Among believers, men are primarily responsible for paying tribute to ancestors, and ancestors affect the fortunes of the living. Without a son, this cycle of interdependence cannot continue, and the patrilineage disintegrates. A woman must have sons because the stability of her marriage depends on it, especially in contemporary monogamous Chagga society. Her son will care for her on his father's *kihamba* in her old age. Sisters-in-law can find themselves in competition with one another over the inheritance of an ancestral *kihamba*, and land shortage intensifies competition. A woman's sons would inherit all the family lands if her sisters-in-law were sterile or had only daughters. Should such a misfortune occur, a sister-in-law who has a son might be suspected of witchcraft or sorcery. Women married to middle sons, who are less likely to inherit land, may be thought especially drawn to causing sterility or the illness and death of children (Moore 1986:258–259).

Many believe that the swelling of a child's body and limbs results from sorcery.[7] It is thought possible to cast spells on children by hiding or swallowing some of their bodily substance, such as hair or feces. Another technique is to introduce some foreign substance into a child's body. As a remedy, family members call an *mganga*, a traditional healer, usually a man whose male authority is expected to counterbalance the indirect power of a malevolent woman. Because parents are responsible for resolving the problem, their relatives may think that there is no point in offering assistance. Isolation of the parents can intensify hardship and generate further bitterness and resentment, leaving some households mired in poverty.

My impression from trips to Kilimanjaro in 1989 and 1993 was that accusations of curse and sorcery had increased considerably. In conversations with medical personnel and friends from my old farming cooperative, people more readily explained problems in terms of the supernatural or said that others were using these explanations for bad fortune. By the late 1980s, AIDS had become a scourge, and some were explaining the outbreak in terms of sorcery.

In general, the situation of women in well-off families has improved since precolonial times. For the majority of women on Kilimanjaro, however, life has become more difficult, and for the poorest women, it has become nearly impossible. They lack sufficient time to accomplish all the work needed for the survival of their families, and they have little control over essential resources. Although cooperation and collective action by women occur, they are rare because of the structurally weak position of women, which results partly from their competition over land and other resources in the lineage. These problems contribute to tension between women, accusations of sorcery, and the likelihood that a child's illness will be explained as having a supernatural cause.

The Predicament of Impoverished Men

A father's situation, as well as a mother's, affects the dynamic of malnutrition among their children. Men, unlike women, have the right to own land, but today there is not enough land to go around. The patrilineage traditionally provided for members in times of hardship, but its erosion over recent decades has left a number of men destitute, in some cases even when they have wealthy relatives. Hardship frequently raises the possibility of spiritual harm-doing among brothers and between fathers and sons.

1974

⌒ Reports of heavy drinking among the parents of malnourished children, especially fathers, began to concern me. One evening, on my way home from visiting Richard Moshi's family, I asked Francis what had caused Richard, his neighbor and coworker at the mission coffee plantation, to become an alcoholic. Francis, a nondrinking Muslim, touched me with his compassionate response. "After a hard day's work in the field," he said, "*pombe* makes the pain go away."

Two children of Richard had been at the nutrition center and were still malnourished. I was surprised to learn, however, that it was not Richard who was singled out as a failure; instead social disapproval fell on his father, Elikana Moshi. What was judged to be immoral in Elikana's case was that he had refused to divide his farmland with his sons, who were left with no place for their wives to grow food for their families. ⌒

Father-son conflicts typify a large number of family land disputes, now the most common form of litigation on Kilimanjaro. I found that of the ten families I investigated in the NURU study, four had a dispute between father and son over land. For Richard, the dispute over land had far-reaching effects on his children.

⌒ My first encounter with Elikana, the father of Richard, came during my search for a malnourished child. Upon arriving at his home, I asked about help among neighbors and relatives, and his first answer was, "It's the same as before," affirming traditions of mutual aid.

He later asserted in an extremely defensive manner, undoubtedly thinking of his own wealth, "You can't give out support during the famine because you have your own problems." He continued, "You can ask once for food or help but not a second time. People have changed. Before, there was much more cooperation. If you need help these days, you can go to KNCU [Kilimanjaro Native Cooperative Union], where the *balozis* have sent the names of those in need of food."

Elikana was typical of a growing number of older men on Kilimanjaro who once enjoyed greater affluence but suffered some financial reversal because of fluctuations in the coffee market. His children estimated that he had about eight thousand trees, enough to ensure comfort during his later years. Elikana definitely had problems. His compound had a number of buildings, but the main house, which had once been a fine home, was in a state of disrepair. The clearing was filled with debris and clutter — uncommon for an apparently wealthy owner of a substantial coffee plantation. Elderly people all around him were complaining that their sons and daughters were neglecting to bring them food. No one could predict how long the drought and low coffee prices would last. Like many other elderly persons during the period of *njaa*, Elikana was anxious. As far as he was concerned, why should he partition his land to a son who had proven to be so unreliable? Elikana told me later that Richard should seek food not from him but from the cooperative union, which was distributing food relief.

Located on the far edge of his father's estate, Richard's compound was one of the most destitute dwellings I had entered. Made of mud and thatched with banana leaves, the house badly needed repair. There were no chairs or other movable pieces of furniture. The house sat in stark contrast with nearby dwellings, not only his father's but also a neighbor's, a fine old stone structure that was well furnished.

On my first visit to Richard's house, I spoke with Elikana's oldest son, who was visiting. When I told him that I wanted to find out the cause of his niece's malnutrition, he answered that Elikana had refused to partition his coffee land, even for cultivating food crops to feed his own children. Elikana had given his oldest son a plot to build a home, but that son had moved with his wife to the lower slopes. The youngest son was married, living at his father's compound. Richard was one of two middle sons, the other having moved into Moshi town.

To refuse grown children a space to grow food crops is an affront to Chagga values of lineage solidarity, and the ongoing drought added to the community's sense of outrage. With such a clear case against their father, the sons took him before a court of elders. Elikana was judged in error and told to partition his land, but he later refused.

Elikana felt especially self-righteous in his treatment of Richard. Two neighbors explained that Elikana had loaned Richard *chimbia* (bridewealth) and had selected a bride for him from a friend's family. Richard, however, had squandered the money on *pombe* instead of making the series of bridewealth payments to his father-in-law at the proper intervals, and his irresponsibility cast shame on the marriage. It seems that Richard did not make the agreed-upon bridewealth payments before the birth of their first child, as required for a proper marriage contract. The neighbors emphasized Richard's difficulties during times of scarcity, and they clearly sided with him despite his irresponsible behavior. For a man to refuse his son a means of livelihood when it affected the well-being of his grandchildren was an even greater shame—one that stood as an immoral violation against lineage solidarity.

The neighbors described Elikana as *kali* (mean), saying his meanness was behind his actions. When I asked if Elikana was unconcerned about *tambiko* (offerings to the ancestors), which would ensure his perpetuity in the afterlife, they answered affirmatively, adding that he had recently begun to read the Bible, an alternative to the traditions of *tambiko*. ⁓

At the time, I did not see the potential for conflict between Richard and his father involving the supernatural realm. According to custom, Elikana could have cursed Richard and his children to force him to complete the bridewealth payments. Richard could have responded with curse to force his father to divide his land. No curse or sorcery accusations were mentioned in their court case, however. I assumed at the time that each man's involvement with the Catholic Church would have excluded the use of curse, but I was wrong. Elikana, like many others, was concerned about *tambiko* and the world of the ancestors, which was not wholly incompatible with Church teachings. He might have drawn on both in a time of crisis.

If Elikana had held solely to Chagga tradition, he would have hoped that his sons would observe *tambiko* on his behalf. Apparently, in turning to Christianity, Elikana anticipated their unwillingness to do so. Richard pursued the dispute with his father rather than following his brother to live on the lower plains, where he might have had better economic opportunities.

Neighbors did not discuss this family's problems with me in terms of spiritual harm-doing but rather in emotional and material terms. Richard was said to drink too much *pombe*, which his wife blamed for the children's lack of food, but his neighbors defended him and said that he drank out of despair. They added that a solution to his problems, which they defined as poverty, would result in less drinking. At the time he was working at the mission for three to five shillings a day, not enough to support a family.

⁓ On the few occasions Richard was home for my visits, he generally stayed clear of the conversations I was having with Elizabethi, his wife. A tall, robust man, he gave me the impression of being too busy to concern himself with my research. Unlike Francis and some of the other fathers with malnourished children, Richard seemed shamed by public scrutiny and attention to his failings. My questions were an embarrassment, and he was fighting to preserve his dignity.

On one occasion, I went too far, saying to Richard, "Do you think that perhaps your father is expecting you to be *kujitegemea* [self-reliant]?" I was referring to the Tanzanian government's radio campaign promoting self-reliance.

Richard became outraged. Walking up to me, he responded loudly and directly into my face, "Everyone knows of the stinginess of this man. He's willing to watch his own grandchildren die just because he thinks his sons should be like him. We can't afford to purchase land at the price he paid years ago. He said he had no help in starting his coffee grove. I doubt that. He's too clever."

Seeing that he had sufficiently intimidated me with the force of his statements, he added, "And if you're interested in helping, why don't you find me work with a decent wage?"

Since I had already taken action after a similar challenge made by another father, I was happy to tell Richard of the cooperative venture under way. I invited him to the first meeting. He agreed to come but failed to appear. When I asked others why Richard was missing, the widow next door again spoke in his defense, explaining that the heavy rains forced him to stay at home. She then pleaded with me, saying he badly needed a break. I was impressed with her concern, and I had noticed that every time I came to her house, Richard's children were about; she said they often ate with her family.

The rain could have been an obstacle to Richard's attendance, as the neighbor suggested, or there might have been extenuating circumstances of which I was unaware. More probably, however, Richard felt ambivalent about joining such a venture. Since his family's deprivation illustrated to others the extent of Elikana's moral failing, participation in a successful cooperative might weaken his stance against his father.

On the other hand, as Richard was already besieged by misfortune, participation in an unsuccessful venture would have wasted precious energy and could swing community sentiment against him. He also might have felt anxious about joining a group of people stigmatized by past misfortunes and united on the basis of a common mark of failure—the malnutrition of their children. Richard chose to retain his strong community support and hoped to benefit all his family in due time, even if the risk involved temporarily going hungry. His job as a wage laborer at the mission simply perpetuated his dependence and fortified his reluctance to change.

Richard's family was caught between a stubborn father pitted against a stubborn son. At the time of my visit, two of Richard's children, Yasinta and Rose, still had signs of malnutrition and were plagued with diarrhea.

One year earlier, their baby sister had died at twelve months of age, while the oldest child, an eight-year-old girl, was healthy and without a history of chronic illness. Richard's wife, Elizabethi, expressed gratitude for what she had learned at the hospital for malnourished children. On the other hand, she must have been frustrated by her inability to apply her new knowledge. With their compound completely surrounded by the coffee trees of Elikana, she had no room to develop a small vegetable garden.

During my visits, I observed Elizabethi's renewed efforts to plant flowers and to help Richard build a latrine. It was completed with the assistance of neighbors who lent Richard money to buy wood for the housing. Elizabethi cultivated a small maize and bean garden miles below their home, and she had to leave the children in the care of their eight-year-old sister most of the day. I left the family convinced that their neighbors' compassion for Richard largely reflected their affection for Elizabethi. ⌒

Elizabethi's relationship to her husband's father had been weakened when Richard had squandered the money for bridewealth payments. The payments help to tie a wife to her father-in-law and the rest of her husband's patrilineage. Because Richard had not paid, all of his children were illegitimate, a status believed by some to provoke the wrath of their father's ancestors.

Because of their illegitimacy, the children belonged to their mother's patrilineage, not their father's. The maternal alignment implied that the children were to some extent intruders in their father's family compound. Under such circumstances, Elikana would not allow his wife to go to care for her grandchildren, and in general, Elizabethi was isolated from members of her husband's lineage.

Landlessness placed Richard and similarly impoverished men in a dependent position much like that of the majority of Chagga women. Adding to their despondency, the impoverished men tended to have poor health, further burdening other family members. In the NURU study, out of forty-two families with malnourished children, five fathers had chronic illnesses, viewed by family members as a cause of the children's malnutrition. People saw the link between the loss of productivity by the father and malnutrition in his children.

Changes in Men's Authority

Richard and his father each justified his own actions by choosing among customary and contemporary values to fit their situations. Christianity, colonial government policy, and other European influences reinforced male authority in the patrilineage in some ways, but they also weakened many traditional sources of male prestige. In the early twentieth century, German administrators had outlawed the age-grade system, the major institution that once socialized young men; as the system that created the warrior age grade, it was a political and military threat. No longer does each man, by right of his birth, grow into a position of authority as he matures. Rites of initiation for men have also disappeared; circumcision is no longer practiced as a mass public rite that defines the members of an age grade. Instead, young men, often already in their twenties, have the operation performed at a nearby clinic or hospital, devoid of most customary symbolism.

Coffee production and the benefits that accrue from money, namely education, professional careers, and wage employment, have become the new realm of manhood. People say that men must control coffee money because only they know how to deal with the complicated technology of coffee pruning, spraying, and processing. Business matters, however, push coffee farmers off the *kihamba* into town, and much farm labor has actually been left to women. Men are in charge of managing coffee production by arranging for loans, the use of equipment, transportation, and sale of the crop.

All activities associated with butchering, purchasing, and distributing meat are also supposed to be controlled by men. Maize, introduced by immigrants and returning migrants, involves cultivation and weeding by both sexes, but its sale is arranged by men. Since many men are employed away from home, however, women often trade in meat and maize, even though people persist in seeing it as men's work.

As land becomes scarce, some men find themselves in the unfortunate predicament of owning few or no coffee trees, which curtails their opportunities to provide educations to their sons, who then are limited to low-paying jobs. The men often become day laborers on large estates, along with women and youths, a degrading alternative for adult men. Three to nine shillings (U.S. $0.42 to $1.28) for a ten-hour day hardly provides for a family. The degradation takes on added intensity because cash is the new symbol of men's authority and dominance over women, part of the fundamental social order of the patrilineage. Without cash and the visible presence of the necessities and luxuries it buys, men may be considered failures by their communities and themselves.

The Use and Abuse of Alcohol

Richard did all his drinking at the local *pombe* shop, the usual place where men congregate. Men gathering at a *pombe* shop in the morning to await its opening at nine o'clock is as normal a sight in the community and as emblematic of the morning as groups of women advancing down the slopes to cut grass for cattle or to cultivate lower *shambas. Pombe* shops may open daily or on a rotating basis, depending on the owner.

The *pombe* drinking community is a repository for many older Chagga customs. Formal exchanges over the *pombe* calabash reinforce status differences, with deference given to old or otherwise honorable men. The beer club also gives men information about job openings and provides a place for business transactions and discussion of community disputes. Many clubs are equipped with a radio, allowing government and world news to enter discussions, giving many humble men a sense of connection with broader political spheres of power. More important, however, people gossip about goings-on in the neighborhood, which is the focus of their worldly concerns. Even though people from all social levels attend, the beer club provides the greatest opportunity for men on the brink of failure to support each other in difficult times.

There are costs related to this neighborhood institution. Money that could be used to purchase food for the family buys *pombe* instead. Day laborers can easily consume a day's earnings in one visit to the beer club, especially when they indulge in roasted meat and *aspro* (a blood and meat mixture). People told of inebriated men returning home and demanding additional meat, neglecting to divide it with their dependents.

Problems related to heavy use of alcohol, including domestic abuse and child neglect, were hardly mentioned in descriptions written in the 1920s and 1940s, but they have been a common topic of conversation for the last

Table 6   *Fathers' Drinking Habits*

	Father of malnourished child		Neighbor father	
	N	(%)	N	(%)
Drinks excessively	12	(38%)	8	(16%)
Drinks moderately	11	(34%)	31	(62%)
Drinks a little or none	9	(28%)	11	(22%)
Total	32	(100%)	50	(100%)
(No information)	(8)		(16)	

Source: Swantz et al. 1975.

Compared with neighbor fathers, more fathers of malnourished children drink excessively (Chi square = 6.93, d.f = 2, alpha = 0.05).

twenty years.[8] In the NURU study, my research team found that neighbors cited excessive consumption of alcohol by the father for 38 percent of families with malnourished children, significantly more than the 16 percent of neighboring fathers (Table 6; see also Swantz et al. 1975).

Men have rights to drink *pombe* and to control the distribution of meat in their households. Their abuse of these rights in some cases appears to be an expression of frustration over economic failure. Although public drinking is acceptable, public drunkenness can ultimately compound an alcoholic's shame, as the community blames him for his neglect. Today, Chagga openly lament when they see one of their own kin or neighbors fall victim to this self-destruction. Stripped of traditional sources of power, some men express their frustration in destructive acts. Love and aspirations for a better life turn to guilt, anger, insistence on male dominance, and sometimes physical abuse of women and children.

Family Conflict and Malnutrition

Families all over the world experience conflict from time to time, and the people who live on Mt. Kilimanjaro are no exception. Throughout their history, Kilimanjaro families have had to deal with strife and hardship—war among chiefdoms, raiding by the Maasai, drought, pestilence, lineage disputes over land, and demands from the chief. These difficulties at times involved widespread change and brought about conflicts in families. In some ways, adversity spurred people to reach ingenious resolutions and innovations. A complex irrigation system, the age-grade system, the organization of the chiefdom, trade with outsiders, and openness to new ideas all developed partly in response to adversity and conflict.

With colonialism, people adopted a new religion and outlook on life. This new moral order altered the local forms of birth spacing and contributed to explosive population growth. Many men now lack sufficient land to distribute to their sons. Competition has increased between fathers and sons, among brothers, and among women who have married into a lineage. People feel envy, resentment, and bitterness, setting the stage for accusations of unjust behavior, of failure to meet customary obligations to kin, and of sorcery and other forms of spiritual harm-doing.

One way to deal with some conflicts as they developed in the early twentieth century was to take up coffee farming. Money from coffee built sturdier homes and purchased equipment to make work more efficient and life more comfortable. Coffee income brought a more secure existence for the majority for some period of time. It could buy consumer goods, which gave power and prestige to their owners. As land became scarce, parents with enough money could send their children to school in the hopes of access to well-paid employment.

Money also brought problems. Not everyone could accumulate money at the same rate, and the gap between wealthy and poor grew. Expensive housing materials, clothing, household appliances, and ownership of automobiles raised the expectations of everyone even though very few could purchase these items. Money could be banked and thus more easily hidden than cattle and other goods used in barter. Better-off people could avoid some public scrutiny of their holdings and public pressure to share their wealth. If a man had many cattle, his wives could not care for all of them, and he would loan animals under contractual agreements to relatives. When he could convert cattle to money, he no longer needed to rely on relatives, and they lost some of the resources that had once come their way. Part of women's labor shifted to the coffee groves, reducing their time for growing vegetables, thus limiting the harvests that they controlled while increasing those of their husbands. Gender inequality was further exacerbated, sometimes unintentionally, by colonial policies regarding money.

Conflicts in families developed between the needy, who tended to press for customary privileges, and the wealthy, who often sought to accumulate money to the exclusion of their kin. Daughters-in-law sometimes could not obtain the customary child care from their mothers-in-law. Sons were sometimes left without land by their fathers.

At times, farmers were hard pressed to make profits, especially when prices of farm supplies increased and the international coffee market took a downturn. When their own incomes declined, wealthier people grew reluctant to meet traditional obligations to needy relatives, and some exploited their poorer kin. Wages for farm labor tended to be low and lag behind inflation. Both men and women were pushed to find other means to earn money.

Many men migrated to urban areas in search of work. Others stayed at home and took on demeaning daily work with wages too low to feed their families. Migration of men increased the farm work required of already overworked women. Seeking more cash, women intensified the marketing of their vegetables, hiring out their labor, and making *pombe* and gin.

In seeking to explain child malnutrition, some blamed the economic and environmental crisis or the mean-spirited attitude of better-off kin. Others blamed the parents. When the emotional climate was filled with envy, resentment, and bitterness from chronic unresolved conflict, sorcery or curse could be invoked. Such accusations led to claims that the child's illness had been brought about through ill will.

These changes have had real consequences for the health of children. Poorer families with ongoing misfortune often cannot afford adequate diets for all their children. Conflicts with kin can cut them off from access to food customarily obtained through exchange or kin obligation. Mothers have less time to supervise the care of younger children. Children are further jeopardized when one or both parents turn to alcohol for comfort.

A patchwork of customary and newer practices has eroded the patrilineage, widened the gap between wealthy and poor, and in many families increased women's work and diminished the availability of child care. Although some members of the community have benefited from changes in the last half of the twentieth century, others have suffered losses. Growing inequality and erosion of mutual support have contributed to conflict in families, to the considerable detriment of small children.

Chapter Nine

Child Favoritism and Malnutrition

*～ A serious childhood illness draws the concern of kin and neighbors.
Parents use their child's behavior as a basis for deciding how to proceed in
dealing with the illness. Severely malnourished children withdraw from
eating and social interaction, making it difficult for parents and kin to
know what to do. ～*

1974

～ I was concerned about six-year-old Hamisi, Francis and Bibiana
Lema's oldest child. I entered the compound and found Hamisi standing
alone next to the house, picking straw from the dilapidated mud wall. He
seemed uninterested in Matthew, and I never saw him play with his
younger siblings. I was distressed over his condition and my inability to get
his attention during daily visits to his home.

"Such a child has no hope," Phillipe commented about her little neighbor. Her statement was perplexing to me, especially because I had never
heard anyone else talk this way about an ailing child.

"Look at Bibiana," she said as we glanced across the path at Francis's
house. "She has a newborn daughter and three other children besides
Hamisi. If she doesn't keep on tending her beans and maize, what will the
family eat? Francis tries to care for the children when Bibiana's gone, but
Hamisi's needs are too much for him. Such a child." She gestured in the
direction of Hamisi and shook her head with pity. Phillipe seemed
concerned about her neighbors but could not intervene because of her own
family. She had nine children, who were all enrolled in primary or secondary
school. They left her little time and energy to take on Hamisi. ～

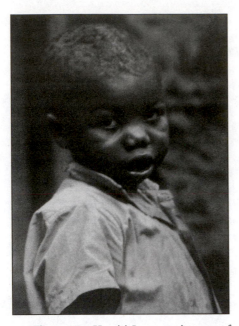

Hamisi had all the symptoms of severe malnutrition, including puffy, flaky, discolored skin and thinning, discolored hair. His petulance drove the other children away, and he rejected even the touch of his own mother as he teetered on the edge of survival. He could not stand to be touched because of his painfully swollen, sore-ridden skin. He had severe diarrhea but no longer much hunger, and he generally refused to eat. Once these symptoms and responses appear, this form of malnutrition tends to lead to death.

~ Figure 17 *Hamisi Lema at six years of age. He did not survive the time of* njaa *in 1974.*

When confronted with "such a child," most people want to leave them alone, and local ideas about kwashiorkor reinforce this reaction. Diarrhea is viewed as a disorder polluting the child's body, especially the digestive system. Diarrhea is also understood to drain the body of necessary substance; Hamisi's refusal to eat thus seemed entirely contradictory. The diarrhea of a severely malnourished child also repels people in other ways.

~ I sometimes detected a telltale foul odor coming from Hamisi that hangs about older malnourished children. When they soil their clothes because of chronic diarrhea, children from poor households have no other pants to change into.

As the eldest of five children, Hamisi should have been helping Bibiana care for the other children and fetch firewood and water. In his free time, he could have fashioned a hoop and rolled it with a stick, as did other little boys his age. He might have joined a group of children singing or playing *bao* (a game like checkers) on a game board scratched on the ground. He did little, however, except whimper when asked to speak. As even his mother pulled away from him, he seemed to sense the lack of support and withdrew even further. ~

Children with kwashiorkor often have an appearance that suggests death to the people of Kilimanjaro. The dead are supposed to be light-haired and light-complected, and the lightening of Hamisi's hair and his light patches of skin, symptoms of kwashiorkor, probably hinted to those around him that he was dying. The swelling of a child's body with kwashiorkor suggests the swelling of a corpse, and Hamisi's puffy skin suggested that he was approaching death. A few months later, he died, at seven years of age.

Severe malnutrition presents many difficulties for a Chagga family. Childhood illness derived from problems that a household cannot solve increases the anxiety of family members. People tend to see kwashiorkor as signifying moral failure on the part of parents or as a child's rejection of the responsibility to thrive and give affection. Some women who have already lost infants seem to withdraw more abruptly and earlier than others when another infant becomes seriously ill. A cycle may develop in which the mother responds to the child's lack of affect by withdrawing herself; the child, in turn, senses the mother's withdrawal.

Under conditions of extreme crisis, furthermore, adults tend not to engage in games encouraging children to eat and not to offer bites of food. I frequently observed an ill and withdrawn weanling sitting passively before the common food bowl to be shared with siblings. The child lacked energy, had lost its appetite, and acted as though trying to eat would be futile. It seemed that when Bibiana ignored Hamisi rather than coax him to eat, Hamisi simply gave up.

Once a child's health fails, a mother begins to lose self-confidence and prestige, impeding her efforts to deal with the problem. Because a mother can anticipate no relief from this situation, particularly under conditions of famine, she may restrain her generosity toward her child.

Hamisi's story involves a physiological state that drove him to rebuff others with refusal to eat, interact, and be touched. Customary notions intensified the perceptions about "such a child." The tragedy of Hamisi's story was repeated in countless other households during my stay on the mountain. Even so, some parents persisted against the odds in trying to prevent their children's deaths.

Ill Favor: Past Criteria for Abortion and Infanticide

Responses in precolonial situations may have been similar in terms of attempting to save or letting go of a child. Earlier ethnographies noted that certain situations might have resulted in abortion or infanticide (now illegal in Tanzania). In the past, the people of Kilimanjaro thought that some

Table 7   *Reasons Given in the Past for Infanticide*

1. An infant conceived out of wedlock.
2. An infant conceived while the mother was still breastfeeding a previous child.
3. An infant conceived within two months of the death of the previous child.
4. An infant conceived by a woman after her daughter had married.
5. Abnormal infants including:
   a. an infant born in a breech delivery or another specific abnormal position, during abnormal labor, with premature expulsion of the placenta, or with the amniotic membranes intact;
   b. an infant born with teeth or without mouth or anus, or covered with body hair, or appearing to be a hermaphrodite; those perceived to have cried in utero during delivery;
   c. one of a pair of twins (the weaker or the child with a sex already represented in the family);
   d. an infant whose upper incisors erupt from the gums before any other teeth.

Source: Raum 1940:88; see also Gutmann 1926:212–217.

children faced inevitable death in early life. Deliberate abortion and infanticide were acceptable and even required under specific, limited circumstances. Voluntary abortion evoked a serious supernatural threat because of a vague sense that a reincarnated ancestor inhabited the body of a fetus or newborn baby. Abortion or miscarriage obligated the family to make sacrificial offerings to the ancestral spirit to protect themselves from danger.

Justification for infanticide included parental wrongdoing as well as abnormalities in the pregnancy, the labor, or the infant. Parental wrongdoing included a breach of sexual morality on the part of parents. Parents, for example, were prohibited from engaging in sexual intercourse together while the mother was still breastfeeding a child. Children conceived under these circumstances could be killed immediately after birth to avoid shame (see Table 7). Similarly, it was a disgrace for a woman to become pregnant after one of her children had been circumcised (i.e., reached adolescence). Children conceived under these circumstances might be aborted or killed at birth (Raum 1940:88).

Specific abnormalities evident at birth were also said to justify infanticide (see Table 7). They ranged from phenomena that were not particularly unusual (e.g., a breech presentation) to rare conditions such as an infant lacking an anus.[1] On the other hand, protection was extended to albino children or those with hunchbacks, clubbed feet, or extra fingers and toes because they were considered sacred (Raum 1940).

Some birth abnormalities were believed to threaten the whole community. To remedy the situation, the chief ordered a purifying rite, including sacrificing the abnormal child. According to one account, it was thought that a spirit had created the deformity to threaten the fertility of the patrilineage. The sense of danger, evil, and impurity associated with an extraordinarily abnormal child thus had ramifications for the entire community. Infanticide in these cases may have been seen as a way to forestall other possible tragedies on a grand scale, including drought, famine, and plague.

According to an account from the 1930s, relatives had to be consulted prior to any infanticide (Raum 1940). The father, or a midwife representing his family, could not kill the child without permission of the mother's family. Ignoring this custom would have entitled the wife's father to recover damages from her husband, unless the chief was convinced the infanticide had been justified.

Reports vary on past methods of infanticide. One account asserts that a child was wrenched by the neck until dead (Gutmann 1926:89); another, that it was suffocated (Gutmann 1926:216). A third states that midwives would drown a child in a pot of water to avoid shedding blood (Raum 1940:90), thus symbolically returning the child to the womb. From the local perspective, the spirit had entered the particular child's body at the wrong time and was being sent back to the ancestors. According to one report, children were purposefully eliminated through neglect:

> A favorite method was simply to neglect the child, which caused fatal consequences during one of the many infantile illnesses. It must be feared that this method is still being employed, especially in the case of twins. (Raum 1940:90)

Raum mentioned the case of twins. Of the forty-seven malnourished children in the NURU study, four were two sets of twins, implying that twins may still present a problem. According to Raum, the problem with twins was the feeling of "bewilderment at excessive productivity," that is, the birth of two children at once (Raum 1940:80). In one instance, he said, the weakest was killed; in another, a boy, since he was held to have more power; and in still another, the child of the sex that was already represented in the family. He added that for the same reason, it was thought unlucky for cowives or sisters to become pregnant at the same time.

The customary indications for infanticide may not have always caused people to directly kill a child, but may have given relatives reason for neglect, as stated by Raum. Neglect may have been the last resort under conditions of extreme hardship and women's exhaustion from heavy workloads.

> The underlying motives for infanticide were said to be an immediate
> reaction to extreme disappointment of high hopes, to perplexity over
> an unexpected turn of events which is desirable to control, and to irri-
> tation at the stultification of professional skill or parental exertions.
> (Raum 1940:89)

Past accounts portrayed abortion and infanticide as expected and justified
under specific conditions.

Qualities of Children that May Influence Favoritism

Neighbors and relatives of families with children who had been in NURU
and the nurses who cared for them insisted that specific malnourished children were given less care than other children in the same families.
Favoritism for a certain child in a family seems to be common on the
mountain, as in many other societies. The older ethnographies noted cultural criteria that influenced preference for some children, although they
did not determine parental behavior. The criteria were simply part of a
range of values and ideas that people drew from in different ways under
varying conditions.

Appearance

On Mt. Kilimanjaro, as in most parts of the world, an attractive appearance
is a reason to value a child.[2] According to an account from Kilimanjaro in
the 1960s, some people followed specific procedures to ensure that a child
would be beautiful. One account said that to obtain an attractive child, a
man, after his wife had conceived, was to avoid all conversation until he met
someone with the desired characteristics. After talking to him, the husband
could return to normal social exchange. If a woman considered her husband
unattractive, she could leave the house after intercourse, stay in the woods
looking at flowers, and return only after her husband had left. Her baby
would then acquire her features, not her husband's (Marealle 1963, 1965).

In an earlier account, children were said to always take some characteristics from the father's family (Gutmann 1926). Their likeness assured men
that the children were theirs, a necessity considering the danger of bringing
other men's children into the lineage. Pregnancy was said to vary from nine
to eleven months, depending on the father's family. If a woman from a lineage with an eleven-month gestation period married a man whose lineage
had nine-month pregnancies, she would be prohibited from visiting her
family in the first month of pregnancy. The characteristics of her husband's

lineage would thus pass to the fetus and bring about a shorter pregnancy (Gutmann 1926:4).

Gender, Birth Order, and Lineage Alignment

Chagga relationships to children also involve the interaction of gender, birth order, and lineage alignment. These dimensions of social relations could draw parents to favor some children over others. Lucas Towo, for example, had two daughters who thrived during the famine of 1971 to 1975, while his two sons died.

1974

⌁ Francis, Nathaniel, and Paulo called me in for a discussion. I thought they wanted to talk over their ideas about a cooperative, but I was wrong.

Paulo began. "Do you think I have problems?" he asked, referring to his terrible health problems, one of his children who was malnourished, and the loss of many of his other children.

"Yes, of course you do," I replied, and waited to see what would follow this rather curious beginning of our conversation.

"Then you must visit the home of Lucas Towo. His two sons are very ill. Perhaps you can help them too?"

The compassion and concern of the three cousins, Nathaniel, Francis, and Paulo, for one another inspired me. To help an impoverished neighbor who was not a relative, and perhaps to bolster my spirits after our failed effort with the cooperative, they sought my involvement. The men led me along a trail over a deep ravine. The trip took almost half an hour because the rains had made the path treacherous. Since I was eight months pregnant and had my small son with me, we walked carefully. Sometimes my feet would stick in the mud; my companions actually had to pull me out.

I was relieved when Francis yelled out the greeting "*Hodi!*" as we approached a compound hidden by banana trees. With visions of warm tea to take away the early morning chill, I was eager to meet Lucas's family.

We found a depressing scene. Outside a banana-thatched house stood two small boys who were obviously starving. They had large heads on emaciated bodies and legs with protruding, knobby knees. Francis called out for Lucas while Paulo asked for their mother, Hildegunda. She had been relieving herself in the banana grove behind the house and shyly approached us while covering her mottled teeth with her hand. Lucas slowly emerged from his house and Francis and Paulo assisted him onto a log. His bony frame was shaking from illness. The family had no visible material belongings.

Paulo explained our purpose. With hand outstretched, Lucas called forth his sons to introduce them. Johani was eleven years old but appeared to be about seven. Patrice was ten years old and, although a bit taller than his older brother, looked like an eight-year-old. Both boys were said to be mentally slow, and I learned later that all the children had chronic hookworm infection.[3]

~ Figure 18 *Lucas and Hildegunda Towo and their four children. The younger daughter, age eight, stands between her ten- and eleven-year-old brothers. Both boys died, and the girls survived.*

Berta, an eight-year-old daughter, returned from collecting wood, and Constancia, the eldest child, age fourteen, returned from picking coffee at a nearby plantation. The two girls appeared to be thriving and were of normal height and intelligence. In fact, Berta was nearly a head taller than her two older brothers! I wondered what factors might have led to such an astonishing difference in health between the Towo boys and their sisters. ～

The good health of the girls and the ailments of the boys suggested that they might have been treated differently on the basis of gender,[4] as noted in earlier accounts (Raum 1940:86).[5] In the past, fathers had reason to prefer boys; a son held the promise of becoming a family priest, who would elevate his father's status, and an heir, who would secure the future of the patrilineage. A son was primarily responsible for ritual offerings of *tambiko* that assured perpetuity of the spirits of the ancestors. A son also contributed to his father's social and political influence through support during judicial hearings or, in former times, in war.

A mother felt that she had "done her duty" when she had "given birth to one son" (Raum 1940:86). His birth brought her legitimacy and authority in her husband's patrilineage and promised security for her in her old age. On the other hand, women were said to prefer daughters because of their companionship and assistance with household chores. Daughters were also welcome to both parents because of the alliances and bridewealth to come with their marriages (Raum 1940:86). Gender-based preference was normal but depended partly on other complex influences.

These influences may have resulted in preferential treatment of the Towo girls.

～ Lucas was a middle son who had practically no promise of inheriting farmland from his father, a poor man. The small clearing surrounding his house was the only land he owned. He had married Hildegunda quite late in life. She was mildly mentally retarded, and neighbors suggested that Lucas had been unable to pay the greater bridewealth that would have been required to marry a woman of normal intelligence.

Under better circumstances, Hildegunda's retardation would not have been a factor in her sons' illnesses because neighbors and relatives would have assisted a woman who was considered slow. Neighbors gave a mother's mental retardation as a cause of child malnutrition in two out of forty-two cases (Swantz et al. 1975:26). It may have become a significant contributing factor during the period of drought and food crisis between 1973 and 1975.

Constancia, the firstborn, gave tremendous assistance and comfort to Hildegunda. Constancia made major contributions not only by working at home but also by contributing earnings from day labor on nearby estates. She had been the only source of income for the whole family since Lucas had become ill four years earlier. Both she and her younger sister could be expected to bring future security in bridewealth payments. The sons, who had little land to inherit and were already mentally slow, could hardly provide future security for their mother. They were unlikely to be productive workers, and Lucas and Hildegunda would not be able to afford bridewealth for their marriages. ∿

When we visited the Towo family in 1994, only Hildegunda and her daughters were alive. Constancia had opened a beer shop and received some financial support from the father of her only child, a daughter who was eight years old. Neither she nor her younger sister, who also had a child, had married. Hildegunda wept as she spoke of the loss of her sons and blamed it on *uchawi* (witchcraft).

The mild mental retardation of Patrice and Johani Towo may have both resulted from and contributed to their malnutrition. The girls might have had greater access to food while helping their mother prepare the family meals, and as healthier, more alert children, they may have taken more food while sharing a common bowl with the others. Mild mental retardation also reduced options for marriage. As long as handicapped youths could do heavy manual labor vital to rural life, however, they could still lead productive lives in their community.

A woman could expect to be taken care of by her oldest and youngest sons when they each inherited a piece of their father's land. If the father's

∿ Figure 19   *The Towos' two surviving children show off their own children in 1989.*

land holdings were too small to divide, however, or if he was landless, a son would find it difficult to meet his obligations to his mother. If poverty forced a parent to assess a child's worth, a daughter may have been viewed as more promising because of the help and companionship she would bring her mother and the bridewealth she would bring to the household.[6]

Of the forty-nine malnourished children in the NURU study, thirty were girls and nineteen, boys. Customs that regulated reproductive behavior persisted to some degree in certain families, and children born under circumstances viewed as negative may have been subject to ill favor. If there was ill favor toward some children, it may have tended to vary by gender and age for cosmological and practical reasons. Some boys may have been victims of neglect during early infancy because of the ability of an illegitimate boy's spirit to bring harm. The higher rates of malnutrition among weanling girls, however, appear to show some favoritism toward males. In contrast, if a child survives to an older age and the household falls on hard times, boys are more likely to end up living on the streets than girls, who customarily make important contributions to the household by working in the compound and the fields.

Birth order could also combine with gender and play a significant role in putting certain children at risk. Birth order is a factor that helps to determine lineage alignment, the affiliation of a child with either the mother's or father's lineage. Alignment of some children with the mother's lineage strengthens ties begun at marriage between patrilineages. It also helps distribute children's labor, which may in part symbolize a return on the bridewealth paid by the maternal patrilineage. Lineage alignment is a different dimension of kinship from lineage membership and incorporation. A child belongs to the father's lineage from birth and is incorporated into it as a full member through various rites of passage. With alignment, a firstborn son and a firstborn daughter are given special ties to the father's lineage and the second-born of each gender to the mother's lineage. Subsequent sets of children are alternately aligned, the third set with the father's side and the fourth set with the mother's, and so on. Lineage alignment was a customary notion on Mt. Kilimanjaro, and it is still recognized in many families.

Normally, a household resided with the husband's lineage, who might favor children aligned with them. Children who were aligned with their mother's lineage were frequently weaned by sending them to live temporarily with their mothers' parents. This was seen as the ideal time for them to get to know their maternally related kin. Ancestral spirits of the lineage would protect the children, and the living relatives would give them gifts during important rites of passage.

Various difficulties sometimes limited parents' time, energy, and ability to deal with their children. Children sent to live with their mother's kin might have been recently weaned and emotionally upset. Their presence in their grandparents' household might also have indicated marital conflict or illegitimacy. In these situations, if any of the children from the father's lineage were staying with the mother's lineage, they might suffer disadvantage due to fear of their powers. Gender, birthorder, and lineage alignment do not determine children's fates but have a situational effect on their treatment that is influenced by many other factors as well.

A Mother's Social Standing

Social standing could also shape the community's perception of a child. The community's reaction to a woman's actions and the circumstances of her marriage determined her social standing. As young men became landless and were forced to migrate to find work, they often had to delay marriage. Traditionally, a young man was supposed to acquire land and build a home before marriage. In recent years, bridewealth payments have risen, further delaying marriage in many cases. One result seems to be increased rates of illegitimate birth (Cook and Kerner 1989:63). With delays in marriage, many young women have premarital sexual relations while working outside the region. They often bring their illegitimate offspring to Kilimanjaro to be raised by their parents with contributions from money they earn (Cook and Kerner 1989).

Living together without formal marriage can result in loss of social support. Parents' economic status can influence community sentiment regarding a child's marriage and any grandchildren. It was reported that one woman in the NURU study abandoned her children, and although we lack further information about this case, it is doubtful that she was from a household that was well-off.

In a polygynous marriage, a man might have a stronger emotional attachment to a particular wife. I observed instances in which the favorite wife's children were given better food, shelter, clothing, and education than the children of less favored wives. From all reports, this pattern was typical. Generally, the senior wife was favored, and her children often had a distinct advantage over children born to the second wife.

Overcoming the Consequences of the Death of a Previous Child and Failure to Follow Tradition

The experience of a child's death can devastate a family's capability to love and care for subsequent children as well as severely disgrace and publicly shame the parents. A sense of shame was evident in the Shuma family. It did not, however, result in the death of another child.

1974

~ During the course of my research, I made frequent visits to Catherine Shuma's extended family compound. Gabriel, twenty months old, was Catherine's second youngest child and was ill with malnutrition. He was aligned with his mother's lineage and received little attention from adults in the compound other than her. Never did I see Gabriel being held except by Catherine, after her return from work in the fields.

The Shumas' closest neighbor expressed pity over the social isolation and economic crisis experienced by Catherine. The neighbor blamed Elifatio for his son Gabriel's malnutrition and claimed that he had spent all the available cash in the household on *pombe*. Elifatio earned only nine and a half shillings (U.S. $1.35) a day as a laborer cutting coffee trees on nearby estates.

The Shumas' compound adjoined that of Elifatio's youngest brother, Steven, who lived with his family in his mother's house. The main houses of the two families were only about twenty feet apart, separated by large dracaena hedges. Steven's house was deteriorating, but he was building a new cement block addition. He worked as a driver for Kilimo (the Ministry of Agriculture) in Arusha, sixty miles away, and had a sizable wage of 340 shillings (U.S. $48.50), about 50 percent more than Elifatio's 228 shillings a month. Steven's wage enabled him to improve his house and to keep his four children, his wife, Helena, and his mother in good health. The older woman, Grandmother Shuma, exerting a powerful influence on these two families, preferred to stay in a traditional thatched roundaval close to her younger son's house.

Because the two families shared a *kihamba* of only six hundred coffee trees, there were already potential conflicts over resources when Elifatio began his family. Elifatio and Catherine's first child was born in 1951, a daughter who died during infancy from unknown causes. Catherine had a very difficult time discussing it. Death of the first child is a bad omen that can signify ancestral displeasure with the parents' behavior, and Catherine seemed devastated and ashamed of her loss. The next child born to her was Eusta, who survived and came to be her close companion. From 1956 to 1959, Catherine had four more children. No more children were born in the compound until Catherine's young sister-in-law, Helena, started having children in 1967. Catherine's last cluster of births (five between 1970 and 1974) overlapped with the births of Helena's four children and that of Catherine's first grandchild in 1974.

Grandmother Shuma apparently had her own reasons for being irritated with Catherine and Elifatio. It is possible that her relationship with Catherine could have turned sour when Catherine's first child died. Elifatio's meager wages were embarrassing compared with his younger brother's. Elifatio squandered his money on *pombe* and neglected to provide meat for his mother.

Grandmother Shuma may have faced an emotional dilemma regarding Elifatio as her eldest son. Customarily, a woman's eldest son is her most cherished child. Through him, she gained legitimacy in her husband's lineage. Her eldest son customarily would take the position of authority in the extended family upon his father's death. When the father had sufficient land holdings, the eldest son inherited the largest portion of farmland and was ultimately responsible for his mother's welfare, even though she traditionally resided with the youngest son.

Grandmother Shuma seems to have felt ambivalent toward Elifatio, and she expressed open hostility toward Catherine. She was warm and cooperative toward Helena, her other daughter-in-law, who she hoped would side with her against Catherine. When Grandmother Shuma was not present, Helena expressed sympathy for Catherine while bemoaning the lack of cooperation: "Women can no longer expect help with a new baby or child care. Other women have too many responsibilities to their own families." Later, in her mother-in-law's presence, Helena remarked, "Grandmother Shuma helped me for four months after each birth and takes care of my four children when I work in the fields."

Many factors may have caused Grandmother Shuma's overt hostility toward Catherine. The demand of a large, extended family for a grandmother's work may have forced her to limit her efforts in view of her own limited energy. Her younger son, with his much higher income, would provide her with more security. The old woman could find reasons to criticize Catherine and make her feel ashamed of infractions of lineage tradition: the death of her first child, her failure to maintain a postpartum sex taboo, and bearing a child after her married daughter had done so. Finally, Catherine's refusal to act like a chastened woman may have been a last offense. Instead, she held her head high and accepted no blame.

Although Grandmother Shuma might have felt morally justified if she had successfully ostracized Catherine, she had to modify her indignation to keep the support of the younger daughter-in-law. She developed a rigid double standard that may have helped her rationalize mistreating Catherine. Helena had also failed to maintain the postpartum sex taboo—her last two children were born within one year. After specifically blaming Catherine's problems on her excessive childbearing, Grandmother Shuma and Helena later said that the spacing of births was *shauri ya Mungu* (the will of God). If the grandmother opposed one woman, she would have to favor the other, for she could not exist without support from the younger generation. Helena was also in a dilemma. If she befriended Catherine, she risked losing the old woman's assistance and favor. Although she sympathized with Catherine, she did not want to jeopardize her own security.

Catherine remained cheerful and energetic despite a lack of support from her husband's patrilineage. She was one of the most hospitable women I had visited, had a hearty laugh, and tended to emphasize the positive aspects of her life. She managed to plant a small vegetable and flower garden in the clearing that formed her family's compound and expressed pride in that achievement and in her new knowledge acquired from NURU. She maintained an almost sisterly relationship with her daughter Eusta, who returned the affection.

Perhaps by maintaining a cheerful demeanor, Catherine was able to discourage open conflict. Bemoaning her unjust treatment could cause family tensions to explode into dispute. As far as I knew, there were no accusations of curse or sorcery, but conditions were ripe for them.

When Catherine went to cultivate her *pori*, her eight-year-old daughter cared for the four youngest children, all boys. Gabriel, who was aligned with his mother's lineage, was a malnourished weanling, displaced from his mother's breast at several months of age. His infant brother had also been sickly for some time, despite Catherine's attentions.

It was not for lack of their mother's involvement that these children suffered malnutrition. Deprived of her husband's and mother-in-law's support, Catherine did everything in her power to provide food for her young family. She brought home maize from her fields, she went to the cooperative union for handouts to victims of the drought, she accepted any food the neighbors offered, and she brewed *pombe* for sale. Catherine was determined that her children would survive. What *aibu* (shame) she had experienced from other failures would be offset by her being a model of *kujitegemea* (self-reliance). Her burdens were only increasing because of drought, though, and it could not be predicted how long she could continue to persevere. ⌒

Despite his unpromising situation, Gabriel somehow survived. When we visited in December 1993, we found a handsome, healthy young man who was head of his own family. Catherine and Elifatio asked him to stay home from work in Moshi to meet us when we visited. Catherine and her husband were filled with pride when Gabriel posed with his wife and daughter for our photographs. The family's fortunes had improved since the hard times of the 1970s, and we quietly celebrated their son's survival.

Ill Favor, Crisis, and Poverty

During the food crisis of 1973 to 1975, it was clear that malnourished children presented many difficulties for parents and kin. Many children with the symptoms of kwashiorkor may have been perceived as moribund. The NURU study showed that many people still used at least some customary criteria to judge children. Neighbors of families with sick children often suggested that the children were disfavored. Some people charged with caring for malnourished children loosened emotional ties and gave up.

The older accounts presented two primary modes of evaluating children. The first involved events or circumstances of the pregnancy and birth as well as personal or social characteristics of the child that appeared during the course of child development and were publicly scrutinized during rites of passage in early childhood. The child's appearance, gender, birth order, and lineage alignment were additional characteristics that were said to be subject to scrutiny.

The second mode of evaluating children in the past concerned the social standing of the parents, primarily the mother. The marital status of the parents, the favoring of a particular wife in polygynous marriages, the parents' previous experiences with child death, and any parental disregard for Chagga tradition had a bearing on how their children were regarded and treated by their kin.

Individual characteristics of parents also may have been involved in a child's malnutrition. As in any society, Chagga parents varied widely in their involvement with their children. Some parents, such as Catherine, made valiant efforts to preserve their children's lives even when rejection was warranted according to local custom. Other parents, including Catherine's husband, Elifatio, took up drinking and failed to meet their family obligations.

To cast blame on all the caretakers, however, diverts attention from broader economic and political issues. Land shortage, unemployment, unstable returns from cash crops, heavier women's workloads, and reduced time for child care led to hardship in some households. Customary practices of scrutinizing children and judging parents' morality created mechanisms through which the effects of economic inequality could be expressed. These intersecting factors put pressure on some parents and made neglecting children a practical course of action in some households.

Chapter Ten

The NURU Experience

The Nutrition Rehabilitation Unit, known as NURU, opened in 1972 as a state-of-the-art center for curing and preventing child malnutrition. For the next twenty years, NURU saved many lives; however, it did not do well at preventing child malnutrition. Although it closed in 1992, similar units are still being initiated in other parts of the world, warranting a close look at NURU as a model of hospital-dominated approaches to child malnutrition and expert-designed development programs.

The flier announcing NURU's opening said of a mother who goes through the program:

> She will get a certificate at the end of her training. She can bring this home to show her family and it will remind her of the weeks she spent at the unit treating her own child. We hope she will feel happy.

The flier bearing the above passage summarizes NURU's approach to the mothers of malnourished children with a typical tone of optimism and naiveté (Table 8, no. 13). Specialists from Tanzania, Europe, and the United States designed NURU with President Julius Nyerere's socialist ideals about local participation, cooperation, and cultural sensitivity in mind.

Those who designed the center, however, did not understand that a malnourished child could be a source of shame for a woman and that the shame might extend to her husband and possibly the entire lineage. No woman on Kilimanjaro would welcome publicity about the treatment of her child for malnutrition. She certainly would not "feel happy" about a publicly awarded certificate.

Table 8   *Flier Announcing the Opening of NURU*

1. Many children around us do not look very sick, but they are much smaller than they should be, less active. If they get a disease, they will suffer for a longer time or they may even die. We call these children malnourished because they have not been getting food that would have been good enough to build them a strong body. Some may become more malnourished and will then be either small and thin or swollen and miserable. We call these conditions *marasmus* or *kwashiorkor*. This kind of a condition is very dangerous and many of these children die. The best thing is therefore to detect the malnutrition before it is too late to try and treat it.

2. The treatment of malnutrition is best done by the *mother*. If she prepares the right food for the child and if the child eats enough of this good food, he will be a healthy child again.

3. The mother must *learn* exactly what good food is, how to prepare it and how to give it to the child.

4. At the Nutrition Rehabilitation Unit the mother is therefore shown in detail how to cook good food. She will learn what kind of food that is good for building the child's body strength. She will also learn what kind of foods give energy and which foods protect the body from certain diseases.

5. The mother will be shown how much to take of each kind of food, how to mix the food and how to cook it. She will also be told how often the child needs food.

6. The nurse will help the mother and explain to her why it is important to do all this in the right way. After a few times the mother will know it very well herself.

7. In the *shamba* that belongs to the unit there is a variety of food like maize, beans, groundnuts, bananas and many kinds of vegetables and fruits. The gardener who has several years of training in farming will help and advise mothers in *shamba* work. Staff from Kilimo will also give some teaching.

8. There will also be rabbits and chickens and the gardener will show the mothers how to take care of such animals. We hope it will be possible for the mother who is interested to get some animals with her to take home.

9. Every afternoon there are lectures about good child care. The nurse will explain and advise about good food, the importance of cleanliness, breast-feeding and weaning, antenatal care, home delivery, immunization and Under-Five clinics, diarrhea, worms, fever, and care to sick children, measles, skin disease and accidents in children. The mother can ask questions and discuss with the nurse and other mothers about problems she may have.

10. The mothers will also be taught how to sew simple clothes for children. Each mother can make at least one new dress for her children. She will also learn how to repair clothes.

11. On admission the child will be examined by a doctor from the child department of KCMC [Kilimanjaro Christian Medical Center], who will find out if there is

any disease that needs treatment. The doctor will also make rounds two times a week to see that the children are growing well.

12. Even if the mother will have to work much with learning new things, cook food, work in the *shamba*, sew and wash, there will be time for having a nice time together with the other mothers. Sometimes student nurses will come to entertain the mothers. We also hope that it will be possible to show films.

13. If the mother has been through all the lectures and knows well how to cook and care for her child, she will get a certificate at the end of her training. She can bring this home to show her family and it will remind her of the weeks she spent at the unit treating her own child. We hope she will feel happy.

14. Anybody is welcome to come and visit the Nutrition Rehabilitation Unit at KCMC any time. *Karibuni* [welcome all]!

The planners saw NURU as a pilot project for integrating the rehabilitation of malnourished children with nutrition education for mothers (Table 8). It also taught farming techniques for food crops and fostered the raising of rabbits for their meat. NURU's planners anticipated that once the programs had been refined, they would be replicated by similar units throughout the region. One of NURU's first priorities was to learn more about the causes of malnutrition on Kilimanjaro to improve its programs. Based at the Kilimanjaro Christian Medical Center, a teaching hospital, NURU was also supposed to educate medical professionals about the problems of malnutrition.

I began to confront the shortcomings of NURU when I assisted a woman with a sick child to gain admittance.

1974

⌣ Francis and Nathaniel Lema were sitting by Francis's house, waiting for me to pass by as I returned from a visit. When I appeared, Nathaniel rushed out to meet me on the road and said, "We wish you would come to see a sick child who is a relative of ours. He's two and a half years old and cannot yet walk."

"How far away is his house?" I was exhausted from a day's walking, and my son Matthew, who was with me that day, was hungry and tired as well.

"Not far. Just beyond Francis's *kihamba*. We've spoken with the child's parents, and they want to meet you."

I agreed to the visit, and on the way Francis explained that the child, Revocarte, was the son of Paulo Lema, his cousin. Revocarte had not been doing well for some time and had almost died a month earlier. Francis and Nathaniel were quite concerned.

The narrow path we took wound through groves of coffee and banana trees, with occasional breathtaking vistas down the mountain across hundreds of miles of plains shimmering with heat. When we got to the open ground before Paulo's house, we saw a small roundaval, its golden thatch contrasting starkly with the rich green of the surrounding trees. There were no barns, cooking shelters, or other outbuildings. I didn't see any tables, chairs, or other belongings about.

Hearing our approach, a man emerged from the house carrying a baby. He wore a torn shirt and pants cut off at the knees. He looked elderly, and his legs were quite swollen. An old woman followed him, and I thought that they were the child's grandparents.

Nathaniel introduced them as Paulo and Paulo's mother. Later, I learned that a chronic kidney infection was causing the swelling in Paulo's legs.

After some conversation, Paulo asked me, "How old is your son?"

"Two and a half," I replied.

"Let's hold the boys up so that we can see the difference," Francis suggested.

Matthew struggled to get loose as I hoisted him up close to Revocarte. I had noticed that even though he was normally drawn to small children, he was uncomfortable with them if they were malnourished. To me, he

∼ Figure 20 *Paulo Lema and his son Revocarte, with me and my son Matthew. Both boys are two and a half years old, but Revocarte's illness had delayed his growth. He survived a serious infection and the food crisis of the 1970s but was severely stunted.*

seemed to be reacting to their sadness. He was nearly twice Revocarte's size even though they were the same age.

"See, he's just not growing as he should," Paulo lamented. "I'd be most grateful if you could get him some *dawa* [medicine]."

I took Revocarte on my lap and examined him. He had no strength in his legs at all and had not yet begun to walk. He could barely pull himself into a sitting position. His skin was dull but not flaky. He was slightly edematous in the legs, his hair growth was poor, and he had a moon face. He was miserable and apathetic.

"What does he eat?"

"*Ndizi tu* [bananas only]. Our two chickens lay only three eggs a week, and we must feed the older children. We keep a cow, but because of the drought, she doesn't produce any milk."

Nathaniel added, "One shilling and twenty cents for a pint of milk is more than they can afford."

During our conversation, Revocarte's mother, Sylvia, arrived with a huge bundle of firewood on her head. Wrapped in tattered clothing, she was perspiring heavily and was clearly exhausted. Everyone said, "*Pole* [my sympathies]!" as the full-term pregnant woman dropped the thirty-five pounds of wood to the ground. She was aware of my presence but made no acknowledgment. Instead she sat quietly, holding her head while listening to more words of commiseration. As is expected of women on Kilimanjaro, she didn't voice any complaints.

After quite a few minutes of silence, she said in a low monotone, "I heard you might come to our house and that you're studying health problems. You've met my son Revocarte. He's had such a bad time."

"Do you have other children?" I asked.

"Oh, yes!"

Sylvia told me that she had given birth to eleven other children; the oldest was about twenty. She went on to say that five had died in early childhood. I was surprised that she enumerated her living and dead children; to me, it was a striking breach of local ways. In Sylvia's case, it was particularly notable because a woman is often blamed for the loss of her children. Perhaps her misfortune had brought her to the point at which she could afford to ignore local custom.

"Why do you think Revocarte became ill?"

"Only God really knows. We've had many misfortunes. Our trees have coffee berry disease, and they've not been bearing well for three years. Without money, what can we do? And as you can see, my husband is not well and can no longer work *kibarua* [as a day laborer]."

"Has Revocarte been to the mission clinic?"

"Three times. For his shots."

"Would you like to take him to NURU? You would stay with him for about a month. There's no cost and they can give Revocarte all the food he wants. You look as if you could use a rest, *Mama* Sylvia!"

"And don't be worried about the cow," added Paulo. "I'll be sure to feed her."

"Yes. That is good," she responded. "Thank you. Thank you very much."

I thought I caught a glimmer of a smile as she came to her decision. As a forty-two-year-old woman who would soon give birth to her thirteenth child while still working the fields and coming home late in the day to complete her household chores, Sylvia definitely was in need of a break.

Two days later, I was sitting on the veranda of the clinic where I was supposed to meet Sylvia at noon to drive her down to NURU, but she did not arrive.

In the early afternoon, Bibiana walked up the steep road to the clinic and informed me that Sylvia and many neighbors were waiting for me by the car, parked at the marketplace about half a mile below. When I arrived, I learned that Sylvia had been there since early morning. She had been on her way back home when neighbors stopped her and sent Bibiana for me.

At first sight, I was glad not to have let her down. She wore a pretty dress, borrowed for the occasion. Appearance was important to a woman who was about to publicly present herself with a child whose sickness was a mark of failure. She had bathed Revocarte, who looked much better, although he still had symptoms of kwashiorkor.

"Where have you been, *Mama* Maria?" she said as she stepped into the car. Paulo handed Revocarte to her along with a bundle of clothing wrapped in *kitenge* cloth. It was the first time I had seen her hold her son.

The six-mile dirt road down to Moshi town was muddy and treacherous from a heavy downpour the night before. Streams of water from the rain had carved deep ruts into the mahogany-colored soil. On the way, Sylvia and I developed the comradeship of two women in late pregnancy as we slid uncomfortably from side to side on the muddy road. Sylvia went through a change from her previous quiet, tired, disinterested stares. She began a nonstop discussion of her life, much of which I could not follow in my attempt to concentrate on my driving.

"So many, many *shida* [problems] these past few years! There is too much work, and it's never finished."

"Is there anyone to help you?"

"Oh, yes. Paulo's mother. But she's very old. Sometimes Bibiana helps, but she has her own problems these days as well. Mostly my sister; my sister will come and help after the baby's born."

"And Paulo?"

"Oh, he's a good man. He shares what little he makes at the mission, but that's not enough these days. If I didn't sell the maize from the lower *shamba*, none of us would eat."

"What about your other children?"

"*Tembeau tu* [walking about]," Sylvia said, referring to unemployment and possibly prostitution. "Those in town are useless. The others at home aren't much help either." Sylvia grew silent for a while. Then she said, "I'm very hungry. Will they have food at the hospital for us? I haven't eaten all day and neither has Revocarte."

We stopped at a local restaurant when we got to Moshi and ordered *ndizi na nyama* (a dish of plantains and beef) for ourselves and milk for Revocarte. He wouldn't eat, but by then I wasn't surprised at his reaction. Loss of appetite was a common symptom of kwashiorkor.

After our meal, we headed for NURU. It was located by the main road and next to the long driveway to the hospital, Kilimanjaro Christian Medical Center. The famine was at its height, and NURU was crowded with patients. The staff was granting admittance to Sylvia as a favor to me.

I watched anxiously as she surveyed her new "home." The staff occasionally referred to NURU as a village, but it was only two large buildings that were one story tall, made of concrete. The whitewashed outer walls bore signs announcing that it was the Nutrition Rehabilitation Unit for children with kwashiorkor. The signs would only magnify the shame of having a malnourished child for any mother who brought her child there.

A nurse dressed in a white uniform and cap came to greet us and took Sylvia's bundle from me for safe storage. "She'll have to register at the main building first, but why don't I show you around a bit for now?"

She led us to the sleeping quarters.

As we entered, the other women stared, making Sylvia uncomfortable. Beds for women and children were lined up along the walls in two rows, giving the room the appearance of army barracks. The privacy cherished by most Chagga was completely absent in this dormitory-style room. Listless children of all ages hung by their mothers' skirts. Only a few children looked healthy and active.

The nurse took us to a large outdoor canopy stretched over an area with firewood stoves and said, "These are the cooking areas." Smoke from the stoves had already darkened one wall and the canopy. Another section had benches facing a blackboard. The few offices at the back were for the nursing staff and the doctor who came twice a week to examine each child. The offices and uniforms clearly separated professionals from patients.

The nurse took us outside. "Here are our agricultural projects. The women who come here are attempting to follow the government call for *ujamaa na kujitegemea* [cooperation and self-reliance]. All the vegetables we use in the kitchens will soon be provided through the mothers' efforts."

This idea seemed to disturb Sylvia a little.

"Of course, for you, *mama*, we'll find something you can do in your condition. Over here, we've started poultry and rabbit pens; we'll have six hundred laying hens that we hope will cover many of the expenses of the unit. The mothers do all the work and learn animal husbandry."

When our tour was over, we drove to the main hospital building for admittance. One of the largest buildings in the region, it was still stark white with newness and smelled strongly of antiseptic. Sylvia found it forbidding. The staff had a way of rushing that was a startling contrast to the more relaxed pace in the countryside. We were required to visit three offices before our arrival on the pediatric floor, where Revocarte was to be examined by a physician.

"I think this little fellow should stay the night in the hospital," the doctor told me in English. When I translated for Sylvia, she grew alarmed.

"But where will I sleep?" she asked. "There are women on the floor, and I didn't bring a mat. What about my things at NURU?"

"I'll get them," I responded. "Don't worry. I'm sure they'll get a bed for you."

"Will you be staying too? I'd be pleased if you stayed. I don't know anyone here."

"I'm sorry, *Mama* Sylvia, but I have to leave. A friend of mine has promised to visit you while I'm gone. She'll let us know if you need anything. Everything will be all right. Please don't worry."

I was too tired to drive back to the mission, so I slept in town. I confessed to myself that I was not quite sure I had done the right thing. Perhaps I had merely absorbed Sylvia's apprehensions and misgivings. Then, on the other hand, the staff had seemed rather cold and callous in dealing with a woman in her ninth month of pregnancy bringing an ill child for treatment. ⌒

Admittance procedures had taken three hours and were not finished until 9:00 P.M., sapping Sylvia of her hope and excitement. Everyone on the staff, including custodians, conveyed authoritarian attitudes toward Sylvia. They assumed a curt manner with a kindness that was often patronizing, and they frequently discussed Sylvia with me, right in front of her. At the time, I thought that Sylvia's discomfort probably resulted from some misunderstanding and that as soon as she could come to see the hospital as I did, her suffering would disappear. Sylvia was experiencing more than simple discomfort with the exhausting bureaucracy, though; it may have been the first time she had ventured out of her lineage territory, and she was probably afraid of strangers. Like most people, she may have feared the Medical Center because of its mysterious doings with patients and their bodily substances. She had already been humiliated by the stares of other women at NURU and may have begun to feel the burden of stigma from being there.

Two weeks after Sylvia and Revocarte were admitted, she left the program on foot and carried him six miles up the mountain, despite being nine months pregnant. Sylvia's departure shocked the staff at NURU. In their view, the unit provided a comfortable environment for the women of Kilimanjaro because it was patterned on local customs: stoves and food were provided where women could cook their own food, they were supposed to work in the fields as at home, and they resided in a one-floor building away from the formal clinical atmosphere of the multistory hospital at the Medical Center. Mothers residing at NURU with their children were supposed to observe that their children recuperated with nothing more than appropriate feeding.

The nurse in charge was a well-educated, progressive Chagga woman who was understanding, communicated well with other women, and wanted to empower the participants in the program. Indeed, many mothers in the NURU study remembered her fondly twenty years after their discharge and some continued to stay in touch with her. The design and administration of NURU incorporated many of the features that late-twentieth-century expertise could provide. In all aspects, NURU was supposed to be culturally sensitive. It was troubling that Sylvia had withdrawn from the program.

I had thought that many factors would encourage her to stay. She faced a great deal of work at home, with three children in addition to Revocarte still living there. Five of her children had died, and she must have felt some apprehension about her current pregnancy as well as about Revocarte. She had been offered care during the coming birth at the hospital where NURU was housed. Sylvia was not alone, however; as many as 45 percent of women in our study (nineteen of forty-two) withdrew their children early or left the program before being discharged. Despite full funding, sophisticated and sympathetic administrators, and the emphasis on cultural congruency in the program, NURU seemed to drive mothers away in great enough numbers to call for a reexamination of the program.

NURU and Medical Pluralism

Medical staff often complained that home remedies and treatment by the *mganga* (traditional healer) kept children from getting to NURU in a timely fashion. A close look at how parents coped with childhood illness, however, revealed that the day-to-day problems of poor households and the enormous workloads of women were greater impediments. Because kwashiorkor is usually characterized by a slow, insidious onset, its initial symptoms do not present clear criteria for choice of action. Parents react in many ways to the symptoms of malnutrition, from passive acceptance to active intervention.

While acute ailments may be treated at home or by the *mganga*, once parents recognize that an illness is life-threatening, they usually take their child to a clinic. In the 1970s, people tended to avoid hospitals not only because so many patients were said to die there but also because hospitals took specimens for clinical tests, including blood and feces, that otherwise were useful only to sorcerers. People may have felt anxious that the specimens would become available to those with sinister intentions. Taking a gravely ill child to the hospital was, therefore, seen as risky and was done only as a last resort.

One of the first efforts to treat a child within the family compound involves a soup of grasses believed to reduce swelling.[1] If home remedies do not work, the family may take a child to a nearby *mganga*, who has the power to counteract any *mafusa* (witchcraft, evil eye, or sorcery) suspected in the child's illness. A sorcerer can do harm by applying a potion to a child's urine, stool, hair, or clothing and then disposing of it in a tree, in the earth, in a flowing river, or by ingestion. The *mganga* begins by trying to discover the cause of the illness; if he discovers the cause before the child breaks out in sores, he is believed to have a chance of curing the child. Once the sores break out, he has no treatment to offer; the child has become moribund.

In the past, a local Chagga *mganga* was usually physically and emotionally closer to his clientele than staff in hospital settings far removed from home. He gathered information from the neighborhood, assessed sources of family conflict, and attempted to undo the harm that made the child ill. This form of healing sometimes contributed to social tension through accusations of sorcery, and its biomedical efficacy varied. Today, many healers on Mt. Kilimanjaro have come from elsewhere and have little training in local indigenous practices. European and Tanzanian doctors at the Medical Center view all local healers as "quacks" whose main goal is to make money.[2] In spite of their limitations, though, many customary healing practices on Kilimanjaro still give families greater control over the whole process than Sylvia had during her stay at NURU.

The time required for home treatment and the efforts of the *mganga* did not account for delays in getting most children to NURU. There were other barriers that posed greater obstacles. Some parents lived miles from a clinic and needed a whole day to make a visit. At the clinic, people often had to wait for a long time to be seen. There was an increase in clinic attendance during the rainy season, perhaps because of reduced farm work, leaving people more time to deal with medical problems. A clinic visit could require leaving some small children alone at home if their mother could not find a relative or older sibling to care for them. To carry a sickly, unhappy child without much hope of a cure to a clinic required extra energy that many parents did not have.

With her admittance to NURU, Sylvia had overcome obstacles involving a public appearance with her malnourished child. Her rapid withdrawal from the Nutrition Rehabilitation Unit was for reasons related to NURU itself. Revocarte had been brought to the unit after a long period of chronic malnutrition; he may have been treated earlier with home remedies and by an *mganga*, but these actions were not responsible for the long hiatus between the onset of serious illness and his arrival at the unit.

Medicalization of a Social and Economic Problem

In their approach to malnutrition, the staff at NURU was engaged in a process of medicalization, the extension of biomedicine to issues that do not inherently involve disease or other medical pathology. "The science of biomedicine itself . . . contain[s] intrinsic assumptions about society and about the nature of reality that are, at best, disempowering and, at worst, harmful to body and society" (Rhodes 1990:169). Examples of medicalization in the United States include the incorporation of pregnancy, birth, menopause, alcoholism, and spouse abuse as processes to be treated by the medical establishment, through "asserting and establishing the primacy of a medical interpretation" (Freund and McGuire 1991:213).[3] Pregnancy, for example, normally requires no medical attention, although medical intervention in some cases clearly saves lives; nonetheless, prenatal care is viewed as a universal requirement in the United States (Davis-Floyd 1992; Jordan 1978), not simply as a screening process to identify those who might need life-saving medical intervention. Alcoholism is routinely seen as a disease amenable to treatment with drugs and individual therapy, although it certainly involves a complex of factors beyond the physical or emotional state of the individual. The biological aspects of these processes have encouraged medicalization, and "biomedicine's aura of factuality" is "precisely its source of power" in such matters (Rhodes 1990:168).

Colonial regimes have extended the biomedical domain throughout the world, and the growing power of the medical establishment to reach into every aspect of life in Europe and the United States is becoming a reality in less developed countries as well. European and U.S. physicians direct research, medical institutions, and medical school curricula in many less developed countries. The grasp of biomedicine has also broadened through wider definitions of health and primary health care. For example, the World Health Organization defines health as "a state of complete physical, mental, and social well-being," a view useful for its comprehensiveness but misleading if it is taken as an agenda for biomedicine to "treat" people to create that state of well-being (see Brown and Inhorn 1990:189; Rhodes 1990). The redefinition of primary health care to recognize the link of poverty to poor health has put addressing poverty onto the agenda of physicians. Biomedical authorities have in some cases eagerly embraced broadened responsibilities, but it is difficult for them to address broad social and economic problems resulting from structural factors, such as regional economies.

There are serious shortcomings in medicalization. In many countries, doctors are trained to focus on and treat the individual (for a contrast, see Morgan 1990). With a problem such as child malnutrition, the parents are often seen as the problem. Clearly, biomedicine is crucial to saving the lives of severely malnourished children; however, medical treatment is not able to address the underlying causes of their illnesses. "Medicine may function to conceal the social origins of sickness and to suppress the possibility of protest" (Rhodes 1990:167). Medical programs to prevent illness often ignore larger structural social, economic, and political problems, particularly poverty. In becoming dependent on medical expertise, people tend to cede their autonomy.

NURU tended to blame mothers for child malnutrition, as did many people in the regional government and others with responsibility for health issues. Parents' behavior, particularly that of mothers, was seen as lacking; their relationships to their children were seen as a pathology in need of fixing. Similarly, local customs were also viewed as problematic.

Medical staff viewed the *mganga* as a major reason for parents' delays in bringing their children to clinics. In addition, staff members said that the unpresentable clothes of extremely poor people discouraged them from using clinics, because local communities expect people to dress well in public, unless working in the fields. The parents of a child obviously suffering from kwashiorkor already faced shame and stigma, and many people not wishing to make their failure even more public may have kept gravely malnourished children out of sight at home. We do not have observations to show whether these pressures actually kept people from resorting to biomedicine, but it is clear that the medical staff saw them as barriers. The staff thus blamed local people and customs for NURU's lack of success.

Doctors carried out their work with dedication, and they saved many lives. At the height of the famine in 1974, doctors and nurses were reduced to tears over the number of malnourished children they could not save, but they did not seem to see that the issue of prevention was too complex to be solved by clinics modeled on NURU. They did not see their own views of local customs and ways of life as part of the problem. The focus on mothers as uninformed individuals remained.

The Development of Child Health Clinics

The Kilimanjaro people have an advantage over other rural Tanzanians in access to health services, even though they are still underserved.[4] In the 1960s, many new child health clinics opened on the mountain. The Kilimanjaro District Council supported twenty-one prenatal clinics, child health clinics, and health centers. The child health clinics run by the District Council and Catholic missions received medical supplies and food irregularly, however, and they were out of easy reach of many farm households.

With the opening of the Kilimanjaro Christian Medical Center in 1967, plans were developed to refer all new cases of malnourished children there for short-term treatment.[5] The rate of severe malnutrition on Mt. Kilimanjaro prompted the physician in charge of the Department of Pediatrics at the Medical Center to plan a rehabilitation unit. He had previously served at Mulago Hospital in Kampala, Uganda, and had participated in the nutrition education program there.

In 1970, the Department of Pediatrics and the Department of Community Health (in which I was involved as a consultant) planned a thorough investigation of knowledge, attitudes, and practice in health and nutrition on Kilimanjaro. The information was to guide the development of health education in the area (Lindner 1972:1). The Lutheran minister in charge of hospital religious services helped to secure a U.S. sponsor to fund our research, a network of mobile health clinics,[6] and the rehabilitation unit (NURU) to open in 1972.[7] This three-part package relied on the assumption that malnutrition could be eradicated through education. Our study was to test the assumption, while the mobile clinics were to target the malnourished for treatment and their mothers for intensive education at NURU. After returning home, women would be able to prevent malnutrition in their own families. They were also to help prevent malnutrition by providing general health education to the community.

All of the maternal and child health clinics, whether run by the local government, the Catholic missions, or the hospital mobile units, had similar routines. Staff weighed children and gave them medical examinations, vaccinations, and medicine. They gave mothers food supplements for the children and instructions on nutrition and health care.

The stationary clinics provided an additional array of preventive measures. They gave agricultural advice through demonstration gardens and instruction about local health problems. The staff were also to make home visits and become involved in helping families cope with the political and economic problems facing them. Funding, however, tended to be sporadic, and preventive measures took a backseat to programs that delivered medical treatment and food.

Centralization of health care and increased dependency on outside donors developed at the Medical Center, despite government policies to discourage these tendencies and to promote prevention. Mawenzi Regional Hospital had originally been charged with spearheading preventive health care, but the heavily funded Medical Center and staff were able to create a more effective service, which the Ministry of Health was reluctant to restrict.

Research and Evaluation

The research planned by the Medical Center's Departments of Pediatrics and Community Health aimed to provide baseline data for program evaluation as well as for other studies (Baldin et al. 1972). The staff wanted to examine the underlying assumptions of the programs; however, the results of the baseline research were not tabulated until a year and a half after the interviews with mothers. By this time, the mobile clinic was already in service, and NURU had been constructed. Unfortunately, the quantitative analysis showed that nutrition education did not significantly reduce childhood malnutrition. In fact, in comparing areas on Kilimanjaro with high exposure to health education to those with low exposure, we concluded:

> So, with better health facilities, with more knowledge about health and with better education, they still do not succeed in overcoming malnutrition and child mortality. One wonders whether the answer to these problems lies in health education at all. (Lindner 1972:58)

In 1972, two hundred children were admitted to the rehabilitation unit at NURU, only about one tenth of the two thousand children with severe malnutrition annually on Kilimanjaro at that time. (The population of children under the age of five years was about forty thousand.) A severe malnutrition rate of 5 percent implied that a much larger pool of children had mild malnutrition, which could become life-threatening with a common health problem such as diarrhea or a cold.

Even though NURU was not filled to capacity, the staff began to feel overwhelmed. No one had anticipated the level the food crisis would reach by 1974, and the staff knew that they were treating only small numbers of

the children who were dying, only two hundred of the thousands of malnourished children.

In the eyes of NURU staff members, the small numbers would not have
been a problem as long as mothers accepted nutrition education and child
care instruction, disseminated NURU's teachings in their communities, and
kept their children well-nourished after discharge. On each of these points,
however, the staff was worried and called for an evaluation of the program.

Women's Views of NURU

To assist in evaluating NURU, I gathered material through participant
observation at the nutrition unit and in the community. Although staff
members lacked confidence in some of the unit's programs and mothers
were obviously upset by them on a daily basis, it was not obvious how to
correct the initial design. Women varied in their views of programs at
NURU. Some felt grateful to have time away from heavy workloads and
family demands at home. They were relieved to observe their children's
gradual and sometimes dramatic return to health, and at least they had
enough food to eat. Some women made friends with the other women in
residence and felt comfortable with the nursing staff, especially the Chagga
nurse in charge, who had a warm and wise disposition and was good at psychological counseling. She was perceptive about the nature of the women's
problems and actively solicited their ideas. In the seventeen years of
NURU's operation, she became a critical observer of her own society and
biomedical institutions and worked at devising other ways to assist impoverished women to provide adequately for themselves and their children.

Not all relationships between the mothers and staff were harmonious,
however.

Sylvia at NURU

∼ I was in Moshi town and decided to visit Sylvia, who had been at
NURU for about ten days.

Sylvia was alone outside the dormitory with Revocarte sitting on the
ground by her side. He was tinkering with some donated toys and appeared
a bit better.

"How are things going for you, *Mama* Sylvia?" I asked as she rose to
greet me. She seemed pleased that I had come.

"Oh, okay, I guess. Revocarte is better. He's been eating some." She
started to fidget with some clothes she was sorting on her lap, and to put

her at ease, I decided to ask her what it was like to live at NURU. A string of complaints followed.

"Most of the mothers are in the gardens now. I stay here and help watch the children. But I've been sick. They gave me *dawa* [medicine] to prevent malaria, but I got it anyway. We don't have so much malaria at home."

She then blurted out that she was being forced to work.

"*Mungu Wangu* [my God]! Doing what?" I asked. "You're not supposed to be working."

"*Mama* Sylvia's been excluded from agricultural duties," said a nurse who was listening.

"That's true but you have me washing the floors!" She looked pleadingly at me and began weeping. "I refuse to wash the floors. *Mama* Maria, I don't have any cement floors to wash at home. This work is killing me."

"*Dada* [Sister, as the nurses were called], why is Sylvia being put through all this?" I asked.

"Because everyone must contribute. This isn't a vacation. Besides, she'd be resented by the other women."

Participation seemed a sensible goal of the program and well within the orientation of Tanzania's goal of *kujitegemea* (self-reliance), I thought, but couldn't a woman in her ninth month of pregnancy be one exception? ⌒

The mother and child were to stay at NURU until the child was considered cured and the staff decided the mother had acquired the correct "knowledge and attitudes" to take care of her child. Many women left the unit beforehand, however, to avoid neglecting their children and other responsibilities at home and to stop doing the work required by NURU, which they experienced as pointless and demeaning.

According to a nurse who formerly worked at NURU, when women returned home, they often found their other children in worse health than before. When staff members assumed that relatives would care for the other children, they did not realize that poor women often lack not just cash but social resources as well. In fact, lack of assistance with child care often had helped to create their children's malnutrition in the first place.

At NURU, the women were required to tend the gardens; however, each woman stayed for only three or four weeks and could not consume any of the crops that she had tended. From the women's point of view, the reward for working in the fields went only to the harvesters. Although the women were supposed to improve their farming techniques, work on the demonstration farm only stirred most of them to anxieties over their own gardens at home. Other required work was unfamiliar or culturally inappropriate. Sylvia, for example, was required to scrub cement floors, something she had never done in her life.

Women at NURU experienced additional indignities. Tours of the unit by Europeans and wealthy Tanzanians embarrassed resident mothers. The tours frequently involved the public exposure of personal information about a woman, often in front of other residents. Also, the nurses regularly chastised the residents openly in front of visitors.[8] This behavior was congruent with hierarchical relationships in Chagga society, and it was consistent with the nurses' training. The women, however, could not hide the painful loss of face experienced in these encounters.

The wives of European doctors held weekly sewing classes, but they may have imparted a condescending air as well-dressed, white, successful women, making the failures of the women at NURU more apparent. While the women of Kilimanjaro readily seek to improve their sewing, cooking, child care, and reading, the unit was imposing this education on mothers who felt like captives and were branded as failures; it was tolerated at best, accepted ambivalently, or rejected outright as an insult.

Some residents of NURU disliked the enthusiastic socialist dogmatism of the staff regarding the government's campaigns for self-reliance and cooperation. Staff sometimes referred to NURU as an *ujamaa* village—a concept many women rejected vehemently. One woman told a neighbor that she was so frustrated that she would never return to NURU again. "Let the NURU people come and take me to *ujamaa* villages if they want. To hell with all their teachings!"

Although the nurses were well-intentioned and increasingly capable under the supervision of the nurse in charge, they were discouraged by what they saw as the women's lack of compliance. Large numbers of children returned, again malnourished, making many staff members exasperated and angry at the mothers themselves. On the other hand, the mothers often became defensive and reacted against their treatment by expressing antagonism toward health care workers.

The staff criticized some women for "absconding"—taking their children and leaving the program before they were discharged. The staff had originally projected that the average length of stay would be twenty-one days. Of the forty-two women in the NURU study, the average length of stay was twenty-four days. Three were said to have "absconded" even though their stays were twenty-one, forty-one, and forty-three days; sixteen other women remained less than twenty-one days but were not charged with that offense. They may have adopted compliant attitudes that gave them more success in obtaining early discharges. In using the term "abscond," the staff gave some recognition to their power struggle with some mothers over issues of autonomy, medical authority, and responsible parenthood.

Mothers' Refusal to Be Community Educators

After being discharged from NURU, women were expected to return home and become community educators. They were expected to instruct other women in the lessons they had learned, especially child nutrition. It became apparent, however, that this goal contradicted one of NURU's central principles, cultural sensitivity.

I became acutely aware of this problem through visits with Eliminata Lyimo, who was the mother of a malnourished girl, Amalia. One day, I went to visit her at home to finish going through the nutrition questions for the NURU study. I knew I was walking into a difficult situation. Eliminata had married into a crowded lineage compound occupied by the two wives of her father-in-law. I had heard that Eliminata had once abandoned her daughter after an argument with her husband that had led her to leave the compound for a while. (It would have been a grave breach of custom for a woman to take her children away with her unless she had her husband's permission.) I had found Eliminata to be somewhat reserved on my other visits, at least when we were in earshot of others.

Eliminata, Mother of Amalia

⌒ As I began to talk with Eliminata, she stood about seven yards away from me. No one offered me a seat, and a crowd began to gather, transforming the occasion into a public spectacle, much to my disappointment. Both of Eliminata's mothers-in-law were in the crowd. At the time, I felt I had to complete the interview, and there was no way to change the awkward situation.

"As you know, *Mama* Eliminata, the doctors at NURU are trying to understand the problems facing families these days. They want to know what foods mothers consider to be good and how much they cost. Could you tell me about everything Amalia ate yesterday, starting with breakfast?"

"*Ndizi tu* [bananas only]!"

"How about lunch?"

"*Ndizi tu!*" She glanced aside to see if others were watching.

"Well, then, what did she have for dinner?"

"*Ndizi tu!*"

"Really?"

Conversation in the crowd grew loud, and a few had started to snicker.

"Then tell me what you consider to be good food for little children."

"*Ndizi tu!*" she responded again as she struggled to keep from laughing. Looking about, she saw one mother-in-law put her hand over her mouth to restrain her laughter.

The other asserted, "Bananas are our food! All Chagga people grow strong on bananas!" ⁓

Eliminata's defiance was not based on lack of knowledge. It was, instead, an assertion of the local view that bananas are good food. For families without money to purchase milk, meat, and eggs, bananas were thought to be able to at least sustain the life of a child.

The compound's traditional styles in housing and clothes and its polygynous structure led me to think that its residents were relatively reluctant to adopt ideas from outsiders. Eliminata had already been daring or desperate enough to leave her husband for a while, but then her daughter, Amalia, had become severely malnourished. Her husband's family blamed her. She had taken Amalia to NURU, where she would have encountered many ideas contrary to the customs in her husband's family compound. Following their customs was particularly important for Eliminata in her position as a daughter-in-law; any display of knowledge from the unit, including new cooking recipes, new ways of handling an infant, new methods of birth control, and even a new skill such as sewing, might have been cause for suspicion and ostracism.

I later realized that answering my questions and repeating the NURU lessons in the presence of her mothers-in-law would have defied their authority. By repeating the lessons, Eliminata could have chanced loss of support in the compound to which she had returned to regain her position as daughter-in-law and mother to her children.

Through her defiance, Eliminata dramatized her allegiance to her mothers-in-law and their customary ways of raising children. Her responses to my questions revealed her resentment of NURU and probably of my study as well. Her experience at the unit could not, in her circumstances, make her an authority on proper nutrition and child care. Most women lost credibility as mothers because of a stay at NURU. Their children's malnutrition was a major stigma.

All of the women who had been at NURU expressed hesitancy to teach the nutrition and childcare lessons to other women. "*Sistahili kufanya hiuyo* [it would not be my place to do so]" was the most common response. NURU was to prepare the women in a nonformal method of sharing information, but women do not ordinarily teach one another. They only teach their children. The women would have had to assume authority as mothers when their own children's health testified otherwise.

Even women from somewhat better-off families, who were not as highly stigmatized by chronic misfortune as others, found it best to keep quiet about a malnourished child.

Marietta and the Role of Community Educator, 1973

⌒ During a visit to NURU's mobile clinic, I met Marietta. She was strikingly beautiful according to local standards—tall, with a dignified bearing and a light complexion. She had six years of education, and it seemed to me that she might be an ideal grassroots community educator.

I was surprised to hear later that one of her children had been in NURU. She was living at her own parents' compound, where her mother cared for the two children while Marietta worked. The compound was picturesque and well-kept, and it showed signs of affluence.

Marietta proved to be bright, motivated, and appreciative of her stay at NURU. She was the first woman I met who had been at the unit and took the initiative to direct my attention to the problems of other women. She led me to Richard and Elizabethi Moshi's house. In Elizabethi's presence, however, she remained relatively quiet, even though Elizabethi shrugged in response to most of my questions. Had Marietta been a woman with better standing, she probably would have prompted Elizabethi. ⌒

I continued to reflect on Marietta's situation long afterward. She had failed to secure a legitimate marriage, and both of her children had severe kwashiorkor. A certificate for "graduating" from NURU was not a prize but a cause of shame for her failure. To ask those who had been through the training to teach other women about nutrition would be somewhat like asking criminals to teach civics.

Some women sought admittance to NURU despite the risk of embarrassment and criticism. In part, their choice was supported by Chagga values favoring *maendeleo*, or technological progress. The unit was viewed as part of high-technology approaches to illness, which were already held in high esteem partly because of the success of antibiotics in the cure of many acute illnesses.

Additionally, even self-respecting people such as Marietta may be forced by stressful conditions to trade loss of face for a chance to improve their condition. The weight of stigma varies among families and individuals. During my visits to families fifteen and twenty years later, most people expressed gratitude for their experience at NURU. (Eliminata was a singular exception.) I wondered, however, whether this expression came mostly out of politeness and hospitality to me as a long-lost visitor from far away. Families of children who had been "rehabilitated" sometimes conveyed the notion that a well-intentioned clinician had "saved" them from their own ill-chosen ways. Eliminata and her kin, however, did not find solace in assuming such a stance and still seemed indignant about the intrusion into their privacy.

The Long-Term Impact of Nutrition Rehabilitation on Children's Nutritional Status

The health education lessons at NURU emphasized that each former patient was to be checked monthly at the mobile clinic. Each woman was to leave the unit with a well-baby card to be used by clinic staff to chart her child's development and immunizations. Only eleven of the forty-two mothers, however, brought their children to the mobile clinics for checkups. The NURU staff had not taken account of the obstacles women faced in attending the mobile clinics.

The clearest indication to the staff that health education lessons were not preventing further malnutrition was the large number of children readmitted to the program. Of the forty-two families with malnourished children in the NURU study, eight had one or more children readmitted at least once. Among other children who were not readmitted, the mobile team found some who were moderately malnourished, but they were sent home for lack of space in the hospital; only severely ill children were readmitted. Of the forty-nine children who had been in NURU, thirty were in poor health at checkups following their discharge, according to assessment by my research team.

Members of the research team asked women who had been residents of the unit what food they considered nutritious for children and what food the child had eaten the day before. Of the twenty-nine women whose responses were noted, twenty-four mentioned food recommended by NURU and reported that their child had a nutritious diet. The women, however, may have given those responses out of respect and hospitality toward the visiting researchers; what they actually fed their children may have been different.

There was no way to determine whether women's knowledge of nutrition had actually improved because their nutrition knowledge was not assessed when they first entered the program. Their knowledge, whether improved or not, had not led to improved health of their children. The

researchers agreed that the women generally did understand the importance of a nutritious diet but could not afford to buy enough of even the
least expensive protein food, beans.

Moreover, lack of community support, familial discord, neighborhood
conflict, limited land, and unstable economic resources are problems that
cannot be altered through nutrition education and farming lessons. If anything, the assumption that educating poor mothers can solve the problem
of malnutrition merely adds to the frustrations and burdens of those who
face chronic crisis.

Transitions at NURU

Until its closing in 1992, NURU sustained allegiance to its founding principles. Local participation, cooperation, and cultural sensitivity increased
over the span of the unit's existence, and the unit remained committed to
curing and preventing malnutrition. Evaluation of the effectiveness of the
programs continued, and NURU also trained health professionals in
issues of malnutrition at the Medical Center. Other major components of
its programs also continued. For example, instead of simply curing malnutrition and sending children home, the program demonstrated that
the children could be healed with adequate food rather than by medica-
tion.

Throughout its existence, NURU continued to look upon mothers as the
primary caretakers of children. Planners ignored other people who took
care of their children, including grandmothers and older siblings, and others responsible for their welfare, such as fathers and other male relatives.
The programs changed enormously, however, over its twenty years. The
staff learned of the association of shame with kwashiorkor and stopped
awarding women certificates for "graduating" from the unit. They also
changed the educational emphasis from nutrition and child care to farming
techniques and income generation.

Well-designed new programs gave women resources—cows, seeds,
seedlings, chickens, and rabbits—so that they could produce nutritious
food (Figure 21). Although they helped many people at difficult points in
their lives, the programs did not succeed in extending food security to poor
families in general.

NURU offered financial support for a woodworking cooperative of
fathers and the hospital carpenter to train them. Staff members came to
understand that unemployment of fathers was one of the key factors in
child malnutrition. NURU also persuaded the hospital to lend land, with-

Figure 21   *NURU programs and their problems*

Program		Problems
Provision of cows to provide free calves and milk to the poor and milk at a reasonable price to others	→	Maintaining cows too expensive for poor people; local government took ownership but failed to care properly for the cows; some died and others were given to better-off people who were to sell milk at a reasonable price
Provide seeds for home vegetable gardens	→	Neighbors' chickens ate the seedlings
Communal nursery for poor women to grow vegetable seedlings to plant at home	→	Women responsible for watering had other, more pressing work responsibilities; other people stole seedlings
Provision of a hen and rooster to poor women for egg and chick production	→	Chickens had to be penned in to keep them out of neighbors' gardens; poor families could not afford feed and had no table scraps to give them
Provision of rabbits to schools, new young to be distributed to poor, who were to distribute new young to other poor households	→	Rabbits stolen and slaughtered, though some people continue with the program

out charging rent, to landless or land-short families for farming. Even though it could address the needs of only a few families, the lending of farmland symbolized a better understanding of the causes of kwashiorkor. Many of the unit's new programs assumed that poor people would cooperate efficiently with one another, even with nonrelatives, and that other people would not exploit new resources flowing into the community. The programs failed to take account of the severe limitations imposed on people by stark poverty.

Over the years, NURU made other transitions. The NURU study had found that nutrition programs had to be closer to people's homes to allow easier access of parents to the clinic and to permit staff to make home visits to give support and education in a familiar environment. Mothers would therefore be able to deal with their young children's health without neglecting their responsibilities at home. The unit was closed in 1992 with the idea of addressing malnutrition through community-based income-generation programs.

With the shift away from socialism in Tanzania, the government returned administration of the Medical Center to the Lutheran Church with an agreement of several years of funding divided between the government and the church. The transition is still under way; staff numbers have been reduced, salaries have been kept constant for several years, and no funding is available for new programs. Currently, some of the food production and income-generation programs begun by NURU continue in some Kilimanjaro neighborhoods. In most areas, though, they have vanished. Children with severe malnutrition who are brought to the Medical Center are hospitalized with a diagnosis of "diarrhea"; one ward is full of malnourished children. Some of the staff formerly at NURU plan to work on community-based efforts to deal with poverty; however, they must first obtain funding. In 1993, NURU's buildings were being used as storage space for hospital supplies.

In Search of Dignity

Throughout this volume, we have shown how outside institutions played varying roles in social and economic change on Mt. Kilimanjaro. Colonial powers ushered in a cash economy and coffee farming. Christian churches attacked most customary Chagga religious ideas involving ancestors and weakened lineage ties. Catholicism undermined traditional birth control and contributed to a decrease in intervals between births. The resulting population increase gave rise to landlessness and a surplus of very poor laborers for the production of cash crops. Years later, Kilimanjaro's social life and economy were further constrained by a cash-poor socialist government that jailed farmers for planting food crops in place of their coffee trees.

Together, colonialism, capitalism, socialism, and Christianity undermined the authority of the lineage and unraveled Chagga safety nets for the poor. While promoting the coffee trade and the hegemonic notion of *maendeleo*, these institutions unintentionally attached shame to poverty and isolated poor people from social and economic resources.

Most of the Kilimanjaro farmers with malnourished children were not passive in the face of these changes. Curse and sorcery, as "weapons of the weak" (Scott 1990), may have defied customary, Christian, and secular political authority even while coercing some to fulfill customary obligations to kin. These actions expressed the frustrations people felt in times of adversity, whether or not they were effective against those who were more powerful.

Poorer women's options were more constrained than those of their better-off female kin and neighbors by the changes brought by the cash economy and by the reinforcement of female subordination by all of Kilimanjaro's institutions. The risks women took in distilling alcholic beverages and other illegal activities may be considered a response to growing economic constraints and dwindling rights. Such work also helped secure cash for the needs of their children.

The illegal informal market of the late 1970s and early to mid-1980s developed, in part, as a protest against the price controls set by the socialist government. On a smaller scale, the parents of malnourished children also protested by resisting NURU programs, which were designed to be compatible with the socialist ideals of the 1970s. As shown by several stories in this book, families resisted the research process and my attempts to organize a men's woodworking cooperative partly because of paternalistic decision-making processes of NURU planners, staff, and reserchers, including me.

In the 1970s, nutrition rehabilitation was a concept new to East Africa. NURU promised a holistic, innovative solution that would take indigenous ideas into account and integrate them with biomedical approaches to decrease rates of child malnutrition. The planning staff knew that many families with malnourished children were poor. They knew that most families still had access to some food, such as plantains from their banana groves; the staff assumed that poor planning, ignorance, alcoholism, and family breakdown were the main reasons for child malnutrition. Of all these obstacles, the unit's staff tended to focus on poor planning and ignorance because they seemed the most manageable. The assumption that education was the key to change required that NURU combine it with medical treatment. The emphasis on education resulted in a systematic attack on customary Chagga notions and the program often unwittingly increased the already heavy burden of shame borne by members of a sick child's family.

Despite NURU's stated allegiance to the principle of cultural sensitivity, there was an initial failure to recognize the stigma that residence at the unit could bring to mothers. Furthermore, educational programming centered on biomedical ideas about diet and child care. Most of the staff thought of local perspectives on causation, especially ideas about curse and sorcery, as errors in logic, backward holdovers to be eliminated. None of the foreign staff and only some of the local staff appreciated the significance, widespread nature, and broad effects of these ideas in daily life as supporting customary obligations in Chagga society and providing a means for poorer people to assert themselves and gain access to resources.

A significant shortcoming of NURU was its initial patterning after Euroamerican approaches to institutionalized welfare. Like the St. Vincent de Paul Society and Moshi Poor House, the unit provided a Band-Aid solution for families of malnourished children. Better-off people could assume that if their kin really cared about their children, they would take them to the clinic for treatment. The staff explained children's illnesses, families' lack of compliance, and NURU's ineffectiveness as the results of alcoholism, family breakups, "selection for failure" of fathers (Moore 1975) and children, and fathers' failure to find work. These problems were involved, but the unit was not designed to tackle them. Poverty and parents' reactions to it would continue to produce malnourished children, leading to rapid burnout of staff as they became frustrated and angry at the parents of their patients.

While kwashiorkor needs medical attention, the relationships of women to their children do not. Like many aspects of life in the Europe and the United States, however, women's roles as mothers were taken up by NURU and medicalized. Medical staff saw mothers as causing their children's malnutrition out of apathy and ignorance and treated them accordingly.

Views of medical staff, better-off Chagga, and government bureaucrats unwittingly serve to delegitimate impoverished people in the creation of programs designed to assist them. In failing to recognize that impoverished people have limited control over their lives because of large-scale social and economic shifts, these perspectives divert attention from the structural causes of poverty. Medical, commercial, religious, and political organizations generally have added to the shame of child malnutrition on Mt. Kilimanjaro in assuming that impoverished parents are culpable.

NURU, like many other health and development projects, did not include poor people in the planning or decision processes. Its focus on parents, particularly mothers, as the major cause of child malnutrition undercut Chagga women's credibility in the dramas played out in their lineages and neighborhoods. Many women, therefore, deeply resented institutional help in spite of the good intentions of planners and staff.

Like many women, Sylvia Lema rejected the affront to her dignity and challenged the common view that mothers of malnourished children are passive and apathetic. Near time for the birth of her thirteenth child, she left the unit and walked, carrying Revocarte, six hours up the mountain to her home.

In her defiant departure, Sylvia cast scorn on the institutions of biomedicine and government, and with her trek home, she sought to preserve her dignity. Like other parents on Mt. Kilimanjaro, Sylvia knew the vital link between her dignity and the survival of her family.

Endnotes

Preface

1.   The second and third groups would be called "peasants" by many anthro-
     pologists (see Hewitt de Alcantara 1994; see also Tilly 1978).

Chapter 1

1.   Throughout this book, the names of the people of Kilimanjaro are changed
     in respect for their privacy.
2.   In this work, the terms "patrilineage," and "lineage" are used interchange-
     ably, following Moore (1986:17–18) instead of technical anthropological
     usage. Moore allows the context to define the level and size of group being
     discussed as do English publications, British colonial records, and Chagga
     usage of the term for patrilineal kin groups, *ukoo* or *kishari* (ibid.).
         The gender emphasis of this book changes with the focus of each sec-
     tion. In discussing poverty, we focus primarily on experiences of men, and
     our approach to child malnutrition emphasizes those of women. These
     approaches grew out of my field experience and derive from local views of
     gender.
3.   The increase in the responsibilities of women to provide food for them-
     selves and their children is reported throughout Africa and in many other

parts of the world as well (Funk 1991; Gladwin 1991; Linares 1993; Obbo 1976; O'Brien and Gruenbaum 1991; Schoepf and Schoepf 1990; Spring 1990; Swantz 1985; Turshen 1991; see also Coles and Mack 1991 on the interesting case of Hausa women; Cohen 1993; Collier and Yanagisako 1987).

4. See Edgerton 1992 for a critique of the tendency of anthropologists to romanticize the communities they study.

5. These figures are derived from estimates based on my participation in a broad economic survey on Mt. Kilimanjaro. There were many difficulties in getting reliable information on people's incomes in the 1970s, and these estimates should be viewed with skepticism. However, in the study of malnourished children from the nutrition center, we used housing standards as a guide for measuring the levels of income. Chagga place high value on modern housing but not everyone can afford it. Table 9 compares forty-two households whose malnourished children resided in the Nutrition Rehabilitation Unit (NURU) with sixty-nine neighboring households.

6. An important theoretical insight that has influenced our writing comes from Sen (1981). He suggests that to understand food crisis, it is crucial to consider unequal access to food supplies. Most famines occur when food is available but distribution is skewed. While many die from food crisis, others

Table 9   *Housing Standards and Possessions as Indicators of Income Level*

	NURU families		Neighbors	
	No.	%	No.	%
I	1[a]	2	19	28
II	8	19	18	26
III	12	50	30	44
IV	12	29	2	3
	42	100	69	101

Source: Swantz et al. 1975:17, 81

I   Cement block house, glass windows; electricity; well furnished with beds, tables, cupboards, easy chairs, refrigerator; car, motorcycle

II   Cement reinforced mud walls, iron roof, cement floor; 3 beds, 2 couches, 2 cupboards; bicycle, radio.

III   Mud walls, earth floor, iron roof; 2 or fewer handmade beds, 1 cupboard, lantern.

IV   Traditional windowless house of mud walls, grass or banana leaf roof; 1 handmade bed or none, no furnishings.

[a]   Household of a young widow and her two children living in poor circumstances in the compound of deceased husband's better-off parents.

thrive, and some even flourish. Sen uses the term "exchange entitlements," referring to rights to control food supplies or otherwise get access to food. Access to food can vary according to a person's status, age, or gender. It also depends on the system of food production, property rights, inheritance, employment, trade, and state welfare provisions. On Kilimanjaro, for example, coffee pickers earn cash that they can use to buy food, while a coffee producer can set land aside for growing food, or he can sell his product for cash with which to purchase foodstuffs. An older Chagga woman, no longer capable of farm work, is supposed to receive food from kin. Entitlements are not fixed and equal but vary according to a person's position in a wider system of control, exchange, production, and distribution.

When a food crisis occurs, some people are more vulnerable because their entitlements can lose all or part of their value. For example, people who rely on wages from coffee picking may find themselves without work when coffee farmers are short of revenue, or they may find that their wages do not cover subsistence needs if prices are inflated. Coffee farmers become vulnerable when income is insufficient to cover investments for fertilizer, pesticides, and workers' wages. They may have little cash for purchasing food, and on Kilimanjaro, some people go hungry until food crops are ready for harvest. Older and younger dependents (those not actively contributing to household sustenance) become especially vulnerable under these conditions and may lose their entitlement to food. As tensions mount, some children in a family may be at higher risk for malnutrition than their siblings. We attempt to explain how blaming and shaming clear the pathway toward loss of food entitlement.

Chapter 2

1. These languages are known also as Kiswahili and Kichagga.
2. The local dialect of Swahili differs slightly from the standard language, but this volume uses standard Swahili for the sake of clarity.
3. People addressed me in a variety of ways. Usually, less educated persons called me "Maria," which was the more commonly used form of "Mary" on Mt. Kilimanjaro. Those with more exposure to outsiders usually called me "Mary." When I became a mother for the first time, many called me "*Mama* Matthew" to extend customary respect. Occasionally, I was addressed as "Mama Tom" in recognition of my attachment to my husband.
4. Golden provides a careful clinical definition of kwashiorkor and argues persuasively, on the basis of clinical trials with refeeding and physiological studies, that it does not result from protein deficiency (1985).

5.   Numbers of deaths are calculated from Grant (1993:7): 3 million deaths annually from diarrheal disease; 3.5 million from pneumonia; and 880,000 from measles. The "synergistic triad" of malnutrition, diarrhea, and lower respiratory tract infection is estimated to cause 68 percent of deaths annually of children between the ages of two and five years in Mexico (Hull and Rohde 1978; see also Aguirre 1966; Alba 1982; Ehrlich 1983; Martorell et al. 1975; Millard 1985; Millard et al. 1990; Puffer and Serrano 1973, 1975, 1976; Wray and Aguirre 1969).

6.   Franke and Chasin trace the way people have shaped the natural ecology of West Africa, with the effect of facilitating famines (1992; see also Horowitz 1990; Derman 1990; Huss-Ashmore and Katz 1989, 1990). Arnold takes a broad view of famine and relations between more and less developed countries (1988; see also Dirks 1992; Downs et al. 1991; Giddens 1987; Vaughn 1992; Wolf 1982).

      Feierman and Janzen's edited volume provides a panoramic view of the relationships of history, social organization, culture, and economy to the spread of disease (1992), Iliffe deals with poverty in various African regions (1987), Comaroff takes up power and resistance (1985), and Crandon-Malamud deals with power in the context of medical pluralism (1991; see also Janzen 1978).

      Cassidy takes a critical approach to views of malnutrition and efforts to reduce rates of toddler malnutrition (1982, 1987). See also Edgerton 1992; Korbin 1981; LeVine and LeVine 1981; Scheper-Hughes 1984, 1992; and Scrimshaw 1978 on anthropological approaches to issues of child abuse and neglect. On the economic and social crisis faced by the Ik and the collapse of their society under famine, see Turnbull 1972; on a contrasting situation in an intact society in the 1930s and 1940s, see Richards 1939; on foodways, see Ritenbaugh 1978.

7.   At the time of the study reported for 1967 in Table 1, the rate of infant mortality for Kilimanjaro was 95 deaths per 1,000 live births, lower than other districts and considerably lower than mainland Tanzania a whole, with a rate of 143 per 1,000 (Kreysler 1973:22). Infant health was relatively good, and health problems grew after the first year of life, apparently with weaning, indirectly implicating malnutrition.

Chapter 3

1.   Dundas deals at length with chiefly duties (1924:278). The position of chief was hereditary (Moore 1986).

2.   We draw this portrayal and other information about Chagga customs in the early twentieth century largely from the work of Gutmann, a German

missionary ethnographer who lived on Kilimanjaro from 1902 to 1920 (Moore 1986:38). He tended to portray the Chagga as living in harmony, an idealized view reflecting his respect for the precolonial society. It is evident, however, that there were greater differences among people and they were more likely to interpret and negotiate rules than shown in his work. Further discussion of variation in Chagga behavior relative to customary ideals can be found in Moore 1986.

3.   On the development of highly centralized state governments with a material basis in water control in China and Mexico, see Krader 1975; Palerm 1990; Sanders and Price 1968; Steward 1955; Wittfogel 1957; Wolf and Palerm 1955. Lacking region-wide annual floods, Kilimanjaro did not have the same basis for the development of a state. (On relations between economy and society, see Weber 1978.)

4.   Chagga ancestors probably arrived on Mt. Kilimanjaro as part of successive waves of migration by Bantu farmers. Maasai herders, raiding, and trading brought other cultural, political, and economic forces to bear on the Chagga. Chagga organization into patrilineages (also termed "clans"; see Moore 1986) may have come from the Bantu, along with political and religious traditions involving ancestor worship. Chagga and Maasai both have age-grade systems. The Maasai reached ascendancy in the region in the mid-nineteenth century but lost power when drought and disease decimated their herds. According to Stahl, there were about one hundred Chagga chiefdoms at the beginning of the nineteenth century and about fifty at the end (1964; see also Johnston 1886).

5.   Traditionally, polygyny was allowed, but only the wealthy could afford more than one wife. Marriage requires payments to the bride's family, and few can afford them for more than one marriage. Although polygyny is still the ideal form of marriage (despite the predominance of Christianity), only 5 percent of the population was estimated to be in polygamous marriages in the postcolonial period (Moore 1986). Women of lower social standing are taken as second wives, and their children, accordingly, have less favored positions. Compared with those of first wives, children of second wives generally inherit less property and land and will be the first to suffer if the father's resources are limited, except when affective paternal ties override this custom.

Upon marriage, the residence of the couple varies between patrilocal and neolocal residence. The eldest and youngest sons stay with their wives in their fathers' compounds (patrilocal residence), and other sons move with their wives into separate households (neolocal residence; see also Johnston 1946).

6.   According to Iliffe (1979), captives had specific rights, including the right to buy their freedom. According to Moore (1986:100), children working in

the chief's household as servants were considered slaves by Gutmann (1926; see also Stahl 1964), and the German administration outlawed this form of servitude for boys but not girls.

7. Handbook of German East Africa 1920:15–22.

8. Some would argue that because the patrilineage persists and maintains some principles of redistribution and corporate ownership of land, Chagga society should be characterized as having only incipient class formation. Kerner (1988) found, however, that the annual income of one wealthy Chagga man in the 1980s was about two hundred times greater than the average (see also Moore 1986 on landholding differences). To some, differences in wealth of this magnitude and differences in land ownership and relations to the international coffee market suggest that class differences already exist. We agree that the case is ambiguous and refer to the presence of classes in the late twentieth century to recognize extreme differences in access to resources that are systematic effects of Chagga social relations.

9. Iliffe notes the size of landholdings (1979:460–463) and the course of the cooperative movement on Mt. Kilimanjaro (1979:279–280). Accumulation of land by a few and intensification of labor were also accompanied by population increase, which led to fragmentation of holdings and a clear division between the landed and landless.

Raikes (1988) details a pattern of loss of entitlements throughout Africa, which has specific application to Kilimanjaro. He argues that the incidence of child malnutrition is higher in Africa's mountainous areas, which have been favored in the production of cash crops, because such production was less risky in these fertile and well-watered areas. Investments in improved seeds, fertilizers, chemicals, and machinery "hastened the accumulation of land and other resources by rich peasants, businessmen and the politically favored" (Raikes 1988:72). Raikes describes the social costs:

> Prior to the advance of commodity production, food shortage provides the opportunity for leaders to legitimize their control and accumulate sociopolitical obligations when people lack the cash to pay. Hoarding and speculation replace redistribution as characteristic responses of the wealthy to periods of shortage. (ibid.)

The position of Raikes is supported by Kavishe, the managing director of the Tanzania Food and Nutrition Center in 1993 (see NCC/CSPD 1993:17, but also see Ljungquist 1993:233). Surveys show that in areas where the food crop is also the cash crop (e.g., maize), malnutrition rates tend to be higher. Rates tend to be lower, however, in areas with both a cash crop and a staple food crop, such as the coffee-banana crop system in Kilimanjaro. Kavishe qualifies this finding as follows:

> It should be stressed that cash crops have a definite role to play in improving food security provided a balanced approach is taken. This is because cash crops like coffee or tea have a value per hectare several times higher than that of basic staples like maize and can therefore generate higher incomes, especially where land is scarce as it has been noted for Kilimanjaro and Kagera. Thus cash crops can benefit food security in Tanzania if policies which maximize the benefit of cash crops to the poor and food insecure are pursued by continued support to the small farmer; reinvestment of agricultural profits to the rural areas; avoiding profit diversion to luxury consumption; maximizing production linkages and creating more efficient food systems. In order to avoid the price insecurity of few cash crops the present stress on commodity diversification need[s] to continue. (Kavishe 1993:86)

The number of Chagga coffee producers increased from 3,300 in 1923 to 65,000 in 1968, a twenty fold increase that outstripped the rate of population growth, which also was rapid (approximately 100,000 people in 1900 increased to 440,239 in 1967 (Gutmann 1926; Moore 1986).

Since the 1920s, maize and coffee production continued to expand in the north of Tanganyika, where soil conservation was becoming an increasingly important concern (Fuggles-Couchman 1964:19).

10. The physiology of lactation contraception is not entirely understood; physical stimulation of the breast increases the rate of secretion of the hormone prolactin, which has both lactogenic and anovulatory effects (Cowie 1972; Harrell 1981; Jelliffe and Jelliffe 1978; Short 1976).

Data from India show 8.9 pregnancies per 100 woman-years in noncontracepting women who are breastfeeding and have not resumed menstruation; oral contraceptive data from the United States show 4 to 10 pregnancies per 100 woman-years (Simpson-Hebert and Huffman 1981; see also Hatcher et al. 1976; Sehgal and Singh 1966). Jelliffe and Jelliffe (1978) find that the interval from birth to the succeeding conception in nine societies ranges from 11.7 to 53.0 months, with most values in the range from 20 to 30 months. In nonlactating women in the same societies, the interval is only 3.0 to 16.9 months. Women in some societies are not aware of the strength of lactation contraception even when their behavior is prolonging it (Millard and Graham 1985).

11. Dramatic increase in population on Mt. Kilimanjaro is a phenomenon of the last century, a culmination of changes over the last 2,000 years of human habitation in the region (Smidt 1989). According to Maro's estimates, the rate of population growth over the period of 1921 to 1932 was 1.9 percent annually; between 1948 and 1967, it was nearly 2.9 percent

annually (Maro 1974). Gamassa found a decrease in the annual growth rate between 1967 and 1988 that he attributes to growing rates of outmigration. He estimates a mean annual rate of increase between 1978 and 1988 of 2.1 percent, with rapid migration within the region from rural areas to the town of Moshi (Gamassa 1991).

Von Clemm (1964:100) calculated population densities on the basis of the remaining land available for settlement; rural population density is 3,690 people per square mile. It is especially noteworthy considering the dispersed homesteads and lack of towns or households clustered into villages on the mountain.

12. Gamassa 1991; Maro 1974.

Chapter 4

1. The road to the margins was most likely paved during the precolonial era. Differences in cattle wealth and political power in the earlier stratified society strongly suggest that competition existed and certain people failed. Indeed, there were complex rituals for the total ostracism of a lineage member, who would be forced to seek his or her fortunes elsewhere. Simply being born a middle son or being a woman without a husband would ensure a more difficult life. This list has conveniently expanded in recent times of scarce resources to include many more people who happened to have gotten a bad start in life. Children of less-educated, poorer farmers have far fewer chances to gain access to secondary school, ensuring the beginnings of a cycle of poverty. Better-off kin rationalize loss of their poorer relatives' entitlements by shaming them or referring them to newer institutions designed to help.

2. The Lucere area was once *shamba* territory, which has been converted to *kihamba* land. Lower-slope *kihambas* are more open to outsider settlement. That 20 percent of heads of household in Lucere were non-Chagga was a pattern more characteristic of the lower belt of Kilimanjaro than of the middle belt, which included the areas of cultivation highest on the mountain.

   Absorption of outsiders is a typical pattern throughout Chagga history. "Strangers, settling locally, who were not qualified as members [of a lineage] on the basis of birth could be attached to local units as individuals in a kind of auxiliary status and/or could found new patrilineages" (Moore 1986:54).

3. I had two years of nursing at Georgetown University and enjoyed the opportunity to exercise my nursing skills during my stay. Seeing that many visited me for minor infections, a Canadian nurse left me with all of her clinic's contents when her school program closed.

4. There was a movement in the government to keep out influences from Europe and the United States regarded as evil, and laws were passed against specific clothing styles, including miniskirts, bell-bottom slacks, and tight pants. The legislation was inspired in reaction to colonial attacks on African cultures and was supported by Christian and Muslim officials. Union with Zanzibar was relatively recent, and for some time, women have been required to wear less-revealing clothing there than on the mainland.

5. Fleuret shows a similar pattern of marginalization of lowland or plains settlers in her research on a related group, the Taita of southeastern Kenya. She says:

> Continued population growth, in addition to reducing opportunities to control land in a variety of ecological zones, has forced some Taita farmers to become permanent squatters on the semiarid plains surrounding the hills, rather than temporary visitors exploiting the bush for seasonal extensive cultivation, herding, hunting, or collecting such products as honey, gum arabic, and fuel. Permanent plains dwellers also have a tendency to be socially marginal. Often they have opted for plains settlement because of involvement in witchcraft cases as victim or witch, abandonment of a spouse, excessive drinking, loss of pawned land or other resources, pregnancy outside of marriage, or extensive investment in livestock. A number of plains dwellers are non-Taita who have been forced by economic or other circumstances into permanent migration. A few are retired long-term sisal estate workers who no longer possess land ownership or use rights in the hills. Since permanent plains residence is a recent development (post-1960), and the original homes of these people so diverse, there has been little opportunity for the formation of ties of consanguinity and affinity in the area which would bind the inhabitants into networks of cooperation and exchange. (Fleurent 1989:224–25).

6. As a once powerful force in East Africa who had withstood colonial policies, Maasai were respected and feared by their neighbors in the 1970s. With the inroads of industrialization and the decimation of their herds during the drought, however, Maasai society became vulnerable. Many of their neighbors began to hold them in contempt. People were also offended by the fascination of tourists with the "noble savages" and the tendency of guidebooks to group the Maasai with wildlife. Most Maasai who assimilated into more "modern" ways of life were not treated with contempt. In fact, a Tanzanian vice president was Maasai, and his death while in office was widely mourned.

7. There were many tensions among the three African states that made up the East African Community. At independence, Kenya, Uganda, and Tanzania formed an economic union to offset much of the dependency on the West for trade. Most of the large infrastructural developments such as hospitals, universities, and communications and transportation systems were developed jointly. Many factors, however, led to the collapse of this system, including a military coup by General Idi Amin. He claimed some of Tanzania's territory for Uganda and made regular threats followed by bombing. Some of the bombing threats were made toward the Kilimanjaro region, where the country's police academy and other important seats of government were stationed. Occasionally, air raid sirens sent all of us in our *shamba* running for cover. Finally, Tanzania declared war on Uganda and overthrew Idi Amin. The cost of this war was an important factor in Tanzania's economic troubles.

8. As complex emotions, shame and guilt have definitions that vary considerably in the literature (Jacoby 1994; Kaufman 1980; Piers and Singer 1953; Schneider 1977; see also Zoja 1995).

9. Some stigmas are positive and welcomed, such as a medal of honor or beauty, whereas other stigmas are negative and degrading (Goffman 1963).

10. Moore notes:

    > The cash-poor must rely more exclusively than their richer kins-folk on the system of personal relationship since they have not the cash to do otherwise. But as the poor have less to exchange, it is not the cash-poor but often their more prosperous brothers who figure as the mainstays of the traditional system of exchange. Having cash enhances the capacity to transact in both systems. Without cash one cannot afford to be either "modern" or "traditional." (Moore 1986:130)

11. See Kaufman 1980 for a discussion of defensive strategies against shame.

Chapter 5

1. There are many parallels between the threat of supernatural harm on Kilimanjaro and the threat of lawsuits in the United States. Both operate to impose sanctions on wrongdoers, and they can both be taken to a community hearing (court). Their existence promotes a vague sense of fear and activates citizens to protect themselves, with fetishes on Kilimanjaro and insurance in the United States. They can both cause guilt and involve accusation and shame; sorcery on Kilimanjaro and legal suit in the United States often provide the only source of power for the poor in forcing the

more powerful to grant more favorable arrangements. It is also true in both societies that overuse of these remedies can fray the fabric of society.

2. I observed the same deferential treatment of an African-American family who stayed at our farm for three weeks. They were surprised to be referred to as *wazungu*, which usually meant European or, more generally, "white," and also carried a broader reference to "strangers." The deference, therefore, is in some cases typical of the hospitality extended to outsiders. In other cases, it seems related to customs born out of colonial relations and still can be seen in the very old when they extend homage to European visitors. Younger people hardly ever act in this manner.

3. We sought to increase food high in protein in the diet of small children because at the time, kwashiorkor was believed to result from protein deficiency. As discussed in Chapter 2, however, more recent studies show that it is more complicated. See also Maletnlema et al. 1974; Mujwahuzi 1981.

Chapter 6

1. In keeping with general usage on Kilimanjaro, we use the terms interchangeably but largely use *kuvimba* in dealing with lay concepts of the 1970s and "kwashiorkor" for contemporary notions.

2. Infertile women are associated with thinness as well, and they can be accused of evil eye.

3. As do many horticultural and pastoral peoples, the Chagga consider human beings to be influenced by the same governing forces that affect nature.

4. The mythological anal plugs of adult men exempted them as superior beings from the earthy, polluting process of defecation. Beans are also humorously associated with flatulence. Because of the male anal plug myth, a wife is supposed to claim responsibility if her husband passes gas. Supposedly Chagga men neither defecate nor fart. Women are responsible for keeping the secrets of male defecation from children. The anal plug myth is still told by elderly women, who traditionally were responsible for passing it on to children. In the past, their custodianship of the secret was linked symbolically to their traditional sources of power. The myth is still told but causes embarrassment to many men who have a more modern outlook.

5. Obsidian is an excellent surgical instrument; when first struck from a larger piece, it is extremely sharp and sterile. It is being used for certain eye surgeries in the United States because its edge is sharper than the edge of any metallic instrument.

6. In this procedure, called "infibulation," two deep cuts remove the labia majora, labia minora, and clitoris, and then the two sides are sewn

together. Infibulation causes significant gynecologic complications, painful intercourse, and in some cases death of the girl. In societies very protective of women's chastity and male family honor, the operation was seen as a way to inhibit the sexual drive of the woman and to prevent premarital sex. This was not the case for the Chagga.

7.   Female circumcision has become an international concern and is now seen as a human rights violation by many groups, including the United Nations. At circumcision festivals in East Africa, the sexually suggestive dancing, which involved techniques of heightening sexual pleasure, must have also caused colonial Europeans embarrassment and perhaps revulsion toward a public festival focused on female genitalia and sexuality (see Strobel 1995:111 on Maasai dancing). Opposition to stopping the custom has solidified the protest of some women from African countries against the meddling of outsiders (see Gruenbaum 1996).

Those who try to appreciate the cultural context and the variability in female genital surgery note that many more women are harmed and die in birth than in circumcision, and that women in many societies, including Europe and the United States, go to great lengths to "redraw" bodies to fit some aesthetic mold. European and U.S. women routinely undergo cosmetic surgery, including eye lifts, chin augmentation, breast implants, liposuction, nose reduction, and breast reduction (some would include episiotomy and cesarean section in this category as well); all entail physical risk to women (see Barnes-Deon 1985; Gruenbaum 1991; Hosken 1979; Kaw 1993; Turshen 1995).

8.   Political conflict among researchers was pervasive in the 1970s.

9.   There is reason to be dubious about polygynous marriage constraining fertility by providing a man with another sexual partner while other wives were still breastfeeding their children because a number of wives would be necessary, and observations of polygynous societies show that few men can afford more than one.

10. Reports on earlier practices may imply a preoccupation with sexual satisfaction of the husband and the expectation of responsible behavior on the part of the wife; however, it is worth noting that the early ethnographers were all European men, and their writing may reflect their own biases about male and female sexuality.

I observed young men and women who talked about actively seeking and courting partners. There was a lot of joking and conversation about sex as we processed seventy-five chickens each weekend for the market. Young women on the farm had ideals for masculine beauty and expectations about skillful lovemaking, and they were as interested in sex as young men. Women also projected strong, often forceful selves in social interaction.

Chapter 7

1. Birthing was considered the greatest challenge a woman would ever face and was seen to be a time of terrible pain and great valor, the equivalent for women of men's going to battle. By assuming command of this turning point in her daughter-in-law's life, the mother-in-law reasserted the strength of the social system that attributed authority to older women in the lineage, as well as her own authority over her daughter-in-law and newborn grandchild.

    The following paragraphs summarize Raum's observations (1940:Part Two). At the birth, many women congregated to comfort the new mother and her mother-in-law. The number of people gathered was a sign of the family's social status. If the husband's mother could not be present, then the woman's own mother or sister took charge. The chief midwife had to be a trusted relative because the midwife had power to harm the newborn.

    Difficulties during birth were believed to be caused inadvertently by the expectant parents. The wife, being from another lineage, was the first one suspected. The mother's crying out with pain during the birth could kill the child or harm her parents; not obeying orders from the mother-in-law, who was in charge, was seen as a sign of pride and as harmful to the newborn.

    The most important rule was that the mother was to endure the pain in silence to avoid harming the child. A girl was trained from childhood to face her ordeal with composure. During labor, her adherence to these guidelines was strengthened by the presence of relatives who pressured her to conform.

    The parturient woman was also held responsible for any delay in the delivery. If the delay was attributed to a quarrel with her parents-in-law, she sent her necklace to be spit upon by her mother-in-law, thus removing any curse. If it was said that the woman's misbehavior had offended an ancestral spirit, who retaliated by obstructing the birth, her husband had to mediate between the living and the dead to reach reconciliation.

    The husband's role was to assist his parturient wife in case of emergency and to defend the infant by means of prayers outside the house. Although custom forbade him to witness the birth, initiation and marriage rites had educated him on the birth process so that he could assist in an emergency.

    The husband was suspected of causing harm if the placenta was retained. If he had, for example, argued with his father, and if the father had since died, a sacrifice had to be offered. If the father-in-law was alive, he was asked to take the birthing woman's necklace into his mouth to cause the placenta to be ejected. If the wife died in her first confinement, the husband was unquestionably guilty and had to pay the full brideprice to his wife's family as retribution. If the newborn died, the husband and wife were held responsible. Her relatives said, "Look, it is his spear!" or accused him of kicking his wife, thus attempting to place the blame on him.

The birthing woman's own mother was also present but had to stay in the background. She wore a bead necklace as an amulet so that she could not be used as a medium for evil powers. It was believed that her inactivity made her liable to emotional displays, and therefore custom allowed her to cry out in place of her daughter, who had to contain her emotions.

If the baby was born alive, the celebration noted at the beginning of this chapter occurred, and the paternal grandmother spat upon the umbilical cord prior to cutting it to prevent it from bleeding. She tied it with a banana bast, placed it on a stick, and severed it with a grass knife. For a boy the bast was taken from the species *mchare*, the noblest banana, and for a girl from the less-valued *mrarae*. Both were planted for this purpose at the wedding ceremony. These "wedding bananas" were considered symbols of fertility, and taking the fiber from other bananas, even for subsequent children, would have resulted in the children's early death.

After the umbilical cord dropped off, it was buried under a banana tree, in the case of a girl, or under a yam, in the case of a boy. The plant's thriving was believed to affect the well-being of the infant. Raum (1940) stated that in some families, the cord was placed in a receptacle and put in the attic to dry. After two months, it was ground up with millet and made into a porridge that was eaten by old women to preserve the child's life.

To help expel the placenta, the mother was given a combination of crushed grass, butter, and her husband's wine to drink. After the placenta was delivered, there was another cry of victory. The placenta was then wrapped in banana leaves and kept under the paternal grandmother's bed for the night and in the house's food store during the daytime. The following day, it was buried just as a human would be—in the byre if the baby was a boy and in the food store if it was a girl, thus anticipating future division of labor (Raum 1940:84, 85).

Thus, the context of the birth process and the rites surrounding it expressed the obligations and hierarchical social relationships of kin: that a woman was indebted to her mother-in-law for commanding action under life-threatening conditions; that a mother was obligated to maintain strict discipline and to sacrifice for the sake of her child; that a man was to deal directly with cosmological powers on behalf of his wife and children; and that a woman's own mother would empathize with and support her, as would other female relatives and friends. Both a new mother and her mother-in-law gained status in the lineage from the birth of a healthy baby.

The literature gives conflicting reports on nursing another woman's infant, with accounts by Dundas depicting it as forbidden and other accounts depicting it as acceptable. Dundas stated that if a child was breastfed by a woman other than its mother, it was expected to die. Furthermore, it was believed that an evil woman could nurse another woman's child secretly in order to kill it (Dundas 1924:201). Lema (1973:373) agreed with Dundas's denial of joint suckling and explained that if the baby refused cow's milk, it was left to starve to death.

Raum, however, said that the husband's mother customarily nursed the infant until the mother's milk came in (Raum 1940:96). He agreed with Dundas that there were Chagga rules restricting nursing to the child's biological mother but showed how the rules were circumvented under specific circumstances. For example, if the infant's mother died, the paternal grandmother took her place and attempted to stimulate milk flow through the use of charms and medicines. She would receive the same care and diet as would a postpartum woman in the confinement period. Other acceptable substitutes might be the father's sister or another of his wives. Even a complete outsider—a "runaway woman"—could be entrusted by the father with the care of his infant. She in turn received shelter and protection from him. Raum (1940:104) added that whenever circumstances required a wet nurse, Chagga observed rites sanctioning this relationship. According to him, however, the responsibility of nursing a specific baby never rested on more than one person.

2. Parents could agree on a common name or call the child by different names. According to Raum, a man called his child "Shillingi" (from the English "shilling"), implying that the mother's confinement had cost him money, while a mother named a child "Ndeluakiwa" (I have met bitterness); the intended significance of some names is known only to the parents concerned (Raum 1940:297).

3. It also involved other members of the family; if the ancestor was a man, the petition asked that his wife, sister, and mother's brother give their blessings to the child.

4. In biomedical terms, the colostrum is valuable for infant health, although breast milk also contains a component of colostrum (Jelliffe and Jelliffe 1978). When a woman breastfeeds soon after birth, the stimulation causes her uterus to contract and expel the afterbirth.

5. It is used as a salt in cooking; it is brought from the plains where it is taken and processed for market.

6. In current days, according to a participant in the 1990s, this dish, *kitawa*, has water in it only if the familly cannot afford to buy enough milk; because of the time required to prepare it, women tend to avoid preparing it nowadays and instead prepare *uji* (a porridge of maize and water).

7. Removal to another household would mean the child no longer had access to its mother's breast or the warmth and security of being carried on its mother's body. The lack of warmth during the cold season was especially

acute because weanlings did not wear pants during toilet training. Moving to another household to allow the child's mother's milk to dry up could have resulted in the weanling's anger and depression, and the child might experience being scolded for the first time. For some children, these experiences may have caused a loss of appetite, leading to the initial stage of malnutrition.

8. Raum (1940:127) gave examples showing that as the child matured, it was taught to reciprocate its mother's nurturance and protection by giving her food. For example, fathers taught their sons to reserve portions of meat cooked at the site of the slaughter of animals for their mothers (Raum 1940:135).

9. Scarification was carried out by a specialist for the purpose of warding off sorcery. A series of small cuts would be made near the site of affliction, and the specialist would suck out some of the baby's blood, mix it with herbs, and reapply it to the incisions (Raum 1940:119, 120).

10. *Shikamoo* means "greetings" or "peace" and is derived from *shika moyo*, which literally means "I hold your heart." It is used when younger persons greet their elders or when a person of a lower position greets a person of a higher position.

11. The third child was usually selected and may have joined the household of an older woman whose children had grown or may have been adopted by a childless couple. Parents could back up debts by placing a child with the creditor. Girls were especially useful for this purpose because the creditor would receive the bridewealth when the girl married (Moore 1986:86).

Chapter 8

1. The custom of a man marrying his deceased brother's wife is known as the levirate.

2. Moore cites studies showing that up to 65 percent of men and a higher percentage of women spend most of their time in their neighborhood lineage areas. Even though transportation is readily available, she states that "the focus of rural life is still passionately local" and "there are seldom compelling reasons to go further than one can walk" (Moore 1986:139, 140).

3. Bananas and beans are defined as women's crops but commerce in them is not particularly lucrative. Everything related to cooking bananas, including peeling, cooking, and carrying, must be done by women. The exception is that some men, truck owners, purchase bananas at cut-rate prices near the farms to sell in town at three to five times the purchase price, considerably more than women expect at the small markets on the mountain. Men are not supposed to eat beans. In the 1970s, they would not admit to eating

kibulu, a bean and banana mixture that is a common dish, partly because it is associated with women's food.

4. None of the forty-two mothers of malnourished children in the NURU study were prostitutes; perhaps prostitution provides the means for some other women to keep their children healthy. During the UNICEF study, I interviewed four Chagga prostitutes in Moshi town. All had children and all explained that they became prostitutes as a way to provide for themselves and their children. They had experienced serious problems such as the death of a husband or ostracism, which led them to prostitution as a last resort. I observed Victoria Kwai, a girl from an impoverished family in Lucere, enter the profession. At age fifteen, Victoria was coerced into "marriage," which meant that a certain young man, realizing her powerless situation, felt free to force himself on her sexually. They lived together for a short while, but he left abruptly after she conceived. Despondent, she ran away to hide in the maize fields, where neighbors found her two days later. After the birth of her son, she began to be sexually available to other men, accepting small tokens for her favors. Victoria continued bearing children without formally marrying and continued to live with her mother. When I visited Victoria in 1989, though, she was married, had six children, and was running the most successful beer shop in Lucere.

A relationship of *kuolewa na nguvu* ("marriage by force") may lead to a stable conjugal union and can be an acceptable alternative to a formal wedding for men and women of low status. It makes marriage available to men who cannot or will not pay bridewealth, although they may have to pay a small amount as a fine. There is little social support, however, to keep the couple together.

The professional prostitutes whom I interviewed in Moshi town in the 1970s reported similar experiences. Urban life was their only choice, and it was reportedly a dismal one. Young men who patronized prostitutes said they paid as little as three shillings fifty cents (U.S. $0.50). More-successful prostitutes were immigrants from other areas, including Bukoba or Nairobi, where they received preparation and support from groups of women in their home communities. They reportedly charged twenty shillings or more. For Chagga women in their own environment, however, prostitution involved alienation, shame, and considerably less income. In the 1980s, it also became a major route of HIV infection, which plagues the Kilimanjaro region today.

5. There have been two types of legal beer drinking establishments on the mountain from the 1970s to the present. The *pombe* shops are open-air, mud-walled buildings where the traditional banana-millet beer is sold, mostly to local farmers. The *mwafrika* are finished, closed-in buildings where one can buy bottled beer and other drinks while listening to the

radio. These businesses are more often patronized by men with salaried positions, including teachers and medical personnel (Moore 1986:350).

See Swantz et al. 1975 for a discussion of the means available to male beer club owners to maintain competition among women and hold the price of *pombe* down.

6. The statistical results in this chapter should be taken as indications rather than confirmation of significant differences, as the data do not meet the assumptions of randomness and independence. On the other hand, there is no reason to doubt that the data are representative of the households of malnourished children who went to NURU and their neighbors. We used the chi square test in the absence of a complete set of matched pairs, which would have made a matched-pair test more appropriate.

7. In biomedicine, the swelling is a symptom of malnutrition.

8. Drinking problems among men have increased as wages and jobs available to them dwindled. In 1975, a calabash of *pombe* cost as much as one shilling, making a considerable dent in the earnings of men working as day laborers for one to nine shillings daily. The only tasks that are supposed to be done exclusively by men today are irrigation ditch digging and repair, house building, and community construction projects, including roads and bridges.

Although people note that drinking is a problem, their overwhelming reaction to the Tanzanian government's closure of beer clubs in 1975 was outrage. The government claimed concern about future drought forecasts and lowered productivity as the rationale for this decision, in addition to jailing farmers found guilty of indolence. Most Chagga, however, rich and poor alike, expressed a need to determine their own fate. As costly as the beer club is, it serves as one of the last bastions of customary life, especially in regard to deference to older and higher-status men. It is a place for male congregation and informal conversation, maintaining a sense of Chagga community and tradition.

Chapter 9

1. Of all the reasons for infanticide, only one rare abnormality would have justified infanticide when an infant was already some months old. Lower incisors are normally the first teeth to erupt; but if the upper incisors were the first teeth to come in, a child was supposed to be killed to forestall misfortune. The teeth, which do not decay with the rest of the body at death, are places of concentrated vital force, which partially explains the apprehension connected with their appearance. In general, children were not named until after they had passed through the early trial period and the rite of the first tooth.

2. In U.S. society, for instance, parents might have trouble emotionally attaching to an ugly infant or a newborn with facial deformities. Fat children or children with gross disproportion also may lose favor with their parents. Any sense of rivalry between spouses may result in favoritism toward children who resemble oneself or one's close family members. Or conversely, a lifetime of disappointment in one's own appearance could result in a preference for children resembling one's spouse.

3. The children were tested at the Catholic clinic and found to have hookworm.

4. It is also possible that there was a sex-linked genetic difference.

5. Gender as a criterion for preference comes out clearly in the following:

> The warmth with which a child is received depends to some extent on its sex. To the father, the birth of an heir as the first child is a moral rehabilitation; it confirms that his premarital sex life was unimpeachable. A son, moreover, is of great religious significance, because after this father's death he becomes the family priest, perpetuating his ancestors' memory and maintaining their authority through prayer and sacrifice. Without a son, the family vanishes "like smoke in the morning wind." Conversely, a man's social and political influence increases with the number of his sons; hence the proverb: "A quiver with but one arrow is of no use." While the young man's chief desire is to "make firm" his parental dwelling—that is, to continue his family though the birth of an heir—in middle age his attention turns to making his service and influence indispensable at court. This he can do chiefly by rearing sons to carry out his bequests, to be at their chief's disposal in peace or war, to inherit his own property and succeed to his profession and political position. On the other hand, a woman feels that she had done her duty when she had given birth to one son. The greeting which her husband then extends to her, "Welcome, you increaser and owner of the heritage!" sums up her ambitions. She is recognized as mistress of the home and has a supporter for older age. The stability of her marriage having been secured, she earns both the respect of her co-wives and the admiration of her age-mates. A Chagga husband may therefore be heard complaining that his wife began to neglect him when their son was able to herd the goats, for she may consider it more advantageous for her future to ingratiate herself with her son. (Raum 1940:86)

6. This point relates to the following passage:

> On the whole, women prefer to have daughters born to them. They are always welcome, because they will later be able to assist

in field and house, to share in womanly confidence, to inherit personal property and the professional knowledge vested in the female sex. Moreover, girls are much easier to rear than boys since they are considered less intelligent, their work requires less ability, and they do not possess that obstinacy which in young boys expresses itself in naughtiness and in older ones as irreverence. To the father, too, a girl is acceptable; as maiden, she cooks for him, her marriage strengthens his family's influence by allying it to another, and the bride-price is a source of income for a great number of years. Raum (1940:86)

Chapter 10

1. This effort at treatment may have some biological effectiveness, as the grasses are used because they are believed to be antihelminthic (although no medical studies of them have been done). A soup with boiled water would be a means of rehydrating a child and would thus be a healthy course to follow, and from a biological standpoint would at least do no harm.

2. Similar reports about medical doctors did not call the whole system of biomedicine into question.

3. Pregnancy and menopause almost never require medical attention; birth requires it more often, but medical authorities agree that interventions, including cesarean sections, are far more frequent than warranted (see Davis-Floyd 1992 for a contemporary discussion and further references). Alcoholism is often treated with drugs that are supposed to help break the physical addiction; spouse abuse and child abuse are increasingly spoken of as sicknesses, and offenders are required to undergo "therapy."

4. There is, in general, tremendous demand on the mountain for modern medical care. The following rather lengthy excerpt demonstrates Chagga success in procuring medical facilities:

> The general medical services in the district are above national average. In 1970–71 there was already 1 hospital bed to 623 inhabitants of Kilimanjaro District (National average: 1 to 745), 1 health center to 143,000 inhabitants (National: 1 to 9,050). Within the new Moshi District there is now 1 health center to 120,000 people and if one includes the beds at the new KCMC Hospital which are used by the district, the overall ratio would be around 1 bed to 550 people. High population on the one hand and a more equitable spread of facilities across the district allows for a high accessibility and utilization of health facilities. If one compares the medical facilities of 1971 with population in

1967, 40.6% of the population lived within 5 km. of a hospital (National: 12.8%) and 97.9% lived within 10 km. (National: 25%); 25.6% of the people had a health center within 5 km. of their home (National: 5.1%) and 67.4% have to walk up to 10 km. (National: 21.8%). Only 1.5% of the population did not have any health facility within 10 km. of their home (National: 13.1%). If one assumes that 60% of the patients of KCMC and Mawenzi Hospitals, none of Kibongoto (TB hospital) and all from the small hospitals in the district came from inside Moshi district then the rate of new inpatient admittances in 1972 would have been 78 out of every 1,000 inhabitants. (National average of hospital admittances: 35 new inpatients out of every 1,000 people.) . . .

The number of new outpatient cases seen in 1972 at various hospitals, health centers, and dispensaries was more than twice as large as the population. Even before the opening of the KCMC Hospital, public health expenditures per capita in the district were about 16/– and private spending at least 5/00 (National: public 11/–, private 2/–). The facilities of KCMC have increased average public health expenditure on people within the district to at least 18/–. KCMC has been built by foreign donors and according to West German standards for about 31 million shillings to serve as a supra-regional reference hospital. In actual fact, 95% of the patients come from within the region and more than half from within Moshi District. Mothers coming for delivery and children in the pediatric wards come almost exclusively from the district (at least 90%). With seven hospitals (KCMC, Mawenzi, Machame, Marangu, Kobosho, T.P.C., Kibongoto) three rural health centers and about fifty dispensaries, the district was fairly well equipped.

While most people had a dispensary in reasonable vicinity of their home not all of them used the nearest facility available to them. Some do not go to mission dispensaries and walk further to a government facility in order to avoid fees; others walk a longer way to go to a mission center because they hope to get better service if they pay or because the mission staff are attributed with more personal concern for the patients.

In two villages it was rumored that the medical staff at the government center do not give proper medicines to the patients and sell the medicines privately instead. So people preferred the mission hospital. In a number of other places people avoided the local dispensary and went straight to a health center or hospital because the dispensaries were so often without drugs that they felt they were wasting their time. Others considered the dispensary unsuitable because they felt the staff was not sufficiently qualified. While it is difficult to ascertain whether these criticisms are warranted or not the result is that maybe as much as one third of the people walk longer distances to health facilities than statistics would indicate. (Von Freyhold et al. 1973:217–223)

5. Before 1973, most children with malnutrition were sent to Mawenzi Regional Hospital for medical treatment and from there to Moshi Chapel Children's Home to finish recuperating. The home was originally established to treat child malnutrition, and it had developed a program to teach women cooking and child care, but mothers were not required to stay with their children in treatment. Many families came to depend on the institution as an expedient way to support their children, whom they tended to leave there for more than a year. Generally, major changes were under way in Tanzania's approach to community health during the 1970s (Heggenhougen et al. 1987).

6. NURU was built with private funds from the United States, was initially staffed by European doctors, and had the funds to obtain medical supplies and spare parts for the vans.

7. In 1972, both Mawenzi Regional Hospital and Kilimanjaro Christian Medical Center began mobile child health clinics that all eventually came under the jurisdiction of the Medical Center. A very strong competitive element developed between Medical Center and Mawenzi Hospital physicians as the Medical Center gained control of the mobile clinics.

8. To reinforce the message of an often heard government radio advertisement in which a crying baby was being comforted by its mother while the inebriated father belligerently demanded his food, a picture poster conveying the same moral was hung in the center of the instruction room. It had not occurred to the NURU staff that the poster would humiliate the women.

Appendix A

Comparisons of Tanzania, Kenya, Malawi,
the United Kingdom, and the United States[a]

	Tanzania	Kenya	Malawi	United Kingdom	United States
Population dynamics					
1. Total population, 1991 (millions)	26.9	24.4	9.9	57.5	252.6
2. Annual population growth rate, 1980–91 (%)	3.4	3.5	4.3	0.2	0.9
3. Total fertility rate, 1991[b]	6.8	6.4	7.6	1.9	2.0
Standard of living					
4. GNP per capita, 1990 (U.S.$)	120	200	370	16,100	21,790
5. Primary school enrollment ratio, 1986–1990[b]					
Male	64	96	73	105	101
Female	63	92	60	106	100
6. Electronics, no. of sets per 1,000 population, 1989					
Radios	21	95	273	1,145	2,122
Televisions	1	9		434	814

Maternal and child health

   7. Infant mortality rate[b]

1960	249	202	365	27	30
1991	178	75	228	9	11

   8. Under-5 mortality rate[b]

1960	147	120	206	23	26
1991	112	52	144	7	9

   9. Contraceptive prevalence (%), 1980–1992[b]

	8	27	7	74	72

 10. Maternal mortality rate, 1980–1990[b]

	340	170	170	8	8

Food consumption

 11. Daily per capita calorie supply as a % of requirements, 1988–1990

	95	89	88	130	138

 12. % of household income spent on all food, 1980–1985

	64	39	55	12	13

[a] Grant 1993

[b] See glossary for definition.

Appendix B

Household Characteristics, Child Malnutrition,
and Maternal Knowledge:
A Survey at Child Health Clinics in Kilimanjaro, 1972[a]

	Number	Percent

CHARACTERISTICS OF WOMEN, MEN, AND HOUSEHOLDS

WOMEN

1. Ethnicity

	Number	Percent
Chagga	333	(80%)
Other	41	(20%)
Total, women	374	(100%)

2. Religion

	Number	Percent
Catholic	221	(60%)
Protestant	86	(24%)
Muslim	55	(15%)
None	4	(1%)
Total, married women	366	(100%)

3. Education

None	149	(37%)
1 to 4 years	162	(41%)
5 to 8	79	(20%)
≥ 8	9	(2%)
Total, women	399	(100%)

4. Marital status

Married	366	(92%)
Single	14	(3%)
Widowed	11	(3%)
Divorced	8	(2%)
Total, women	399	(100%)

5. Age at marriage

≤ 15 years	33	(9%)
16	40	(11%)
17	31	(8%)
18	81	(22%)
19	37	(10%)
20–24	99	(24%)
≥ 25	14	(4%)
Not reported	31	(8%)
Total, married women	366	(100%)

6. Geographic mobility

Always lived in same area	297	(74%)
Has lived elsewhere	102	(26%)
Total, women	399	(100%)

MEN

7. Education

None	77	(21%)
1 to 4 years	133	(36%)
5 to 8	105	(29%)
≥ 8	32	(9%)
Unknown	19	(5%)
Total, men	366	(100%)

8. Distance between husband's
   and wife's birthplaces

Six miles or less	248	(68%)
More than six miles	118	(32%)
Total	366	(100%)

9. Occupation

Farmer	250	(68%)
Farmer with other work	71	(19%)
Only other work	44	(12%)
Unknown	1	(-)
Total, men	366	(99%)

HOUSEHOLDS

10. Size

2 to 5 members	151	(36%)
6 to 9	209	(50%)
≥ 10	58	(14%)
Total, households	418	(100%)

11. Source of cooking water

Pipe	234	(56%)
Well	63	(15%)
Open streamlet	120	(29%)
Rain	1	(-)
Total, households	418	(100%)

12. Toilet facilities

Outhouse or toilet	380	(91%)
Not available	38	(9%)
Total, households	418	(100%)

HOUSEHOLDS IN THE MIDDLE
BELT OF MT. KILIMANJARO

13. Farmland

None	18	(7%)
≤ 1 acre	52	(22%)

(13. Farmland—cont.)

1 acre	78	(33%)
2 to 3 acres	73	(31%)
4 to 5	11	(5%)
≥ 5	6	(2%)
Total, households	238	(100%)

14. Main crops

Coffee	207	(87%)
Bananas	192	(81%)
Maize	121	(51%)
Potatoes, rice	16	(7%)
Other vegetables	77	(32%)
Other fruit	28	(12%)
Total, households	238	(-)

15. Main crops sold by household

Coffee	194	(81%)
Bananas	71	(30%)
Others	3	(1%)
None	20	(8%)
Total, households	238	(-)

16. Livestock

Cows	150	(63%)
Goats	128	(54%)
Chickens	130	(55%)
Others	9	(4%)
None	38	(16%)
Total, households	238	(-)

17. Livestock products sold by household

Milk	11	(5%)
Eggs	32	(13%)
Meat	7	(3%)
None	197	(83%)
Total, households	283	(-)

REPRODUCTION AND CHILD HEALTH

CHILDBIRTH

18. Number of children

    born per woman

1 child	46	(12%)
2 to 5 children	209	(52%)
6 to 8	113	(28%)
≥ 9	31	(8%)
Total, women	399	(100%)

19. Number of children
    desired per woman

1 to 5 children	43	(12%)
6 to 8	86	(23%)
≥ 9	44	(12%)
As many as God gives	106	(29%)
No more	87	(24%)
Total, women	366	(100%)

20. Birth of youngest child

At home	137	(33%)
At health facility	281	(67%)
Total, women	418	(100%)

21. Malnutrition of children

Protein-calorie malnutrition	8	(2%)
Underweight[b]	83	(20%)
Normal weight	320	(78%)
Total number of children	411	(100%)

22. Child mortality/woman

0 deaths	250	(63%)
1	89	(22%)
2	33	(8%)
3	20	(5%)
4 or more	7	(2%)
Total, women	399	(100%)

HEALTH CONCEPTS OF WOMEN [c]

BREASTFEEDING AND WEANING

23. Age at weaning of youngest child
who had been weaned before
the survey

≤3 months	6	(3%)
4 to 6	3	(2%)
7 to 11	22	(13%)
12 to 17	37	(21%)
18 to 23	48	(27%)
≥ 24 months	60	(34%)
Total, women	175	(100%)

24. Age preferred for weaning

≤ 5 months	6	(1%)
6 to 11	34	(8%)
12 to 17	63	(15%)
18 to 23	95	(23%)
≥ 24 months	197	(47%)
Don't know	23	(6%)
Total, women	418	(100%)

25. Breast milk thought to be bad
for a child when the woman is
pregnant and/or menstruating

Never	19	(5%)
Pregnant	259	(65%)
Menstruating	73	(18%)
Don't know	48	(12%)
Total, women	399	(100%)

26. Stopped breastfeeding because

Mother's new pregnancy	57	(32%)
Mother sick or died	30	(17%)
Mother went to work	6	(3%)
Mother did not have enough milk	6	(3%)
Mother thought her milk was bad	2	(1%)
Child got diarrhea	20	(11%)
Child old enough for other food	45	(26%)
Child stopped itself	8	(5%)
Don't know	2	(1%)
Total, women	176	(99%)

FEEDING SMALL CHILDREN

27. Type of food preparation

Small child needs food prepared specially	118	(37%)
Same as rest of family	197	(63%)
Total, women	315	(100%)

28. Number of times daily to feed weanlings

1 time per day	11	(3%)
2 times per day	43	(12%)
3	207	(57%)
4	68	(19%)
≥ 5	29	(8%)
Don't know	2	(1%)
Total, women	360	(100%)

KWASHIORKOR

29. Cause of kwashiorkor

Did not eat good food	173	(41%)
Sick	52	(12%)
Has worms	25	(6%)
Does not get enough care	7	(2%)
Breastfed when mother was pregnant	1	(-)
Don't know	160	(38%)
Total, women	418	(99%)

30. How to prevent kwashiorkor

Give child good food	130	(31%)
Take child to hospital	89	(21%)
Give child good care, medicine, and keep it clean	22	(5%)
Do not breastfeed child	2	(-)
Don't know	175	(42%)
Total, women	418	(99%)

31. Care required for child with kwashiorkor

Give good food	197	(47%)

(31. Care required for child with kwashiorkor—cont.)

Bring to a hospital	235	(56%)
Give care and medicine	7	(2%)
Don't know	76	(18%)
Total, women	418	(-)

32. Cause of diarrhea

Dirty, poorly prepared food	184	(44%)
Worms	61	(15%)
Dirty stomach	36	(9%)
Mother's milk when she is pregnant	18	(4%)
Child is sick or teething	38	(9%)
Don't know	104	(25%)
Total, women	418	(-)

---

[a] Lindner 1972. The data are from interviews with people who brought children to clinics for patients under five years of age.

[b] Underweight was defined as "less than 80% of the Harvard Standard" (Lindner 1972:48).

[c] The questionnaire was phrased largely in terms of biomedicine; the people who designed it (including me) did not appreciate the importance of eliciting local perspectives on causation or the cultural variation on the mountain.

Appendix C

Research by Mary Howard on Mt. Kilimanjaro:
Participant Observation, Interviews, Survey Research,
and Analyses of Health Statistics

Research Project

Ethnography of child malnutrition and NURU[a]

Researchers

Mary Howard

Dates

1970–1975

Research (Publication)

Carried out participant observation for almost five years as a rural resident, member of an agricultural cooperative; wife; mother of two sons born in East Africa (Howard 1980)

Research Project
Clinic survey[b]

Researchers
Bo Baldin, Irmgard Lindner, Ulla-Stina Henricson, Mary Zalla[c]

Dates
1970–1971

Research (Publication)
Planned questionnaire, analyzed data on survey responses of 418 people, mostly mothers, on child health and nutrition (Lindner 1972)

Research Project
UNICEF study[d]

Researchers
Michaela Von Freyhold, Mary Zalla[c], Katherine Sawaki, assisted by Victoria Kessi

Dates
1972–1973

Research (Publication)
Evaluated programs in education and child nutrition; held focus groups with women; analyzed essays written by standard 7 school children; gathered statistics from hospital, government, and university sources on maternal-child health and demography (Von Freyhold et al. 1973)

Research Project
NURU study[e]

Researchers
Marja-Liisa Swantz, Ulla-Stina Henricson, Mary Zalla[c], assisted by H. Akarro, E. Kileo, C. Kuwite, A. Shuma

Dates
1973–1974

Research (Publication)

Interviewed parents in 42 families who had had children at NURU and parents in 69 neighboring households about children's nutritional status, household economy, mothers' reproductive histories, children's illnesses (Swantz et al. 1975)

Research Project

Women's Beer Production[f]

Researchers

Mary Howard

Dates

1989

Research (Publication)

Returned to study the role of women's work in beer production as a means of supporting their families

---

Research Project

Child health study[f]

Researchers

Mary Howard

Dates

1993–1994

Research (Publication)

Return visit to contact families in the NURU study (Howard 1994)

---

[a] NURU: Nutrition Rehabilitation Unit, located on the grounds of the Kilimanjaro Christian Medical Center (KCMC), a large hospital serving this part of Mt. Kilimanjaro.
[b] Funded by KCMC (see note a).
[c] Mary Zalla was Mary Howard's married name.
[d] Funded by UNICEF and the Tanzanian National Scientific Research Council, Child Health Programs.
[e] Funded by the Bureau of Resource Assessment and Land Use Planning, the University of Dar es Salaam.
[f] Funded by a Thomas E. Winslow Faculty Development Grant, Ohio Wesleyan University.

Glossary

age-grade system	principle of social organization, grouping people according to age; each person enters an age grade through initiation and assumes specific rights and responsibilities; also called "age-class" system
age class	age grade
agistment	loaning cattle to someone else who cares for them and takes part of their products (calves, blood, and milk)
aibu	shame
akili	intelligence
akiwa ndani	period of a new mother's seclusion after giving birth
askari	watchman
aspro	Chagga dish made of cow blood and meat mixture, also known as *kisusio*
balozi	ten-house leader; neighborhood leader
baba	father; adult male
banda	traditional round house
bao	a game similar to checkers
baraza	judicial meeting
bwana	mister

bwana mkubwa	(lit., big man) a man with power and influence in his neighborhood, commerce, or the civil service
child mortality rate	annual number of deaths per 1,000 children under five years of age
chimbia	bridewealth
chungu	sour
colostrum	the liquid produced by a woman's breasts immediately after birth; it is rich in nutrients and antibodies and is replaced by milk in a few days
contraceptive prevalence	percentage of married women ages fifteen to forty-nine using contraception
dada	sister
dagaa	small dried fish
dawa	medicine
eleusine	finger millet
fagia	to sweep; sweeper
fundi	expert
GNP	gross national product
habari gani?	how are you?
heshima	respect
hodi	formal greeting used by visitors as they enter a compound
hohehahe	a derisive term used to make fun of those who fall to the bottom of the social ladder
infant mortality	number of deaths of infants under one year of age per 1,000 live births
kali	strict, powerful, sharp, mean
kanga	piece of cloth
karibuni	welcome
kibarua	day laborer
kibulu	dish made of beans and bananas
kichaaa	crazy (singular adjective)
kihamba	field of the most valuable farmland, in Mt. Kilimanjaro's middle belt, inherited through fathers

kijiji	a village
kilau	plant roots used to prevent infection by worms.
Kilimanjaro	the name of a mountain, a government district, and a geographic region; in this book, the people of Kilimanjaro are rural Chagga who live on the mountain
Kilimanjaro Christian Medical Center	a hospital complex on Mt. Kilimanjaro built in 1967 with the later addition of NURU on the hospital grounds; known locally as KCMC
Kilimanjaro Native Cooperative Union (KNCU)	the cooperative of coffee growers on Mt. Kilimanjaro, formerly the Kilimanjaro Native Planters Association
Kilimo	informal reference to the Ministry of Agriculture, formally named *Wizari ya Kilimo*
kitenge	colorful cloth used as a skirt to wrap around a woman's lower body and as a shawl for her shoulders or for carrying an infant, similar to *kanga*
kujitegemea	self-reliance
kuku	chicken, hen
kupiga chungu	gesture of striking a pot
kuvimba	(lit., to swell) swelling; local reference to kwashiorkor used in the 1970s
kwashiorkor	protein-calorie malnutrition
kyana	type of dracaena plant
low birth weight	weight at birth that is less than 2,500 grams (5.5 pounds)
maendeleo	progress, development
mafusa	sorcery and witchcraft (they are not seen as distinct by Chagga)
mama	mother; adult woman
maskini	poor
masumba	wealthy man
maternal mortality rate	annual number of deaths of women from pregnancy-related causes per 100,000 live births
mavi	feces
mbege	finger millet; also used to mean locally brewed beer made of bananas and finger millet
mchare	a type of banana

mganga	traditional healer
mgeni	a guest
mjinga	foolish
mlaso	a cooked mixture of milk, cow's blood, and butter
mlevi	a drunkard, an alcoholic
mnangu	"the incomplete," used in reference to an infant who is not yet baptized
morani	warriors
mrarae	a type of banana
msesewe	a tree whose roots are used as herbal remedies
Mungu wangu	exclamation, "my God!"
mwafrika	(lit., African) on Mt. Kilimanjaro refers to a type of bar that sells locally brewed banana beer
mwandani	observing the tradition of seclusion and rest at home after a birth
mzee	elder
mzungu	white person, also translated as "European," generally meaning a category of light-skinned people not from sub-Saharan Africa
ndizi	banana
ndizi na nyama	traditional Chagga dish of plantains and meat
ndizi tu	bananas only
ng'ombe	cow
njaa	hunger
NURU	Nutrition Rehabilitation Unit established to combat endemic child malnutrition with nutrition education; it was located on the grounds of the Kilimanjaro Christian Medical Center
patrilineage	a large group of kin with membership by descent through the male line
pole	(lit., slow, slowly) often used to say "my sympathies"
pole sana	I am very sorry
pombe	beer, also known as *mbege*
pori	a field at the base of Mt. Kilimanjaro
primary enrollment ratio	the total number of children enrolled in primary school, regardless of age, expressed as a percentage of the total number of children of ages appropriate for that level

roundaval	English term for the traditional round house (*banda*), thatched with grass or banana stalk peelings
Ruwa	Chagga name for God
safi	clean, neat, cool
sawa sawa	fine, OK
shamba	fields in Mt. Kilimanjaro's lower belt used for growing maize and beans, traditionally redistributed by chiefs but now usually passed on from father to offspring
shauri ya Mungu	God's will
shida	trouble, problem
shilingi	see "shilling"
shilling	Tanzanian monetary unit (*shilingi*); from 1970 to about 1975, the exchange rate approximated 7 Tanzanian shillings to the U.S. dollar
sijui	I don't know
soda	sodium bicarbonate, a mineral found on the plains and used as salt in cooking
tambiko	ritual in which offerings to the ancestors are made
tamu	delicious, nice
TANU	Tanganyika African National Union (the name of a political party through the 1970s)
teknonymy	addressing a parent as "father of" or "mother of" the first child
tembea tu	walking about or wandering without purpose (also phrased *tembea tembea*)
total fertility rate	the average number of births per woman by the end of her reproductive span (projected from prevailing age-specific rates)
uchawi	witchcraft and sorcery; an *mchawi* is an individual witch, either male or female, who attempts to manipulate the supernatural to bring about fortune or misfortune
ugawa	egalitarianism
ujamaa	brotherhood
ujinga	foolishness
ulevi	drunkenness

under-five mortality rate	number of deaths of children under five years of age per 1,000 live births (child mortality rate)
underweight	moderate underweight: below minus-two standard deviations from median weight for age of a reference population; severe: below minus three standard deviations
usawa	social equality
ushirikiano	cooperation
uwiri	a Chagga musical instrument
vichaa	crazy people
wakichaa	crazy (plural adjective)
wazungu	Europeans; white people generally; sometimes used to refer to other outsiders also
Yesu	Jesus

Bibliography

Aguirre, A. 1966. Colombia: the Family in Candelaria. *Studies in Family Planning* 11:1–5.

Alba, F. 1982. *The Population of Mexico: Trends, Issues, and Policies.* New Brunswick, NJ: Transaction.

Arnold, D. 1988. *Famine.* Oxford: Blackwell.

Baldin, Bo, Irmgard Lindner, Mary [Howard] Zalla, and Ulla-Stina Henricson 1972. Proposal for the study of attitudes, beliefs and practices of mothers attending under-five clinics on Mt. Kilimanjaro. Moshi, Tanzania: Pediatrics Department, Kilimanjaro Christian Medical Center.

Barnes-Deon, Virginia L. 1985. Clitoridectomy and infibulation. *Cultural Survival Quarterly* 9(2):26.

Bell, Diane, Pat Caplan, and Wazir Jahan Karim. 1993. *Gendered Fields.* New York: Routledge.

Bennett, Lynn. 1990. An approach to the study of women's productive roles as a determinant of intra-household allocation patterns. In Beatrice Lorge Rogers and Nina P. Schlossman, eds., *Intra-Household Resource Allocation.* Tokyo: United Nations University Press. 35–50.

Bennett, Norman Robert. 1964. The British on Kilimanjaro: 1884–1892. *Tanganyika Notes and Records* 63:229–245.

Berg, Alan D. 1972. Nutrition as a national priority: The lessons of the Indian experiment. In Bo Vahlquist, ed., *Nutrition: A Priority in African Development.* Uppsala: Almqvist and Wiksell. 183–202.

Berman, Peter, Carl Kendall, and Karabi Bhattacharyya. 1994. The household production of health: Integrating social science perspectives on micro-level health determinants. *Social Science and Medicine* 38(2):205–216.

Brown, Lynn R. 1995. Women, food security and structural adjustment in Ghana. Paper presented at the Annual Meeting of the American Anthropological Association, November 17, Washington, D.C.

Brown, Peter J., and Marcia C. Inhorn. 1990. Disease, ecology, and human behavior. In Thomas M. Johnson and Carolyn F. Sargent, eds., *Medical Anthropology*. New York: Praeger. 187–214.

Caldwell, John C. 1982. *Theory of Fertility Decline*. New York: Academic Press.

Caplan, Pat. 1993. Learning gender: Fieldwork in a Tanzanian coastal village, 1965–85. In Diane Bell, Pat Caplan, and Wazir Jahan Karim, eds. *Gendered Fields*. New York: Routledge. 168–181.

Cassidy, Claire Monod. 1980. Benign neglect and toddler malnutrition. In L. S. Greene and F. E. Johnston, eds., *Social and Biological Predictors of Nutritional Status, Physical Growth and Neurological Development*. New York: Academic Press. 109–133.

———. 1982. Protein-energy malnutrition as a culture-bound syndrome. *Culture, Medicine and Psychiatry* 6(4):325–345.

———. 1987. World-view conflict and toddler malnutrition: Change agent dilemmas. In Nancy Scheper-Hughes, ed., *Child Survival*. Boston: D. Reidel. 293–324.

Castle, Sarah E. 1994. The (re)negotiation of illness diagnoses and responsibility for child death in rural mali. *Medical Anthropology Quarterly* 8(3):314–335.

Chavez, Leo. 1992. *Shadowed Lives*. Fort Worth: Harcourt Brace Jovanovich.

Clifford, James. 1988. *The Predicament of Culture*. Cambridge: Harvard University Press.

Cohen, Ronald. 1993. Women, status, and high office in African politis. In John S. Henderson and Patricia Netherly, eds., *Configurations of Power*. Ithaca, NY: Cornell University Press. 181–208.

Coles, Catherine, and Beverly Mack, eds. 1991. *Hausa Women in the Twentieth Century*. Madison, WI: University of Wisconsin Press.

Coles, Robert, and Jane Hallowell. Coles 1989 [1978]. *Women of Crisis*. New York: Delacorte Press/S. Lawrence (reprinted).

Collier, Jane Fishburne, and Sylvia Junko Yanagisako, eds. 1987. *Gender and Kinship*. Stanford: Stanford University Press.

Comaroff, Jean. 1985. *Body of Power, Spirit of Resistance*. Chicago: University of Chicago Press.

Cook, Kristy, and Donna O. Kerner. 1989. Gender and food shortage in Tanzania. *Feminist Issues* 9(1):57–71.

Coreil, Jeannine, Antoine Augustin, Neal A. Halsey, and Elizabeth Holt. 1994. Social and psychological costs of preventive child health services and Haiti. *Social Science and Medicine* 38(2):231–238.

Cosminsky, Sheila. 1985. Infant feeding practices in rural Kenya. In Valerie Hull and Mayling Simpson, eds. *Breastfeeding, Child Health, and Child Spacing.* London: Croom-Helm.

Cowie, A. T. 1972. Lactation and its hormonal control. *In* C. R. Austin and R. V. Short, eds., *Hormones in Reproduction, Book 3.* Oxford: Alden and Mowbray Ltd. 106–143.

Crandon-Malamud, Libbet. 1991. *From the Fat of Our Souls: Social Change, Political Process, and Medical Pluralism in Bolivia.* Berkeley: University of California Press.

Davis-Floyd, Robbie E. 1992. *Birth as an American Rite of Passage.* Berkeley: University of California Press.

Deere, Carmen Diana, and Madgalena Leon de Leal. 1982. *Women in Andean Agriculture.* Geneva: International Labor Organization.

de Garine, I., and G. A. Harrison, eds. 1988. *Coping with Uncertainty in Food Supply.* Oxford: Clarendon Press.

Derman, William. 1990. River basin development: dilemmas for peasants and planners. In Rebecca Huss-Ashmore and Solomon H. Katz, eds., *African Systems in Crisis. Part Two: Contending with Change.* New York: Gordon and Breach. 29–41.

Dettwyler, Katherine A. 1994. *Dancing Skeletons: Life and Death in West Africa.* Prospect Heights: Waveland Press, Inc.

Devereaux, Leslie. 1987. Gender difference and the relations of inequality in Zinacantan. In Marilyn Strathern, ed., *Dealing with Inequality.* Cambridge: Cambridge University Press. 89–111.

DeWalt, K. M., P. B. Kelly, and G. H. Pelto. 1980. Nutritional correlates of economic microdifferentiation in a highland Mexican community. In Norge W. Jerome, Randy F. Kandel, and Gretel H. Pelto, eds., *Nutritional Anthropology.* Pleasantville, NY: Redgrave. 206–221.

Dirks, Nicholas B., ed. 1992. *Colonialism and Culture.* Ann Arbor: University of Michigan Press.

Dirks, Robert. 1980. Social responses during severe food shortages and famine. *Current Anthropology* 21(1):21–44.

District Executive Director's Office, Rombo and Tanzania Food and Nutrition Center. 1986. *Kilimanjaro Regional Profile: A Proposed Program for Child Survival and Development in Rombo District.* TFNC Report No. 1017. Dar es Salaam: Tanzania Food and Nutrition Center.

Donahue, John M., and Meredith B. McGuire. 1994. The political economy of responsibility in health and illness. *Social Science and Medicine* 40 (1):47–53.

Downs, R. E., Donna O. Kerner, and Stephen P. Reyna, eds. 1991. *The Political Economy of African Famine.* New York: Gordon and Breach.

Dundas, Charles. 1924. *Kilimanjaro and its People: A History of the Wachagga, Their Laws, Customs and Legends*. London: Witherby.

Edgerton, Robert B. 1992. *Sick Societies*. New York: Macmillan.

Egeno, Bertel and Roushidi Henin. 1973. *Population Growth in the Population of Tanzania*. Dar es Salaam: Bureau of Resource Assessment and Land Use Planning, the University of Dar es Salaam, and the Bureau of Statistics.

Ehrlich, S. P., Jr. 1983. Selected conditions in the Americas: a guide for health research policy. *Bulletin of the Pan American Health Organization* 17(2):111–125.

Eide, W.B. and F.C. Steady. 1980. Individual and social energy flows. In Norge W. Jerome, Randy F. Kandel, and Gretel H. Pelto, eds., *Nutritional Anthropology*. Pleasantville, NY: Redgrave. 61–84.

Engle, Patrice L. 1990. Intra-household allocation of resources: Perspectives from psychology. In Beatrice Lorge Rogers and Nina P. Schlossman, eds., *Intra-Household Resource Allocation*. Tokyo: United Nations University Press. 63–79.

Eveleth, Phyllis B., and James M. Tanner. 1990. *Worldwide Variation in Human Growth*, 2nd ed. Cambridge: Cambridge University Press.

Feierman, Steven, and John M. Janzen, eds. 1992. *The Social Basis of Health and Healing in Africa*. Berkeley: University of California Press.

Fernandez, Renate Lellep. 1990. *A Simple Matter of Salt*. Berkeley: University of California Press.

Finerman, Ruthbeth. 1994. "Parental incompetence" and "selective neglect": Blaming the victim in child survival. *Social Science and Medicine* 40(1): 5–13.

Finerman, Ruthbeth and Linda A. Bennett. 1994. Guilt, blame, and shame: Responsibility in health and sickness. *Social Science and Medicine* 40(1): 1–3.

Fleuret, Ann. 1989. Indigenous Taita responses to drought. In Rebecca Huss-Ashmore and Solomon H. Katz, eds., *African Food Systems in Crisis. Part One: Microperspectives*. New York: Gordon and Breach. 221–237.

Foster, Phillips. 1992. *The World Food Problem*. Boulder: Lynne Rienner.

Franke, Richard W., and Barbara H. Chasin. 1992. *Seeds of Famine*. Lanham, MD: Rowman and Littlefield.

Freire, Paulo. 1985. *The Politics of Education*. South Hadley, MA: Bergin and Garvey.

Freund, Peter E. S., and Meredith B. McGuire. 1991. *Health, Illness and the Social Body*. London: Prentice-Hall.

Fuggles-Couchman, N. R. 1964. *Agricultural change in Tanganyika 1945–1960*. Stanford: Stanford University Press.

Funk, Ursula. 1991. Labor, economic power and gender: coping with food shortage in Guinea-Bissau. In R. E. Downs, Donna O. Kerner, and Stephen P.

Reyna, eds., *The Political Economy of African Famine*. New York: Gordon and Breach. 205–226.

Gamassa, D. M. 1991. Historical change in human population on Mount Kilimanjaro and its implications. In William D. Newark, ed., *The Conservation of Mount Kilimanjaro*. Gland, Switzerland: IUCN (International Union for Conservation of Nature and Natural Resources). 1–8.

George, Susan. 1983 [1977] *How the Other Half Dies*. Totowa, NJ: Rowman and Allanheld (reprinted).

Giddens, Anthony. 1987 *A Contemporary Critique of Historical Materialism*. Berkeley: University of California Press.

Gladwin, Christina H., ed. 1991. *Structural Adjustment and African Women Farmers*. Gainesville: University of Florida Press.

Goffman, Erving. 1963. *Stigma: Notes on the Management of Spoiled Identity*. New York: Simon and Schuster.

Golden, Michael H. N. 1985. The consequences of protein deficiency in man and its relationship to the features of kwashiorkor. In Kenneth Blaxter and J. C. Waterlow, eds., *Nutritional Adaptation in Man*. London: John Libbey. 169–187.

Gould, Stephen Jay. 1981. *The Mismeasure of Man*. New York: W. W. Norton.

Grant, James P. 1993. *The State of the World's Children 1993*. Oxford: Oxford University Press.

Gruenbaum, Ellen. 1991. The Islamic movement, development and health education: Recent changes in the health of women in central Sudan. *Social Science and Medicine* 33(6):637–645.

———. 1996. The cultural debate over female circumcision: The Sudanese are arguings this one out for themselves. *Medical Anthropology Quarterly* 19 (4): 455–475.

Gutmann, Bruno. 1926. *Das Recht der Dschagga*. Munich. English translation by A. M. Nagler, Human Relations Area Files. New Haven: Yale University Press.

Hai Nutrition Campaign. 1987. Hai: District Medical Officer, Hai, Lyamungo Division, Kilimanjaro Region.

Handbook of German East Africa. 1920. Compiled by the geographical section of the Naval Intelligence division, Naval staff, Admiralty. London: H.M. Stationary Office.

Harkness, Sara, and Charles M. Super. 1994. The developmental niche: a theoretical framework for analyzing the household production of health. *Social Science and Medicine* 38(2): 217–226.

Harrell, B. B. 1981. Lactation and menstruation in cultural perspective. *American Anthropologist* 83(4):796–823.

Harrison, G. A. 1988. Seasonality and human population biology. In I. de Garine and G. A. Harrison, eds., *Coping with Uncertainty in Food Supply*. Oxford: Clarendon Press. 26–31.

Hatcher, R. A., et al. 1976. *Contraceptive Technology 1976–1977*, 8th ed. New York: Irvington Publishers.

Heggenhougen, Kris, Patrick Vaughan, Eustace P. Y. Muhondwa, and J. Ruta-banzibwa-Ngaiza. 1987. *Community Health Workers: The Tanzanian Experience*. Oxford: Oxford University Press.

Herrnstein, Richard J., and Charles Murray. 1994. *The Bell Curve*. New York: Free Press.

Hewitt de Alcantara, Cynthia, ed. 1994. *Economic Restructuring and Rural Subsistence in Mexico*. San Diego: Center for U.S.-Mexican Studies.

Hirschmann, David, and Megan Vaughan. 1983. Food production and income generation in a matrilineal society: rural women in Zomba, Malawi. *Journal of Southern African Studies* 10(1):86–99.

Hope, Anne, and Sally Timmel. 1984. *Training for Transformation*. Gweru, Zimbabwe: Mambo Press.

Horowitz, Michael M. 1990. Donors and deserts: The political ecology of destructive development in the Sahel. In Rebecca Huss-Ashmore and Solomon H. Katz, eds. *African Systems in Crisis. Part Two: Contending with Change*. New York: Gordon and Breach. 3–28.

Hosken, Fran. 1979. *The Hosken Report—Genital and Sexual Mutilation of Females*. Lexington, MA: Women's International Network News.

Howard, Mary T. 1980. *Kwashiorkor on Kilimanjaro: The Social Handling of Malnutrition*. Ph.D. dissertation, Department of Anthropology. East Lansing: Michigan State University.

———. 1990. "We don't have no say in our lives any more": An anthropologist's study of group home life for adults with mental retardation. *Adult Residential Care Journal* 4(3):163–182.

———. 1994. Socio-economic causes and cultural explanations of childhood malnutrition among the Chagga of Tanzania. *Social Science and Medicine* 38(2):239–251.

Hull, T. H., and J. E. Rohde. 1978. *Prospects for Rapid Decline of Mortality Rates in Java: A Study of the Causes of Death and the Feasibility of Policy Interventions for Mortality Control*. Working Paper Series, no. 16, Population Institute, Gadjah Mada University.

Hull, Valerie, and Mayling Simpson. 1985. *Breastfeeding, Child Health, and Child Spacing*. London: Croom-Helm.

Huss-Ashmore, Rebecca, and Solomon H. Katz, eds. 1989. *African Systems in Crisis. Part One: Microperspectives*. New York: Gordon and Breach.

———. 1990. *African Systems in Crisis. Part Two: Contending with Change*. New York: Gordon and Breach.

Huss-Ashmore, R. and R. B. Thomas. 1988. A framework for analysing uncertainty in highland areas. In I. de Garine and G. A. Harrison, eds., *Coping with Uncertainty in Food Supply*. Oxford: Clarendon Press. 469–475.

Iliffe, John. 1979. *A Modern History of Tanganyika.* Cambridge: Cambridge University Press.

————. 1987. *The African Poor.* Cambridge: Cambridge University Press.

Ishumi, A.G.M. 1980. A survey of students at the University of Dar es Salaam. *Tanzania Notes and Records* 84 and 85: 137–147.

Jacoby, Mario. 1994. *Shame and the Origins of Self-Esteem.* London: Routledge.

Janzen, John M. 1978. *The Quest for Therapy in Lower Zaire.* Berkeley: University of California Press.

Jelliffe, Derrick B., and E. F. Patrice Jelliffe. 1978. *Human Milk in the Modern World.* Oxford: Oxford University Press.

————. 1989. *Community Nutritional Assessment.* Oxford: Oxford University Press.

Jerome, N. W. 1980. Diet and acculturation: The case of black American immigrants. In Norge W. Jerome, Randy F. Kandel, and Gretel H. Pelto, eds., *Nutritional Anthropology.* Pleasantville, NY: Redgrave. 275–363.

Johnston, H. H. 1886. *The Kilimanjaro Expedition.* London: Kegan, Paul, and Trench.

Johnston, P. H. 1946. Some notes on land tenure on Kilimanjaro and the *vihamba* of the Wachagga. *Tanganyika Notes and Records* 21:1–20.

Jordan, Brigitte. 1978. *Birth in Four Cultures.* Montreal: Eden Women's Publications.

Kaufman, Gershen. 1980. *Shame: The Power of Caring.* Cambridge: Schenkman.

Kavishe, Festo P. 1993. *Nutrition-Relevant Actions in Tanzania.* Monograph Series No. 1. Dar es Salaam: Tanzania Food and Nutrition Center.

Kavishe, Festo P. and Fatma Mrisho. 1990. *A Summary of the Food and Nutrition Situation and Policy for Tanzania.* TFNC Report No. 1288. Dar es Salaam: Tanzania Food and Nutrition Center.

Kaw, Eugenia. 1993. Medicalization of racial features: Asian American women and cosmetic surgery. *Medical Anthropology Quarterly* 7(1):74–89.

KCMC (Kilimanjaro Christian Medical Center). 1986. *Disease Statistics of Children beyond the Neonatal Period.* KCMC Annual Report. Moshi: Kilimanjaro Christian Medical Center. 29.

Kelly, Valerie, and Thomas Reardon. 1995. Impacts of devaluation on Senegalese households: Policy implications. *Food Policy* 20(4):299–313.

Kerner, Donna O. 1988. *The Social Uses of Knowledge in Contemporary Tanzania.* Ph.D. dissertation. New York: City University of New York.

Kerner, Donna O., and Kristy Cook. 1991. Gender, Hunger and Crisis in Tanzania. In R. E. Downs, Donna O. Kerner, and Stephen P. Reyna, eds. *The Political Economy of African Famine.* New York: Gordon and Breach. 257–272.

Kilimanjaro Regional Development Director's Office. 1991. *The Situational Analysis of Food and Nutrition Problems in Kilimanjaro.* Report No. 1231. Dar es Salaam: Tanzania Food and Nutrition Center.

Korbin, Jill E., ed. 1981. *Child Abuse and Neglect: Cross-cultural Perspectives.* Berkeley: University of California. 35–55.

Krader, Lawrence. 1975. *The Asiatic Mode of Production.* Assen, Holland: Van Gorcum.

Kreysler, J.V. 1973. An analysis of survey data pertaining to protein energy malnutrition. In *The Young Child in Tanzania.* Dar es Salaam: UNICEF Liason Office, under the auspices of the Tanzania National Scientific Research Council, directed by David P. S. Wasawo. 19–46.

Leacock, Eleanor Burke. 1981. *Myths of Male Dominance.* New York: Monthly Review Press.

Lema, Anza Amen. 1973. *The Impact of the Leipzig Lutheran Mission on the People of Kilimanjaro, 1893–1920.* Ph.D. dissertation. Dar es Salaam: University of Dar es Salaam.

Leridon, H. 1977. *Human Fertility.* Chicago: University of Chicago Press.

Leslie, Charles. 1990. Scientific racism: Reflections on peer review, science and ideology. *Social Science and Medicine* 31(8):891–912.

LeVine, Sarah, and Robert LeVine. 1981. Child abuse and neglect in Sub-Saharan Africa. In Jill E. Korbin, ed., *Child Abuse and Neglect: Cross-Cultural Perspectives.* Berkeley: University of California Press. 35–55.

Linares, Olga F. 1993. State and household crops among the Jola (Diola) of Senegal. In John S. Henderson and Patricia Netherly, eds. *Configurations of Power.* Ithaca, NY: Cornell University Press. 160–180.

Lindner, P. I. 1972. Baseline study of mothers and children attending under-five clinics in Kilimanjaro. Moshi, Tanzania: Kilimanjaro Christian Medical Center.

Ljungqvist, Bjorn. 1993. Growth monitoring in health and nutrition information systems: Tanzania. In J. Cervinskas, N.M. Gerein, and Sabu George, eds., *Growth Promotion for Child Development.* Proceedings of a colloquium held in Nyeri, Kenya, May 12–13, 1992. Ottawa: International Development Research Center. 232-258.

Lukmanji, Z., F. Magambo, M. Ngonyani, C. Mayombana, C. Sikane, and R. Rutahakana. 1993. Activity pattern and time allocation of rural women in farming post-harvest seasons in Tanzania. Abstract of presentation at the 15th International Congress of Nutrition, Adelaide, Australia, September 26 to October 1, 1993. *Tanzania Food and Nutrition Journal* 6(1):37.

Lutz, Catherine A. 1988. *Unnatural Emotions.* Chicago: University of Chicago Press.

Maclachlan, Morgan D. 1983. *Why They Did Not Starve.* Philadelphia: Ishi.

Maletnlema, T. N., R. Mhombolage, and G.E. Ngowi. 1974. Family food consumption surveys in rural Tanzania. *Tanzania Notes and Records* 73:43–54.

Marealle, Chief Petro Itosi. 1963. Notes on Chagga custom. *Tanganyika Notes and Records* 60:67–90.

————. 1965. Chagga customs, beliefs and traditions, R. D. Swai, trans. *Tanganyika Notes and Records* 64:56–61.

Maro, Stephen P. 1974. *Population and Land Resources in Northern Tanzania: The Dynamics of Change, 1920–1970.* Ph.D. dissertation, University of Minnesota.

Martorell, R., C. Yarbrough, A. Lechtig, J. P. Habicht, and R. E. Klein. 1975. Diarrheal disease and growth retardation in preschool Guatemalan children. *American Journal of Physical Anthropology* 43:341–346.

Mbilinyi, Marjorie, and Patricia Mbughguni, eds. 1991. *Education in Tanzania with a Gender Perspective: Summary Edition.* Stockholm: Swedish International Development Authority.

McConnel, R. 1918. Appendix 2. *Uganda Annual Medical Report.* Entebbe, Uganda: Government Printer.

Meghji, Zakia Hamdani. 1989. *Malnutrition in Moshi District 1987–88.* Moshi: Tanzania Media Women's Association.

Messer, Ellen. 1989. Ecology and politics of food availability. In Rebecca Huss-Ashmore and Solomon H. Katz, eds., *African Systems in Crisis. Part One: Microperspectives.* New York: Gordon and Breach. 189–202.

————. 1990. Intra-Household allocation of resources: Perspectives from anthropology. In Beatrice Lorge Rogers and Nina P. Schlossman, eds., Intra- Household Resource Allocation. Tokyo: United Nations University Press. 51–62.

Millard, Ann V. 1982. Child mortality and lactation contraception in Mexico. *Medical Anthropology* 6(3):147–164.

————. 1985. Child mortality and economic variation among rural Mexican households. *Social Science and Medicine* 20(6):589–599.

————. 1990. The place of the clock in pediatric advice: Rationales, cultural themes, and impediments to breastfeeding. *Social Science and Medicine* 31(2):211–221.

Millard, Ann V., Anne E. Ferguson, and Stanley W. Khaila. 1990. Agricultural development and malnutrition: A causal model of child mortality. In John Caldwell, Sally Findley, Pat Caldwell, Gigi Santow, Wendy Cosford, Jennifer Braid, and Daphne Broers-Freeman, eds., *What We Know about Health Transition: The Cultural, Social, and Behavioral Determinants of Health.* Canberra, Australia: Australia National University. 285–310.

Millard, Ann V., and Margaret A. Graham. 1985. Principles that guide weaning in rural Mexico. *Ecology of Food and Nutrition* 16:171–188.

Morgan, Lynn M. 1990. International politics and primary health care in Costa Rica. *Social Science and Medicine* 30(2):211–220.

Moore, Sally Falk. 1975. Selection for failure in a small social field: Ritual concord and fraternal strife among the Chagga, Kilimanjaro, 1968–69. In S.F. Moore and B. Myerhoff, eds., *Symbol and Politics in Communal Ideology.* Ithaca: Cornell University Press. 109–143.

————. 1976. The secret of the men: A fiction of Chagga initiation and its relation to the logic of Chagga symbolism. *Africa* 46(4):357–370.

————. 1986. *Social Facts and Fabrications: "Customary" Law on Kilimanjaro, 1880–1980.* Cambridge: Cambridge University Press.

————. 1994. *Anthropology and Africa.* Charlottesville: University of Virginia.

Moore, Sally Falk, and Paul Purritt. 1977. *Chagga and Meru.* Ethnographic survey of Africa. London: International African Institute.

Morsy, Soheir A. 1978. Sex roles, power, and illness in an Egyptian village. *American Ethnologist* 5:137–150.

Mujwahuzi, M. R. 1981. Probable causes of recent food shortages. *Tanzania Notes and Records* 86 and 87:67–71.

Nations, Marilyn K., and L. A. Rebhun. 1988. Angels with wet wings won't fly: Maternal sentiment in Brazil and the image of neglect. *Culture, Medicine and Psychiatry* 12:141–200.

NCC/CSPD (The National Coordinating Committee for Child Survival, Protection, and Development). 1993. *The National Program of Action (NPA) to Achieve the Goals for Tanzanian Children in the 1990s.* Dar es Salaam: Government of the United Republic of Tanzania.

Newbury, David. 1991. *Kings and Clans.* Madison: University of Wisconsin Press.

Newman, L., ed. 1990. *Hunger in History.* New York: Basil Blackwell.

Obbo, Christine. 1976. Dominant male ideology and female options: Three East African case studies. *Africa* 46(4):371–389.

O'Brien, Jay, and Ellen Gruenbaum. 1991. A social history of food, famine and gender in twentieth-century Sudan. *In* R. E. Downs, Donna O. Kerner, and Stephen P. Reyna, eds. *The Political Economy of African Famine.* New York: Gordon and Breach. 177–203.

Page, Hilary J., and Ron Lesthaeghe. 1981. *Child-Spacing in Tropical Africa.* New York: Academic Press.

Palerm, Angel. 1990. *Mexico Prehispanico: Essays on Evolution and Ecology.* Edited by Carmen Viqueira. Mexico: Consejo Nacional para la Cultura y las Artes.

Piers, G., and M. B. Singer. 1953. *Shame and Guilt.* Springfield: Thomas.

Piven, Frances Fox, and Richard A. Cloward. 1993. *Regulating the Poor,* 2nd ed. New York: Random House.

Procter, R.A.W. 1926. Commentary. *Kenya Medical Journal* 3:284.

Puffer, R. R., and C. V. Serrano. 1973. *Patterns of Mortality in Childhood. Report of the Inter-American Investigation of Mortality in Childhood.* Washington, D.C.: Pan American Health Organization.

————. 1975. Birthweight, maternal age, and birth order: Three important determinants in infant mortality. *Pan American Health Organization Scientific Publication* 294.

————. 1976. Results of the inter-American investigations of mortality relating to reproduction. *PAHO Bulletin* 10:131–142.

Raikes, Philip. 1988. *Modernizing Hunger: Famine, Food Surplus and Farm Policy in the EEC and Africa.* Portsmouth, NH: Heinemann Educational Books.

Raum, O. F. 1940. *Chaga Childhood.* London: Oxford University Press.

Rhodes, Laura Amarasingham. 1990. Studying biomedicine as a cultural system. In Thomas M. Johnson and Carolyn F. Sargent, eds., *Medical Anthropology.* New York: Praeger. 159–173.

Richards, Audrey. 1939. *Land, Labor, and Diet in Northern Rhodesia.* London: Oxford University Press.

Ritenbaugh, Cheryl. 1978. Human foodways: a window on evolution. In Eleanor E. Bauwens, ed., *The Anthropology of Health.* St. Louis: Mosby. 111–120.

Rogers, Beatrice Lorge. 1990. The internal dynamics of households: A critical factor in development policy. In Beatrice Lorge Rogers and Nina P. Schlossman, eds., *Intra-Household Resource Allocation.* Tokyo: United Nations University Press. 1–19.

Rosaldo, Michelle Z. 1980. Knowledge and Passion. Cambridge: Cambridge University Press.

Rothman, Barbara Katz. 1982. *In Labor: women and power in the birthplace.* New York: W. W. Norton. (Reprinted as *Giving Birth: Alternatives in Childbirth.* New York: Penguin Books, 1985.)

Rushton, J.P., and A. F. Bogaert. 1989. Population differences in susceptibility to AIDS: An evolutionary analysis. *Social Science and Medicine* 28:1211–1220.

Ryan, William. 1971. *Blaming the Victim.* New York: Vintage.

Samhoff, Joel. 1974. *Tanzania, Local Politics and the Structure of Power.* Madison: University of Wisconsin Press.

————. 1979. Education in Tanzania: Class formation and reproduction. *The Journal of Modern African Studies* 17(1):47–69.

Samhoff, Joel, and Rachel Samhoff. 1976. The local politics of underdevelopment. *The African Review* vi (1):69–97.

Sanders, W. T., and Barbara Price. 1968. *Mesoamerica: The Evolution of a Civilization.* New York: Random House.

Sacks, Karen. 1979. *Sisters and Wives.* Westport, CT: Greenwood Press.

Said, Edward. 1979. *Orientalism.* New York: Vintage.

Scheper-Hughes, Nancy. 1984. Infant mortality and infant care: Cultural and economic constraints on nurturing in Northeast Brazil. *Social Science and Medicine* 19(5):535–546.

————. 1992. *Death without Weeping.* Berkeley: University of California Press.

Scheper-Hughes, Nancy, ed. 1987. *Child Survival.* Dordrecht: D. Reidel.

Schneider, Carl D. 1977. *Shame, Exposure and Privacy.* Boston: Beacon Press.

Schneiderman, Stuart. 1995. *Saving Face: America and the Politics of Shame.* New York: Alfred A. Knopf.

Schoepf, Brooke Grundfest, and Claude Schoepf. 1990. Gender, Land and Hunger in Eastern Zaire. In Rebecca Huss-Ashmore and Solomon H. Katz, eds., *African Systems in Crisis. Part Two: Contending with Change.* New York: Gordon and Breach. 75–106.

Schumann, Debra A., and W. Henry Mosley. 1994. Introduction, the household production of health. *Social Science and Medicine* 38(2):201–204.

Scott, James C. 1985. *Weapons of the Weak.* New Haven: Yale University Press.

Scrimshaw, S. C. M. 1978. Infant mortality and behavior in the regulation of family size. *Population and Development Review* 4(3):383–403.

———. 1990. Combining quantitative and qualitative methods in the study of intra-household resource allocation. In Beatrice Lorge Rogers and Nina P. Schlossman, eds., *Intra-Household Resource Allocation.* Tokyo: United Nations University Press. 86–98.

Seavoy, Ronald. 1989. *Famine in East Africa: Food Production and Food Policies.* New York: Greenwood Press.

Sehgal, B. S., and S. R. Singh. 1966. Breastfeeding, amenorrhea, and rates of conception in women. Mimeographed. Lucknow, India: Planning Research and Action Institute.

Semiti, Godfrey A. 1972. Nutrition and agricultural planning in Tanzania. In Bo Vahlquist, ed., *Nutrition: A Priority in African Development.* Uppsala: Almqvistand Wiksell. 167–175.

Sen, Amartya. 1981. *Poverty and Famines: An Essay on Entitlement and Deprivation.* Oxford: Oxford University Press.

Shanklin, Eugenia. 1994. *Anthropology and Race.* Belmont, CA: Wadsworth.

Shann, G. N. 1956. The early development of education among the Chagga. *Tanganyika Notes and Records* 45:21–32.

Shayo, W. O. 1981. Nutritional status of children of 1–15 years and related factors in Old Moshi Sango Village Moshi District May/June 1981. Files of the authors.

Shields, David L. L., ed. 1995. *The Color of Hunger: Race and Hunger in National and International Perspective.* Lanham: Rowman & Littlefield Publishers, Inc.

Short, R. V. 1976. Lactation: The central control of reproduction. In *Breastfeeding and the Mother.* Ciba Foundation Syumposium 45 (new series). Amsterdam: Elsevier/Exceprta Medica/North Holland. 73–81.

Shorter, Aylward. 1974. *East African Societies.* London: Routledge and Kegan Paul.

Simpson-Hebert, Mayling, and Sandra L. Huffman. 1981. The contraceptive effect of breastfeeding. *Studies in Family Planning* 12(4):125–133.

Smidt, P. R. 1989. Early exploitation and settlement of the Usambara Mountains. *In* A.C. Hamilton and R. Bensted-Smith, eds., *Forest Conservation in the East Usambara Mountains, Tanzania.* Gland, Switzerland: IUCN. 75–78.

Spring, Anita. 1990. Profiles of men and women smallholder farmers in Malawi. In Rebecca Huss-Ashmore and Solomon H. Katz, eds., *African Systems in Crisis. Part Two: Contending with Change*. New York: Gordon and Breach. 107–136.

Stahl, Kathleen M. 1964. *History of the Chagga People of Kilimanjaro*. The Hague: Mouton.

Stambach, Amy. 1995. *Kutoa mimba*: Debates about schoolgirl abortion in northern Tanzania. Paper presented at AERA Annual Meeting, San Francisco.

Steward, Julian, ed. 1955. *Irrigation Civilizations*. Washington, DC: Pan American Union.

Strathern, Marilyn. 1987. Conclusion. In Marilyn Strathern, ed., *Dealing with Inequality*. Cambridge: Cambridge University Press. 278–302.

Strobel, Margaret. 1995. Women in religious and secular ideology. *In* Margaret Jean Hay and Sharon Stichter, eds., *African Women South of the Sahara*, 2nd ed. New York: Longman. 101–118.

Susser, Mervyn W., William Watson, and Kim Hopper. 1985. *Sociology in Medicine*, 3rd ed. Oxford: Oxford University Press.

Swantz, Marja-Liisa. 1969. *The Religious and Magical Rites Connected with the Life Cycle of Bantu Women in Some Bantu Ethnic Groups of Tanzania*. Ph. D. dissertation in anthropology. Turku University, Finland.

———. 1985. *Women in Development: A Creative Role Denied? The Case of Tanzania*. New York: St. Martin's Press.

Swantz, Marja-Liisa, U. S. Henricson, and Mary [Howard] Zalla. 1975. *Socioeconomic Causes of Malnutrition in Moshi District*. Research Paper No. 38. Dar es Salaam: Bureau of Resource Assessment and Land Use Planning, University of Dar es Salaam.

Tanzania Demographic and Health Survey 1991/92 Preliminary Report. 1992. Bureau of Statistics, President's Office, Planning Commission, United Republic of Tanzania, Demographic and Health Surveys. Columbia, MD: Macro International, Inc.

Taussig, Michael. 1992. Culture of terror—space of death: Roger Casement's Putumayo Report and the explanation of torture. In Nicholas B. Dirks, ed., *Colonialism and Culture*. Ann Arbor: Univerity of Michigan Press. 135–173.

Tilly, Charles. 1978. *Historical Studies of Changing Fertility*. Princeton, NJ: Princeton University Press.

Torun, Benjamin, and Francisco Chew. 1994. Protein-energy malnutrition. In Maurice E. Shils, James A. Olson, and Moshe Shike, eds., *Modern Nutrition in Health and Disease*, 8th ed. Philadelphia: Lea and Febiger. 950–976.

Torun, Benjamin, and Fernando E. Viteri. 1988. Protein-calorie malnutrition. In Maurice E. Shils and Vernon R. Young, eds., *Modern Nutrition in Health and Disease*, 7th ed. Philadelphia: Lea and Febiger. 746–773.

Turnbull, Colin. 1972. *The Mountain People*. New York: Simon and Schuster.

Turshen, Meredeth. 1984. *The Political Ecology of Disease in Tanzania*. New Brunswick, NJ:Rutgers University Press.

———. 1995. Women and health issues. In Margaret Jean Hay and Sharon Stichter, eds., *African Women South of the Sahara*, 2nd ed. New York: Longman. 239–249.

Turshen, Meredeth, ed. 1991. *Women and Health in Africa*. Trenton, NJ: Africa World Press.

Vahlquist, Bo. 1972. Malnutrition as a socio-medical problem. In Bo Vahlquist, ed., *Nutrition: A Priority in African Development*. Uppsala: Almqvist and Wiksell. 23–37.

Van Esterik, Penny. 1989. *The Breast-Bottle Controversy*. New Brunswick, NJ: Rutgers University Press.

Vaughan, Megan. 1991. *Curing Their Ills*. Stanford: Stanford University Press.

———. 1992. Famine analysis and family relations: Nyasaland in 1949. In Steven Feierman and John M. Janzen, eds., 1992 *The Social Basis of Health and Healing in Africa*. Berkeley: University of California Press. 71–89.

Viteri, Fernando E., and Benjamin Torun. 1980. Protein-calorie malnutrition. In Robert S. Goodhart and Maurice E. Shils, eds., *Modern Nutrition in Health and Disease*, 6th ed. Philadelphia: Lea and Febiger. 697–720.

Von Clemm, Michael F. M. 1964. Agricultural productivity and sentiment on Kilimanjaro. *Economic Botany* 18:99–121.

Von Freyhold, Michaela, Mary [Howard] Zalla, and Katherine Sawaki. 1973. Moshi District. In *The Young Child in Tanzania*. Dar es Salaam: UNICEF Liason Office, under the auspices of the Tanzania National Scientific Research Council, directed by David P. S. Wasawo. 166–238.

Wallerstein, Immanuel M. 1986. *Africa and the Modern World*. Trenton, NJ: Africa World Press.

Warren, Kay B., and Susan C. Bourque. 1989. Women, technology, and development ideologies: Frameworks and findings. In Sandra Morgen, ed., *Gender and Anthropology*. Washington, DC: American Anthropological Association. 382–410.

Waterlow, J. C. 1948. Fatty liver disease in infants in the British West Indies. Medical Research Council Special Report Series No. 263. London: HMSO.

Watts, Michael. 1991. Heart of darkness: Reflections on famine and starvation in Africa. *In* R. E. Downs, Donna O. Kerner, and Stephen P. Reyna, eds., *The Political Economy of African Famine*. New York: Gordon and Breach. 1–68.

Weber, Max. 1978. *Economy and Society*. Edited by Guenther Roth and Claus Wittich. Berkeley: University of California Press.

Whiteford, Scott, and Anne E. Ferguson, eds. 1991. *Harvest of Want*. Boulder, CO: Westview.

Wikan, Unni. 1990. *Managing Turbulent Hearts*. Chicago: University of Chicago Press.

Williams, Cicely D. 1935. Kwashiorkor. *Lancet* 11:1151–1152.

———. 1973. The story of kwashiorkor. *Nutrition Review* 31:11.

Williams, Cicely D., Naomi Baumslag, and Derrick B. Jelliffe, 1985. *Mother and Child Health*, 2nd ed. London: Oxford University Press.

Wittfogel, Karl A. 1957. *Oriental Despotism*. New Haven: Yale University Press.

Winkler, Cathy. 1995. Ethnography of the ethnographer. In Carolyn Nordstrom and Antonius C.G.M. Robben, eds., *Fieldwork under Fire*. Berkeley: University of California Press. 155–184.

Wolf, Eric R. 1982. *Europe and the People without History*. Berkeley: University of California Press.

Wolf, Eric, and Angel Palerm. 1955. Irrigation in the old Acolhua Domain, Mexico. *Southwestern Journal of Anthropology* 11:265–281.

Women and Children in Tanzania. 1990. Dar es Salaam: Government of the United Republic of Tanzania and United Nations Children's Fund.

World Bank. 1981. *Accelerated Development in Sub-Saharan Africa: An Agenda for Action*. Washington, D.C.: The World Bank.

Wray, J. D., and A. Aguirre. 1969. Protein calorie malnutrition in Candelaria, Colombia — I. Prevalence, social and demographic causal factors. *Journal of Tropical Pediatrics* 15:76–98.

Zalla, Thomas M. 1982. *Economic and Technical Aspects of Smallholder Milk Production in Northern Tanzania*. Ph.D. dissertation, Department of Agricultural Economics. East Lansing, MI: Michigan State University.

Zeitlin, Marian, Hossein Ghassemi, and Mohamed Mansour. 1990. *Positive Deviance in Child Nutrition*. Tokyo: United Nations University Press.

Zoja, Luigi. 1995. *Growth and Guilt*. London: Routledge.

Index

Index of People on Kilimanjaro

Topic Index